# sTORI telling

# TORI SPELLING

## WITH HILARY LIFTIN

SIMON SPOTLIGHT ENTERTAINMENT
NEW YORK LONDON TORONTO SYDNEY

SSE

SIMON SPOTLIGHT ENTERTAINMENT
A Division of Simon & Schuster, Inc.
1230 Avenue of the Americas, New York, NY 10020

First Simon Spotlight Entertainment trade paperback edition February 2009
SIMON SPOTLIGHT ENTERTAINMENT and colophon are
trademarks of Simon & Schuster, Inc.
For information about special discounts for bulk purchases, please
contact Simon & Schuster Special Sales at 1-800-456-6798 or
business@simonandschuster.com.
Designed by Gabe Levine
Manufactured in the United States of America
10   9   8   7   6   5
Library of Congress Cataloging-in-Publication Data
Spelling, Tori, 1973–
sTORI telling / Tori Spelling with Hilary Liftin. — 1st ed.
p. cm.
ISBN-13: 978-1-4169-5073-8
ISBN-10:       1-4169-5073-7
ISBN-13: 978-1-4165-8700-2 (pbk)
ISBN-10:       1-4165-8700-4 (pbk)
1. Spelling, Tori, 1973– 2. Actors—United States—Biography.
I. Liftin, Hilary. II. Title.
PN2287.S664A3 2008
791.4502'8092—dc22
[B]
2007046882

*To Dean and Liam, my beautiful boys—*
*you made all my dreams come true.*

# Contents

# PROLOGUE

When you're a kid, you don't worry what anyone thinks. You go around saying whatever pops into your head or picking your teeth, and it never occurs to you that someone might think you're gross, awkward, or ridiculous. That was me—picking my nose, snorting when I laughed, wearing white after Labor Day—I just was who I was. That all changed one day at the tender age of twelve when I was getting ready for a family photo. We were having a formal family portrait taken with our dogs (doesn't everyone do that?), and I was getting frustrated with my bangs. I couldn't get them to do whatever a twelve-year-old in 1985 wanted bangs to do. So I went into my parents' bathroom, all dressed up, with my hair done as best I could manage, and asked my mother, "Am I pretty?"

She looked at me and said, "You will be when we get your nose done."

I was stunned. My nose, as noses tend to be, was right in the middle of my face, and I had just been told that it was ugly. So long, innocence.

To be fair, let the record show that my mother has absolutely no recollection of making this comment. I know this because in high school I took a class called Human Development, taught by Mrs. Wildflower. In it we had to keep a journal (her name was *Mrs. Wildflower*—what did you expect?), and when Mrs. Wildflower read my story about the nose incident, she called my parents. That afternoon I came home to find my mother crying. She said, "I never said that. I'd never say something like that." I'm sure she was telling the truth as she remembered it.

Nonetheless, I had my nose done the minute I turned sixteen. Or didn't you hear? But what I realized as a twelve-year-old was bigger than that I was destined for the plastic surgeon's chair. I realized that how other people saw me wasn't necessarily how I saw myself. Feeling pretty or smart or happy wasn't all there was to it. What I hadn't considered before was how I was *perceived*. And it wasn't the last criticism I'd hear about my nose.

Little did I know then how huge a role public perception would play in my life. My nose, and pretty much every other "prominent" body part and feature, would be prey to gossip and tabloids in just a few years. But the unwanted attention wasn't limited to my body. According to the press, I was the rich, spoiled daughter of TV producer Aaron Spelling. They claimed I grew up in California's largest single-family residence. They said that my father had fake snow made on his Beverly Hills lawn for Christmas. They said I was the ultimate example of nepotism, a lousy actor who nonetheless scored a lead role in her father's hit TV show. They pigeonholed me as my character on *Beverly Hills, 90210*: Donna Martin, the ditzy blonde virgin. They later talked about my wedding, my divorce, and my second wedding. They reported that I'd been disinherited and was feuding with my mother. They told about the birth of my son. What I learned from my ugly nose was true times a million: The details of my life were and would always be considered public property.

Some of what you may have read about me is accurate (my father *did* hire a snow machine for Christmas), some false (I didn't live in that enormous house until I was seventeen), and some exaggerated (I wasn't "disinherited"). But all the while the life I was living was much more than that. I lived in fear of my own doll collection. I let a bad boyfriend spend my *90210* salary. I planned a fairy-tale wedding to the wrong man. I begged casting directors to forget that Donna Martin ever existed. I was working hard and shopping like crazy. I was falling in love and getting hurt. My life has been funnier and sadder and richer and poorer than any of the magazines know.

Public opinion dies hard. To this day I still look in the mirror and hate my nose. Still, everyone else has been telling stories about me for decades now. It's about time I told a few of my own.

## CHAPTER ONE

# X Marks the Spot

Here's the part of my book where I'm supposed to say, *Sure, my family had lots of money, but I had a normal childhood just like everyone else.* Yeah, I could say that, but I'd be lying. My childhood was really weird. Not better or worse than anyone else's childhood, but definitely different.

Part of it was the whole holiday thing. My parents liked to make a spectacle, and the press ate it up. Like I said, it's true that my father got snow for our backyard one Christmas. But that's only half the story, if anyone's counting—he actually did it twice. The first time was when I was five. My father told our family friend Aunt Kay that he wanted me to have a white Christmas. She did some research, made a few calls, and at six a.m. on Christmas Day a truck from Barrington Ice in Brentwood pulled up to our house. My dad, Aunt Kay, and a security guard dragged garbage bags

holding eight tons of ice into the back where there was plastic cov-
ering a fifteen-foot-square patch of the yard. They spread the snow
out over the plastic, Dad with a pipe hanging from his mouth. To
complete the illusion, they added a Styrofoam snowman that my
father had ordered up from the props department at his studio. It
was eighty degrees out, but they dressed me up in a ski jacket and
hat and brought me out into the yard, exclaiming, "Oh, look, it
snowed! In all of Los Angeles it snowed right here in your backyard! Aren't you a lucky girl?"

I'm sure that little white patch was as amazing to a five-year-old as
seeing a sandbox for the first time, but my parents didn't stop there.
Five years later they were thinking bigger, and technology was too.
This time, again with Aunt Kay's guidance, my dad hired a snow
machine to blow out so much powder that it not only filled the
tennis court, it created a sledding hill at one end of the court. I
was ten and my brother, Randy, was five. They dressed us in full-on
snowsuits (the outfits were for the photos, of course—it was a typical
eighty-five degrees out). According to Aunt Kay, the sledding hill
lasted three days and everyone came to see the snow in Beverly Hills:
Robert Wagner, Mel Brooks . . . not that I noticed or cared. Randy
and I spent Christmas running up the hill and zooming down in red
plastic saucer sleds. Even our dogs got to slide down the hill. It was
a pretty spectacular day for an L.A. girl.

My parents didn't get the concept of having me grow up like other
kids. When I was about eight, my class took a field trip to my dad's
studio. It was a fun day—my father showed us around and had some
surprises planned, such as a stuntman breaking "glass" over some
kid's head. But then, at the end of the day, the whole class stood for

a photo. My father and I were in the back row. Just before the shutter clicked, he picked me up and held me high above the class. My face in the photo says it all. I was beyond embarrassed that my father was lifting me up like that. I just wanted to fit in. When I complained to him, he said, "But you couldn't be seen." He just didn't get it.

And then there were the birthday parties. The setting was always the backyard of our house on the corner of Mapleton and Sunset Boulevard in Holmby Hills, a fancy area on the west side of Los Angeles. It was a very large house—though not the gigantic manor where everyone thinks I grew up—maybe 10,000 square feet. It was designed by the noted L.A. architect Paul Williams, whose many public buildings include the famous Beverly Hills Hotel. A house he designed in Bel-Air was used for exterior scenes of the Colby mansion on my dad's television series *The Colbys*. Our house's back lawn was probably an acre surrounded by landscaping with a pool and tennis court, the regular features of houses in that neighborhood.

As I remember it, the theme for my birthdays was always Raggedy Ann, and there would be a doll centerpiece and rented tables and chairs with matching tablecloths, napkins, and cups. But every party had some new thrill. There were carnival moon bounces, which weren't common then as they are today, and fair booths lined up on both sides of the lawn offering games of ringtoss, balloon darts, duck floats, Whac-A-Mole, and the like. One birthday had a dancing poodle show conducted by a man in a circus ringleader's outfit. Another included a puppet show with life-size puppets. And one year we had a surprise visit from Smidget, who at the time was the smallest living horse. My godfather, Dean Martin, whom I called Uncle Bean, always brought me a money tree—a little tree with rolled up twenty-dollar bills instead of leaves. Just what a girl like me needed.

When my sixth-grade class graduated, we had a party at my house for which my father hired the USC marching band. Apparently, my dad first approached UCLA, but they said no. According to Aunt Kay, who organized a lot of these parties for my parents, my father told her, "Money is no object." Well, it must have been an object to the USC marching band because all one hundred plus members showed up to play "Pomp and Circumstance" and whatever else marching bands come up with to play at sixth-grade graduations. I have to admit I didn't even remember the marching band's presence until Aunt Kay told me about it. What I remember are the things a twelve-year-old remembers: the rented dance floor and the DJ and hoping that the boy I liked would ask me to slow dance to "Crazy for You" by Madonna. I remember swimming in the pool. I remember feeling sad that we were all moving on to different schools. I remember being only mildly embarrassed that my mother was hula hooping on the dance floor, but I'm sure I was truly embarrassed by the marching band.

My parents were endlessly generous, and those parties were spectacular . . . on paper. The reality was a little more complicated. For every birthday and Christmas my big present was *always* a Madame Alexander doll. Madame Alexander dolls are classic, collectible dolls. Sort of like a rich man's Barbie, but—at least in my house—they were meant for display, not play. My mother loved the best of the best, for herself and for me. She was known for her *Dynasty*-style jewelry—quarter-size emeralds dangling off nickel-size diamonds. Most attention-grabbing was the forty-four-carat diamond ring she always wore. That's right—no typo. Forty-four carats. Walking around with that thing must have been as good as weight lifting. I always begged her not to wear the ring to school functions. But that was her everyday style—put together in blouses with Chanel belts, slim jeans, Chanel flats, perfectly manicured red nails, and a heavy load of jewelry worth millions of dollars.

As for the Madame Alexander dolls, every birthday, as soon as I unwrapped them, they were whisked away, tags still attached, to a special display case in my room that had a spotlight for each doll. No way in hell was I allowed to dress and undress them or (God forbid!) cut their hair. Every time I unwrapped a present, my heart sank a little bit when I saw that same powder blue box. I knew that all I had was a new, untouchable doll to add to my expensive collection. But my mother would be smiling with pleasure. She loved the dolls, had always coveted them as a girl, and wanted me to have something special. I didn't want to hurt her feelings, so I always thanked her and acted excited—she had no idea that all I wanted (at some point) was a Barbie Dream House.

So *now* imagine another birthday party. I was four or five. The great lawn was festooned with balloons and streamers. Colorful booths lined the perimeter of its downward slope. And in the center of it all was a mysterious white sheet with a big red *X* painted across it.

In the middle of the festivities a plane flew overhead. I was just starting to read, but our family friend Aunt Kay had spent all morning teaching me how to read *Happy Birthday, Tori*. Not coincidentally, the plane was pulling a banner saying just that. I read it and was thrilled and proud, jumping up and down and clapping my hands in excitement. Aunt Kay waved to the pilot, and he dropped a little parachute with a mystery gift attached to its strings. So dramatic! It was supposed to hit the *X* on the sheet, but instead, it landed in a tree. One of the carnival workers had to climb the tree to get it down. I later found out that Aunt Kay had to get special permits for the plane to fly that low over the house.

As soon as my present was liberated, I ran to the box and pulled away the padding until I got to the present. I tore open the wrapping paper, and there it was. The powder blue box. Another Madame Alexander doll. This one was a surprise, along with the plane, from Aunt Kay. (Some of my most valuable dolls were gifts from her collection.) My friends oohed and aahed, and I fake-squealed with joy. Then I handed the doll over to my mother so her dress wouldn't get dirty.

At some point I wondered if all these spectacular events were actually being done for me. Really, how many sixth-grade girls' biggest fantasy is for a college marching band to play at their graduation? Take Halloween. When I was five or six, my mother decided I would go as a bride. No polyester drugstore costume for me, no sir. Halloween found me wearing a custom bridal gown made by the noted fashion designer Nolan Miller, with padded boobs and false eyelashes. And, like many Halloweens, I wore high heels. It wasn't easy to find heels for a young child, so my mother went through the Yellow Pages until she found a "little person" store that sold grown-up shoes in my size.

Then there was the Marie Antoinette costume my mother had Nolan Miller make for me when I was nine or ten. My five-year-old brother, Randy, was Louis XVI (a costume that actually suited him—even at that young age, he was already showing a taste for the finer

things. We'd go to a restaurant and he'd tell the waiter, "For my appe-
tizer I'll have the escargot.") My Marie Antoinette costume had golden
brocade, a boned bodice, and gigantic hip bustles. It was topped off
with an enormous powdered wig of ringlets so heavy that I got my
first headache. I looked like one of those Madame Alexander dolls of
which my mother was so fond. Meanwhile, Randy got off easy in a
ruffled red coat and a comparatively lightweight wig.

My parents drove their young royals to the flats of Beverly Hills,
L.A.'s prime trick-or-treating turf. The houses were closer together
than those in our neighborhood but still inhabited by rich people
who didn't think twice about giving out full-size candy bars. Not that
we got to keep any of the candy we collected anyway. My mother
was paranoid about hidden razor blades and poisoned chocolate,
so she always confiscated our booty and replaced it with bags she'd
painstakingly assembled herself.

As I wobbled my way down the street trying to adjust to my new
center of gravity, some kids threw raw eggs at me. I barely felt the
first couple—they must have hit my bustle. But then, as if in slow
motion, I saw two eggs coming toward us, one at me, one at my
brother. Randy darted out of the line of fire, but I couldn't escape
because of my enormous petticoats. An egg hit me in the ear. I wish
I could at least claim it was some French immigrants avenging their
eighteenth-century proletariat ancestors, but I think I was just caught
in run-of-the-mill vampire/Jedi knight cross fire.

After the Marie Antoinette debacle, I'd had it. When Halloween
rolled around again, I begged to be anything other than a histori-
cal figure. I wanted to be a plain old bunny. You know, the classic Halloween costume: plastic mask, grocery bag for candy, jacket

hiding the one-piece paper outfit. My mother agreed to the bunny concept. But instead of drawn-on whiskers and bunny ears on a headband, I had a hand-sewn bunny costume, which had me in (fake) fur from head to toe with just my face showing. Who was I to complain? It was the best bunny costume a girl could ever want. Unfortunately, after four houses I had an allergy attack and had to go home.

For all the effort and fanfare my parents put into my childhood, I'm most sentimental about some of the lower-key indulgences, the ones that had nothing to do with how I was dressed or what kind of party our family could throw. We have a beach house in Malibu, and whenever we went there, my mother and I would walk out to the end of our beach to pick shells. (This is the same beach house where Dean Martin, my Uncle Bean, came to stay for a summer during his divorce. He was a huge golfer and traveled with a stockpile of golf balls that had his autograph printed on them. Every morning he'd set up a driving range on the private beach in front of our house and shoot golf balls into the ocean. People from all sides of the beach would be diving into the water to collect those golf balls as souvenirs, but Uncle Bean would just keep hitting the balls, completely oblivious.) Anyway, whenever my mother and I went shelling, she always brought her purse, which wasn't suspicious since she smoked at the time. I'd hunt for shells and she'd urge me on, pointing me to spots I'd missed. It never took me long to find a few big, beautiful, polished seashells. I was always telling my friends that Malibu had the most amazing seashells.

My Malibu illusions were shattered when I was twelve. We took a family trip to Europe, but because my father refused to fly, we took the scenic route. It started with a three-day train trip to New York in a private train car attached to the back of a regular Amtrak train. We brought two nannies, my mother's assistant, and two security guards. From New York we took the *Queen Elizabeth II* to Europe. I loved the boat—it had a shopping mall, restaurants, and a movie theater—but what excited me most was that they had little arts-and-crafts activities scheduled for the kids. It was the closest to summer camp I ever got. (It was also the farthest from home I ever got. Every other family vacation was spent in Vegas, mostly because you could get there by car.) In England we made the tourist rounds: Trafalgar Square, Madame Tussaud's, and so on. Of course, when my mother saw the Crown Jewels at the Tower of London she commented, "I have a necklace bigger than that." It was true. She did.

But I was talking about the breaking of the Malibu seashell mythology. In England I was reading *OK!* or *Hello!*—one of those gossip magazines that were more respectable back in the eighties—and I came across an interview with my parents. In it my mother talks about how she used to buy exotic seashells and hide them for me on the beach in Malibu. Total shock to me. So much for the beautiful seashells of Malibu. You know your family doesn't exactly communicate well when you find out things like this in weekly magazines.

Part of why I was upset about the seashells (beyond normal almost-teenage angst) was that it had only been the year before that I realized there was no Santa Claus or Easter Bunny. All I knew was that every year on the night before Easter, the Easter Bunny would call me on the phone and tell me to be a good girl. And every Christmas Eve the phone would ring and Santa's workers would inform my father that Santa had landed and he was approaching our house. A few moments later there'd be a knock at the door and . . . there was Santa. My brother and I would rush to greet him in our coordinated Christmas outfits. I'd be wearing a red overalls dress with a white shirt and red kneesocks, and Randy would be wearing red overalls shorts with a white shirt and red kneesocks. We'd sit on Santa's lap, one on each knee, and tell him what we wanted for Christmas. Then he'd tell us to get to bed early, that tomorrow was a big day, and he'd ho-ho-ho out the door. It didn't always go so smoothly—like the time that Randy peed on Santa's knee—but for the most part that was what had gone on for years, and I saw no reason to believe the kids at school when they said Santa was bunk. I saw him with my own eyes.

I probably would have kept believing if my cousin Meredith hadn't come over for a sleepover when I was eleven. She was a year older than I was, and that fact alone made her cool. I was really psyched that she was spending the night. It was Easter, and I must have said something about the Easter Bunny's imminent arrival because she was like, "You're kidding that you think there's an Easter Bunny." I said, "Yes, there is." Then she said, "Don't tell me you believe in Santa, too!" The kids at school were eleven like I was— what did they know? Why should I believe them? But Meredith was twelve. She knew stuff. I had to concede. If it hadn't been for her, who knows how long the charade might have gone on. Oh, and after that I never saw Meredith again. I think her disclosures convinced my parents that she was a bad influence.

As a kid I felt deceived to discover my parents had been lying, but now I realize it was pretty lovely. My mother loved decorating for and with us—coloring Easter eggs, carving jack-o'-lanterns, setting up moving Santa scenes at Christmastime. The seashells, the holiday characters, the decorations, these were pure, sweet moments that weren't about putting on a show, they were about making us happy. These were the heartfelt private gifts from my parents for which I never knew to thank them.

Looking back, what I remember with the most affection is being four years old and having a dad who would sit in the Jacuzzi with me and make up stories. My father was a slight man with slouchy shoulders that made him appear even smaller. For all his power in Hollywood, most of the time he'd appear in a jogging suit with a pipe. He spoke in a soft voice with a hint of Texas twang and would come right up to you to shake your hand or give you a hug even if he didn't know you well. The overall effect was very *Wizard of Oz* man-behind-the-curtain—*this* unimposing, gentle guy is the famous Aaron Spelling? People always felt comfortable with him right away.

He and I would sit in the hot tub, and he'd be Hansel and I'd be Gretel and my mom (upstairs with a migraine) would be the witch. (Yes, I now think this is weird, if not psychologically damaging, that my father let me cast my unwitting mother as the villain. At least I can say that on the day I have in mind I kept looking up at the window of my mother's bedroom, hoping to see the shade go up, which meant the witch felt better and might join us at the pool.) Or we'd play Chasen's.

Chasen's restaurant, which is now closed, was a legendary celebrity hangout on Beverly Boulevard in Beverly Hills. Frank Sinatra, Alfred Hitchcock, Marilyn Monroe, Jimmy Stewart, and most of the Hollywood elite were regulars in their day. When I was a kid, the family would go to Chasen's on Mother's Day or Father's Day for a fancy celebration. So my dad and I would recline in the Jacuzzi and say, "We've just arrived at Chasen's. What should we order?"

A few years later I asked my parents for an allowance because the other kids at school had allowances. My father wanted to give me five dollars, but I wanted only twenty-five cents because that's what the other kids got. Dad told me that in order to earn my allowance, I'd have to help out around the house, so he gave me a job and said he'd do it with me. Every weekend we'd go out into the yard to scoop up dog poo and rake leaves.

That's right, every weekend TV mogul Aaron Spelling, net worth equivalent to some small island nation, went out and scooped poo with his daughter. We hadn't yet moved to the Manor—that enormous house that the press can't get over—but we still had a large yard and four dogs. And of course we had gardeners who were supposed to be taking care of all that. But there was always plenty for us to pick up, and I suspect he told the gardeners to leave it be. Sort of like the seashells, I guess—but a lot grosser. No matter, I loved it. I remember spending a lot of time out on that lawn, hanging out with my dad, playing softball, or working in the vegetable garden with him and my mother. One year we grew a zucchini that was as big as a baby. There are photos of me cradling it. My father was very proud—no matter what it was, our family liked the biggest and the best.

For the most part my father thought that money was the way to show love. Where do you think all those lavish jewels my mother wore came from? Every holiday he bought her a bigger and brighter bauble as if to prove his love. When I asked Aunt Kay to help me remember some of the extravagances, she said, "Money was no object. That's how much he loved you. There was no limit to what he would do for you." When my mom and I were planning my wedding, my father said almost the same thing: "She loves you so much. Do you know how much she's paying for this wedding? That's how much she loves you." When it comes down to it, luxury wasn't the substance of my childhood. Love was, simply, the time my parents gave me. What I wish my father had understood before he died is that of all those large-scale memories he and my mother spent so much money and energy creating, picking up poo is what has stayed with me my whole life.

*CHAPTER TWO*

# How to Sell Lemonade

Unlike most kids my age, I never went away for summers—not only did my father refuse to fly, he wouldn't allow me to go to summer camp. (My father was pretty overprotective. I wasn't allowed to sleep out at friends' houses until I was really old. I mean, *really* old. I remember crying to my friends about not ever getting to sleep over—and this was when I was a senior in high school and already owned my first car!) My father said he forbade summer camp because he'd miss me too much. But he worked such long hours. Maybe he was afraid I'd be kidnapped and held for ransom? Who knows. I never questioned decisions like that in our house. I was a polite kid. I never talked back. My parents made the rules and I respected them. So no August evenings spent around a campfire roasting marshmallows and telling ghost stories.

Instead, I spent plenty of summer days at my father's office on the Twentieth Century Fox lot. My dad was a big shot in TV. By the time I was six or seven, he'd created *Starsky and Hutch, Charlie's Angels, Fantasy Island, Vega$, Hart to Hart,* and others, and commanded respect on the studio lot where his production company, then Spelling-Goldberg Productions, had a mini-compound of bungalows out of which they worked. It was like a little town to me—all the bungalows were like little houses, but there were very few cars on the streets. One of my father's assistants would keep an eye on me while he was busy inventing hit shows. Sometimes Dad's driver would zoom me around the lot in a golf cart or let me take a turn at the wheel.

One day I decided to set up a lemonade stand on the lot. I put out Minute Maid lemonade and started selling it along with some little watercolors I'd done on tracing paper. They weren't prodigy art, just fingerpaint-level doodles. It was a hot day and I was doing some good lemonade business, and I must say I was pretty proud of my operation. Then a guy came up and said, "That's a great painting. I'm going to buy that." I knew it was just kid art and was kind of embarrassed, so I said, "You don't have to." He paused, seemed to glance around quickly, then said, "Yes, yes I do."

So I knew. I knew early on that I was Aaron Spelling's daughter and that fact made the people around me act differently. Because of that, I guess, all I wanted was to be normal. (Isn't that the way it always goes? Plenty of children spend their days wishing they were rich, and what do the rich kids do? Wish they were normal. I guess we all glamorize whatever it is that we aren't, but I know we rich kids can't go around asking for sympathy.)

One thing I had going for me was Nanny. I had a nanny for all of my childhood (and beyond). But to call her "a nanny" doesn't come close to doing her justice. For years I thought her name was actually Nanny—I had no idea to be a nanny was a job; I thought there was this woman in our family named Nanny, a confidante and guide and angel with whom I spent almost all my time. In the photos of my parents carrying me home from the hospital, my mother is pushing the pram, and my father and Nanny are on either side of her. And that's the way it was, except that in later pictures Nanny is often the one who was holding me.

Nanny, whose real name was Margaret, was like a mother to me. If we're all a mix of nature and nurture, my parents gave me my nature and Nanny was the nurture. Everything I learned, I learned from her. She was an African-American woman in her fifties, heavyset, with tightly curled hair she had set every week. She was always impeccably dressed in a white uniform, and nobody messed with Nanny, not even my parents, but she had a beautiful warm smile and an easy laugh. Nanny was like a family member and lived with us five days a week— and she stayed on with my parents when my brother and I moved out, until I was twenty-seven years old. Even after she moved out, Nanny was still at every family dinner, every holiday celebration, every Mother's Day. She was a permanent part of our family.

Nanny and I were so close—I'm sure at times it was tough on my mother. In third grade I wasn't doing well in math. It came to a head on one of Nanny's days off. I refused to go to school, claiming I was sick. I must not have been a good actress (who, me?) because my mother saw that I was faking. She sat me down to talk it through, and it finally came out that I never wanted to go to school again because I was afraid of the math teacher. My mother was very understanding, trying to calm me down and telling me we'd hire a tutor. But I got more and more worked up. All I would say through my tears was "I want Nanny, I want Nanny." Finally my mother called Nanny at home and put me on the phone with her. Even though it was her day off, Nanny came over. That was all I needed. Nanny's presence calmed me down. The anxiety about math had transformed—the real issue became needing my Nanny, and when she appeared, I knew everything would be okay. The three of us went out to dinner at Delores', my favorite hamburger joint. My mother couldn't have been thrilled. She'd done everything she could to help, and calling the off-duty nanny can't be a mother's best moment. I can still picture what her face looked like—chin up but not happy—even as a child I noticed her consternation, but only later did I understand what it meant.

I sometimes think this was a turning point for the relationship between my mother and Nanny. It must have hit her then or at another moment that I was closer to a woman she had hired than I was to her. It shouldn't have been a surprise to her—it was a dynamic she created and financed. But from then on my mother seemed to see Nanny as something of a threat. They had an up-and-down relationship. My dad didn't help matters by putting his arm around Nanny and saying, "I have two wives," and then winking and saying, "We all know who the real wife is." But ultimately, I'm grateful to my mother for doing what was best for me. She called Nanny that day. She kept Nanny on for my entire childhood and beyond. She let the relationship exist and flourish. When people ask me what it would have been like to grow up without money, what comes to mind is that I wouldn't have had Nanny. And if that were the case, I'd be a completely different person.

As far as I'm concerned, my time with Nanny was the real world. It kept me grounded. Lots of my childhood memories are with Nanny, and most of them don't match anyone's idea of how Aaron Spelling's daughter spent her youth. Nanny lived in Crenshaw, a mostly middle-class African-American district in South L.A. On weekends when I was young, Nanny would load me, then later me and Randy, into the station wagon, the family house car, and take me to her world. In Crenshaw we'd hang out with her friends and family. I remember spending hot afternoons sitting out on a small square of lawn in Crenshaw running back and forth through the sprinklers with playmates while Nanny chatted with her friends. A familiar jingle would sound and the ice-cream truck would come around the corner. I'd run over to buy a Push-Up, the only white kid as far as the eye could see. I loved going to Crenshaw with Nanny. I liked the small lawn and how all of Nanny's neighbors seemed to know each other. I liked being surrounded by other kids my age, playing whatever games occurred to us. I liked feeling like just another American kid. It made me feel completely safe. I don't know if my overprotective parents knew where we went with Nanny, but I have a feeling that they wouldn't have considered Crenshaw as safe for me as I did.

Like I said, I was stuck at home all summer, and when I wasn't in Crenshaw with Nanny or on the Fox lot inducing my father's employees to drop big bucks on powdered lemonade and over-priced scribbles, I'd hang around our house. Playing with my little brother or watching TV or anything that kids seem to do during long, unstructured summers seemed boring. I couldn't exactly go outside and play with the other kids on the block—our house *was* the block. The most happening thing in my neck of the woods was the housekeepers going about their daily activities. All I wanted was to be a part of it. So I'd ask if I could work with them. They'd scrub floors, I'd scrub floors. They'd clean windows, I'd clean windows. They'd fold laundry, I'd fold laundry. When they broke for lunch, I'd eat what they ate, when they ate, where they ate it. It was the closest to normal I could find.

At some point during the summer I was seven, I informed my mother that I was moving. She gamely asked where it was that I planned to go. It was the laundry room cupboard. I liked the idea of settling into someplace relatively small and warm. So I brought my bedding, my portable TV, and a stock of provisions, including a can of corn—I had no can opener, but a can of corn was somehow critical to survival—into the laundry room and took up residence. I lasted until bedtime.

Actually, it wasn't just my desire to be like everyone else that made me move to a smaller, less decorated, cozy room. The truth is that I didn't exactly feel safe in my own room. See, all those gorgeous Madame Alexander dolls (collectors' items, don't forget!) were lined up in cases along the wall facing my bed. Can you imagine how scary it was for a seven-year-old girl to see all those eyes staring down at you in the darkness? Couple that with the fact that my mom loved horror films and screened them for company. There I was, four years old, sitting on my mother's lap in a big, comfy chair, watching *Invasion of the Body Snatchers* starring Donald Sutherland. I never slept soundly again. Eventually, terror drove me into Nanny's room, where I slept in a twin bed next to hers until I was thirteen. That's right, Nanny and I were roommates.

As for my bed, the one I slept in only sometimes, for some reason it had bed railings to prevent me from falling out of bed. Bed railings. Until I was ten. As far as I know, I had no history of falling out of bed. Nobody ever talked to me about the dangers of falling out of bed or how I might avoid falling out of bed. That's just the way it was. My bed was pretty much a glorified crib. All this bed-sharing and crib-sleeping came to an embarrassing head when I was in the Brownies. I was about seven, and my mom was a troop leader. She may not have been reading me bedtime stories and playing Chasen's with me, but she was an involved parent in the ways that suited her personality. For her, involvement in Brownies was not unlike working at a charity event. She could organize brunches or troop activities.

One of the Brownie traditions was that your troop would "steal" you for breakfast. You'd be sleeping peacefully in your bed when, at the crack of dawn, your troop would surprise you. You'd join the growing group to go traumatize the next girl. Of course, the parents were in on the game, but the girls had no idea if and when it might happen. Now, my mom herself never dressed in any particular way for bed or told me what to wear. But one night she presented me with a frilly nightgown and matching bed coat and insisted that I wear them to sleep. I should have known something was up, but I was a good girl and pretty much followed my mother's word without question.

Early the next morning my Brownie troop came to my house to surprise me. I wasn't the first one pulled, so ten or so girls had already amassed, giggling and armed with flash cameras. They clamored into my room to wake me up. Oh, the embarrassment of what they saw:

There was my room, which looked like a hotel suite with its plum floral decor and complete absence of toys, stuffed animals, or games (all of which were strictly confined to the adjoining playroom). And my bed, holding center stage with its infantilizing bedrails. Even worse, the bed was empty. Where was I? Not in the laundry room cupboard, that's for sure. As my entire Brownie troop was about to find out, I was down the hall in Nanny's room. When they made their second surprise entrance, my heart sank. Why hadn't I anticipated this? Why hadn't I thought it through? And why, oh why, hadn't I figured out why my mother had outfitted me in a matching bedtime ensemble? Note to self: Sleep in own bed whenever presented with a frilly eveningwear set.

I slept with Nanny when I was scared, cleaned the house with the maids on summer vacation, and dreamed of relocating to the laundry closet. But I guess the ultimate story about how closely I identified with the household employees is the story of my first off-screen kiss. When I was fifteen years old, we had a young chef who was a total surfer dude—dark blond flippy California hair, a deep tan, a puka shell necklace, the works. At our house he wore a chef outfit—clogs and palazzo pants—but when he left, he headed to the beach in an OP shirt, board shorts, and flip-flops. He was always flirting with me, and needless to say, I ate it up. What fifteen-year-old wouldn't have a crush on the twenty-six-year-old family chef/surfer boy? My girlfriends and I would parade around the kitchen trying to get his attention, then we'd retreat to my bedroom and talk about what he had said and what I had said back and how well I had flirted and how it clearly meant he was completely into me. And every morning I'd come into school and report on each detail of our interactions: "When he put my sautéed halibut in front of me, our pinkies practically touched. He totally did it on purpose."

Then, on New Year's Eve, I took the bull by the horns (so to speak). As we usually did on New Year's, my parents, Nanny, my brother, and I were gathered in the family room. The TV was on, and we had noisemakers, hats, and Japanese confetti balls. My parents drank champagne, and there was Martinelli's sparkling cider for the kids. I had a friend over, and I was dressed up in a satiny blouse with shoulder pads and a skinny, double-looped belt around it (ah, the eighties). But how could I focus on the same old Times Square ball-dropping when I knew our cute chef was still in the kitchen, cleaning up from dinner? I'd stolen a few sips of champagne, and armed with liquid courage, I commanded my friend: "Stand guard. I'm going back there." I snuck back to the kitchen. He led me to the laundry room (See? I knew my affection for that room was well-founded!) and kissed me up against the dryer. It was amazing. It was huge. It would soon be the talk of the high school. I'd never had a boyfriend and now a twenty-six-year-old—an adult!—was putting the moves on me. How cool was that?

This went on for a couple months. We snuck kisses, and he hid little love notes in my school papers. After a school dance he came to drive me home and we made out in his red pickup truck. Sigh. But my heart was soon to be broken. During recess one day he pulled up to the side of the school. I jumped into his truck and we kissed for fifteen minutes. How cool was I? Then I went back to math class and passed notes with all the girls, reporting what had happened. One of the kids told her mother, she called my mom, and the shit hit the fan. I came home from school that day and saw that his pile of cookbooks was gone from the kitchen. I knew what that meant, and I started to cry. Nanny comforted me, but then she said, "Your parents are in their bedroom and they want to talk to you." They were furious (I can't understand why—just because their fifteen-year-old daughter was involved with a man *eleven years her senior*). I was grounded for five months, a lifetime, although in retrospect that was probably just to make sure I didn't see him again. (I later found out that my mother had us both followed for months.)

After my punishment was meted out, my mother pulled me into her bathroom saying she wanted to talk to me alone. She sat me on her chaise and stood above me, arms crossed. I started to tell her that I was in love with him, that she'd ruined my life by sending him away, and that I wanted to die—you know, the usual teen heartbreak drill. But she broke in and said firmly, "I need you to tell me right now. Was there penetration?" Ew. She used the word "penetration." Who says that? I was so grossed out. I almost vomited. "No, Mom!" Now I *really* wanted to die. My brother remembers walking into my room a few hours later to find me lightly sawing away at my wrists with a letter opener.

The next morning I came down to breakfast with bandages around my wrists. I hadn't actually hurt myself, but, drama queen that I was, I wanted to demonstrate just how miserable I felt. Nobody took any notice of my fake wounds, which just pissed me off more. I never saw the chef again. Actually, I did run into him once, in my twenties, outside a bar. He was kind of like, "Hey [wink, wink], you're all grown up!" And I was thinking: *Boy, you're short.* In my memory he was so tall . . . but now? Not so much. And all that surfing sun had taken its toll. But it was still a perfect first kiss, and to this day my mom is only half joking when she says, "He was the best chef we ever had. Too bad you had to ruin it."

## CHAPTER THREE

# Nepotism Works Both Ways

I'm getting ahead of myself. Let's go back a few years. I was shy. I didn't want to stand out, to make a fuss, to be different. Except when it came to one thing: acting. People always think I became an actress because I could—like my choice of career was just another present that my father had a plane drop in the middle of the lawn for me. Yes, my dad did give me parts and acting lessons, and yes, my name opened doors for me. I'll get to all of that. But *wanting* to act is different from having the opportunity to act, and for me wanting it started when I was only five.

It wasn't my dad who got me my first break. It was my mother's hairdresser. José Eber had long, flowing blond hair and always wore a different cowboy hat to hide his bald spot. José has been a big shot stylist to the stars for decades—at the time he was styling people like Farrah Fawcett, Cher, and Elizabeth Taylor. So José was making an appearance on a talk show called *Hour Magazine,* which was hosted by Gary Collins. They were doing a segment on styling celebrity children. José asked if I was willing to go on the show, and I agreed. I was really excited to be on TV. It was going to be me and Chastity Bono (who was much, much more sophisticated since she was all of nine years old).

On the day of the show my mother brought me to the studio. As soon as we arrived, they led us around the side of the stage to show me where I would be entering. When I looked out, I saw that there was a studio audience. For some reason I hadn't realized that there would be an audience. Suddenly I was terrified. I was shy, remember? As scary as those Madame Alexander dolls were, a whole crowd of *real* eyes staring out at me seemed infinitely worse. I freaked out and started saying I couldn't go out there in front of all those people. My mother, who never would be a pushy stage mother, told me I didn't have to do it. I could try it if I wanted, but it was okay if I wanted to back out. My hair was expertly styled, half up with curls and bangs that started prematurely at the crown of my head. I was wearing a fancy dress from the now-defunct department store Bonwit Teller. I'd promised José I'd do it, and, scared though I might be, I felt obligated.

I walked out onstage and gave the audience a wave and a smile. They applauded. That was encouraging, so I gave a little curtsy. Now, this may or may not be true, but the way I remember it was that when I curtsied, the audience went wild with applause. There I was, smiling and waving, loving the attention. It was my little Sally-Field-accepting-the-Best-Actress-Oscar moment—thinking, *They like me . . . right now they like me!* I'd always said that I wanted to be a veterinarian when I grew up. Or, failing that, a manicurist. But that night I went home and told my dad I wanted to be an actress.

Here's where the nepotism comes in. That summer my father promised he'd put me in one of his shows. As I mentioned, Vegas was pretty much our go-to vacation spot since you could drive there. Dad would rent a mobile home, and one of the drivers would transport us there while we watched movies in the back. For three weeks or so we'd stay in the penthouse at the Desert Inn, where my dad's show *Vega$* was filmed. In those days Vegas wasn't as family-friendly as it is now, but Randy and I loved running around the big hotel, hanging out at the pools, seeing movies during the day, and going to the arcade room. My mother always tried to find stuff for us to do, like visiting ghost towns or water parks. One time she arranged for us to go to a place called the Chicken Ranch. She thought we could see chicks hatching and feed the chickens. Dad had to explain to her that a chicken ranch was a whorehouse. She didn't believe him so she called to check. The woman who answered the phone identified herself as "Bubbles." When my mother asked if it was a kid-friendly place, Bubbles just started laughing.

Anyway, the summer after my onstage debut, my father wrote a small part in *Vega$* for me. I even had a line. I got to say, "Hi, Uncle Dan" to Robert Urich, who played Dan Tanna. Clearly a critical role that was central to the entire episode. On the day we shot "my" episode, my father came to the set. He stood behind the camera, all proud. I said, "Hi, Uncle Dan," the director said, "Cut!" and that was it. I was done. The director turned to me and said, "That's your new nickname. One-Take Tori." I was all impressed with myself.

After that my dad put me in all his shows. During the school year I'd always be gone for a week here and there doing small parts on *Fantasy Island* ("Hi, Uncle Roarke!"), *T.J. Hooker* ("Hi, Uncle T.J.!"), *Love Boat* ("Hi, Uncle Isaac!"), and the others. Just kidding about the actual lines. The truth is that the first time I was on *Fantasy Island,* I had one line with Tattoo. But by the time I made my second appearance, I'd refined my craft. I was one of the guests who came down the walkway out of the plane. My story line was that my parents had been killed in a car crash and I came to Fantasy Island to find God. George Kennedy played a drunk who claimed to be God. I was in the big leagues.

My father used to go over scenes with me before I went to an audition or shot a part. He'd give me direction, and after I did a scene, I'd look up for his reaction. When he thought I had it nailed, he'd say, "That was *plu*perfect," which he explained meant "more than perfect." He never stopped saying that to me. Even after my high school plays, he'd say, "That was pluperfect."

From the time I was really little—younger than ten—I prided myself on being very professional. I'd show up on time, report to hair and makeup, and sit without fidgeting as they prepared me for shooting. For better or worse I always knew my lines and everyone else's. If an actor called out for his line, I'd tell it to him. I had no idea it was annoying. One time on *T.J. Hooker,* William Shatner and I were doing a walk-and-talk scene. I played a gypsy girl who had witnessed her uncle being killed by the gypsy mob. We were walking out of the police station, and he was asking me questions. It was a pretty intense scene. Now, the tough thing about walk-and-talk scenes is that if you forget a line, you have to start over again from the very beginning. Shatner was forgetting his lines a lot, so I was helpfully reciting them to him. Finally he hissed, "That's not nice to do. You shouldn't tell an actor a line. That's why there's a script supervisor." My feelings were hurt—I was barely ten years old!—but I also suspected that he just felt bad because he couldn't remember his lines.

For decades I thought William Shatner was an asshole because of that moment. Then I worked with him on a movie called *A Carol Christmas* for the Hallmark Channel. It was a remake of *A Christmas Carol* where I played a modern-day Scrooge and Shatner played the Ghost of Christmas Present. It was a reversal from our *T.J. Hooker* moment, since now I was starring and he was a supporting character. He was incredibly nice and funny. And very professional. When an actor does a scene, the places where he's supposed to stand are marked with tape. I remember that he hit every single mark perfectly without ever looking down. Anyway, I couldn't believe I'd relied on my ten-year-old self's first impression for so long. Of course, I didn't tell him how he'd traumatized me. I knew he wouldn't remember. I'm pretty sure he was too distracted by the lovely and then-svelte Delta Burke, who was guest starring as my gypsy sister in the episode.

So, yes, it helped to have a father in the business. A lot. Some kids get summer jobs in their parents' offices or businesses. Me, I got bit parts in prime-time soaps. But even then, being Aaron Spelling's daughter wasn't always the ticket to success. At my elementary school the third-grade play was *Hansel and Gretel.* The entire class auditioned by reading the play out loud. When the cast list went up, I discovered that I'd won the coveted role of Gretel. Even though I was only in third grade, I was old enough to feel a sense of accomplishment. The previous year I'd played Becky in *Tom Sawyer,* so I'd gotten the lead part two years in a row! That had to mean something. This—acting—was my special gift. It had nothing to do with being Aaron Spelling's daughter. Or so I thought. It quickly emerged that the other children's parents were outraged that I'd gotten Gretel. They thought it was due to a conspiracy that I was given a lead role two years in a row. It had to have something to do with my father—either he'd given money or the school wanted him to give money.

I knew I'd won the role fair and square, but the parents made enough of a stink that the school just gave up. Did they replace me in the lead role? Nope, they simply canceled the play. Every other grade did a play, but ours was canceled. I was shattered. So much for believing in myself. So much for achieving something independent of my father. The irony was that while everyone thought my family was inflating my success, in fact it was hindering me. Little did I know it then, but this pattern would show up over and over again in my life: I achieve something; people think it's all because of my father; and ultimately, I come away with nothing, back at square one.

Around this time I started coming out of my shell a bit. Pre–Surfer Chef Incident, I was always a perfect child, very respectful, very polite. But somehow I began to realize that I could make my friends laugh by being funny and acting kind of nutty. I graduated to Westlake, a private all-girls' school, in seventh grade. As I came out of my shell, I started telling jokes and acting out stories, and the other kids seemed to like it. Eventually I started doing characters for them. My friend Dawn and I had an act where we were Roger and Ethel Spielonger, a married nerd couple. As Roger I wore glasses, a bow tie, and a pocket protector. Roger snorted whenever he laughed.

Mostly, we just performed for our friends. We'd announce that Roger and Ethel were going to make an appearance. They'd gather round, and we'd come out in our accessories, put on a show, and everyone would laugh. At the weekly school assembly we'd stand up as Roger and Ethel and announce what was going on that week in the drama department. It became kind of a cult thing at the school, where Roger and Ethel would be brought in to lead various events. Finally I wasn't just a girl with a famous father.

Meanwhile, I was trying to be a real actress outside of school. I'd been taking private acting lessons since I was eight, and after a couple years my coach decided I was ready to start auditioning. I may have been young, but I knew that acting exclusively in my father's shows didn't really count. So I got an agent and a manager. Then, when I was around eleven, the guy who'd been my manager for a year dropped me. According to my mother, he said I wasn't hungry enough. I always reflect on that comment. It was one of those defining moments that pushed me to take acting even more seriously. Being told I can't do something always makes me want to succeed. I'd show him. I still fantasize that if I ever win an award for anything, he'd be one of the many people I'd thank for telling me I couldn't do it.

Undaunted, I put together my very own acting résumé that had my name at the top, and below—well, it was pretty much a list of all my dad's shows, the only experience I had. Oh, except for a listing at the very bottom of the single school play I'd done. The first time I went in to audition for a school play at Westlake, I handed the drama teacher a head shot and a résumé. All the other kids came in and sped through some lines between classes. I thought I was being professional. I was twelve and totally clueless.

At home I started to voice my opinions about my famous father's work. I was opinionated about casting and dailies—the rough footage of his shows that he brought home every night. That year alone he had an unimaginable number of shows on the air—the workhorses: *Love Boat*, *T.J. Hooker*, and *Hotel*; the miniseries *Hollywood Wives* (based on Jackie Collins's book); *The Colbys* (a spin-off of *Dynasty*); a short-lived cop show called *Hollywood Beat*; and a couple TV movies. My dad was beginning to see me as more of an individual, a person with valid thoughts and ideas. I'd always been interested in casting. Even at the age of five when I'd see a movie with a child actor I thought was good, I'd run out of the room to fetch pen and paper. When the credits rolled, I'd write down her name and hand it to my dad, saying, "You should hire her." My father always paid close attention to my suggestions for edits and casting and took them seriously. In fact, Emma Samms is always saying she owes her career to me. I'd seen her as Holly on *General Hospital* and recommended her to my father for Fallon on *Dynasty*, a lead role that she had for five years. And it's not like my dad took advice from everyone. We'd be talking about a scene, my mother would start to interject, and he'd cut her off, saying, "Candy, please." Needless to say, this sort of behavior wasn't great for my relationship with my mom. But more on that later.

Eventually all the auditioning I was doing paid off. I did a movie with Shelley Long called *Troop Beverly Hills*, had a guest appearance on a show called *The Wizard*, and I appeared on the sitcom *Saved by the Bell*. When I auditioned for the part of Violet Bickerstaff on *Saved by the Bell*, I pretty much did my Roger Spielonger character, snorting when I laughed, and got the part. The producers of *Saved by the Bell* were happy enough with my performance that they kept bringing back my character. I even had my first kiss on that show. It was with Screech. It's true. My first kiss wasn't with the cool surfer/ chef eleven years my senior. It was with Screech, the biggest dork on national television. My dad had nothing to do with any of these jobs, and I was really proud of that. (I know, *Saved by the Bell* isn't *Citizen Kane,* but it was a well-earned paycheck.)

Then I made an interesting discovery while rooting through my father's briefcase. I liked to read his scripts and make casting suggestions, but this time I picked up a script for a pilot—the first episode of a TV show—called *Class of Beverly Hills.* As I started reading it, I realized that every single part called for someone my age. I was blown away—it was the first script I'd ever seen of his that had all teenage characters. At the time there weren't any hour-long dramas that had an all-teenage cast. I didn't really want to ask my father for a part—I was doing pretty well on my own. But I called my agent and told her about it. She said, "Do you want me to get you an audition?" I told her that I was embarrassed to go in as the boss's daughter. If I got the part, I wanted it to be because I deserved it. I said, "Can't you just tell them a fake name?" I'm sure she thought that was adorable. Here I was, a tenth grader, a kid actor trying to make it. No question she was going to drop my father's name. But she humored me, saying, "Okay, what fake name would you like me to give them?" I wanted to keep Tori—I knew if they called "Susan" or "Marie" up to the stage, I'd forget my alias and blow the whole audition. I'd just seen a TV movie of my dad's called *Rich Men, Single Women* in which Heather Locklear played a character named Tori Mitchell, so I just went with that. Subtle, huh? Next thing I knew, I had an audition set up with the director and casting director. There's not a shot in hell that they didn't know it was me.

I read for the part of a character called Kelly in *Class of Beverly Hills*. I didn't get Kelly, but they offered me the consolation part of Donna, a small character who had all of three lines in the pilot. Clearly, my dad had said, "Just give my daughter some small role." But I was happy to accept any part. Eventually it was all over the press that I'd auditioned for the role with a fake name but that everyone had known it was me. How exactly did that story get out? Oh, my father thought it was so cute that he told it all over town. And why did he have so many opportunities to tell it? Because *Class of Beverly Hills*, which was renamed *Beverly Hills, 90210*, would become a hit.

## CHAPTER FOUR

# They Hated Me at Hello

We shot the pilot for *Beverly Hills, 90210* when I was in tenth grade, and by the time eleventh grade started, the show was up and running. On the first day of work I arrived at the set an hour early, parked a block away, and sat there waiting—for an hour in my car—until the time I was scheduled to show up on set. The cast and crew knew I was the producer's daughter. Undoubtedly, they assumed that was why I had the job, and they weren't wrong. I had everything to prove. I was terrified, but I was used to being scared. Maybe it was growing up with the Madame Alexander dolls. Regardless, I was there early the first day; I planned to be early every day thereafter; and I was determined to say every line perfectly so nobody could find anything bad to say about me. I didn't expect they'd pay much attention to me anyway—I was just a bit player.

I was intrigued by my costars, but for a long time I was too shy to be myself around them. From the moment we met while filming the pilot, I had an insta-crush on Brian Austin Green, and there was always a little spark between us, through all the years of the show (more on that later). I thought Jennie Garth and Shannen Doherty seemed cool, but I barely spoke to them until a week into shooting the pilot, when we were almost done. There was a party scene with me, Jennie (who played Kelly), Shannen (who played Brenda), and a guest cast girl. The shoot went late, until midnight, and I started acting goofy and self-deprecating. Jennie said, "You're funny! You seemed so shy." It doesn't seem like much, but that was a turning point. From then on Shannen, Jennie, and I were friends. Ian Ziering (Steve) and Jason Priestley (Brandon) somehow seemed much older than I was, and we really only became friends years later. And as for Luke Perry (Dylan), when I first started, he was just the cool, inaccessible older guy. He was always flirtatious. He called me "Camel" because he said I had long eyelashes like a camel. Trust me, Luke Perry can call you "Camel" and make it sound sexy. When you were with him, he made you feel like you were the only other person in the world. But either because he was a guy or because of the age difference, it was tough for me to have a true heart-to-heart with him. Only later would I realize what a loyal friend he really was.

When the show first started, I had a really small part. Donna had about two lines per episode, and those lines were mostly complex dramatic encounters wherein I had to say something as deep and meaningful as "Hi, Brenda" or "See ya later, Kelly." Sort of the sixteen-year-old version of "Hi, Uncle Dan." Thank God for all those acting lessons.

So few lines, and yet in response to my delivery of them, the press had a field day. Maybe I should have known they'd target me because of my father, but it was my first real taste of negative press, and it was brutal: I couldn't act, and I was unattractive to boot. At first I was hurt, then a little annoyed. I mean: "Hi, Brenda." How could they possibly hear me say two words and conclude that I was a lousy actress? Seriously, anyone who could speak could do the lines I was doing. They were against me because of who I was. They hated me at hello. My dad advised me to stop reading the tabloids, but it was easier said than done. I was young and the criticism felt very public. But it also motivated me.

Having so few lines meant I had lots of time to think about what I could do to grow my part. *90210* was a drama, but I'd always been more of a clown. So I tried to find ways to stand out in the crowd. When Donna was in a group, I'd give her a funny reaction—rolling my eyes or grimacing or pursing my lips. The writers and producers noticed that I was something of a ham. They asked if I liked comedy, and when I said I did, it gave them a direction for Donna. They decided to make her ditzy, giving her plenty of physical comedy stuff. Stuff like Donna on Halloween: Everyone is going to a costume party and Donna is dressed like a mermaid and can't walk. Or Donna at the school formal: She comes in a *Gone with the Wind* dress and can't get out of the limo. All this was old hat to me—my Marie Antoinette costume and the other Halloween getups of my youth had given me plenty of practice with wardrobe-inflicted catastrophes.

Fitting in on the set didn't come quite so easily. Brian Green, who played David—my on-screen on-again, off-again, on-again boyfriend—and I were the youngest cast members. When the show started, they told us we'd have to have a tutor on the set to meet Screen Actors Guild standards. Great. Might as well wear a T-shirt saying DON'T BOTHER TALKING TO ME—I HAVEN'T GRADUATED HIGH SCHOOL. Then I found out that if I took the GED, I wouldn't have to have a schoolteacher on set. Bingo. I took and passed the GED. Now I no longer needed a tutor. No chaperone. Unfortunately, it also meant that there were no legal limits to how many hours I could work at one stretch. Sometimes our workdays were seventeen hours long. On top of that I was trying to keep up with my classes at Westlake because I wanted a degree from there. I'd spend all day on the set, get home at midnight, and have to do my schoolwork. But that was okay with me. I just wanted to be treated like everyone else, to hang with the older kids. And not to be seen as the producer's daughter. Whatever it took to fit in.

Little by little Donna became a bigger part of the show. The press could say whatever they wanted about how my father got me the part. I knew that Donna's character grew because I worked on her. The truth about my father was that he was perfectly content with me having a token role with two lines an episode. In fact, I was low-balled money-wise because he was embarrassed about the nepotism. Even during the second year on the show, when I was one of the leads, I still got paid the Screen Actors Guild minimum for a series regular—far below the escalating salaries of my costars.

*90210* wasn't an instant hit. But during the second season, just as I was graduating from high school and getting more mileage as Donna, it started to take off. As soon as we were big, the press followed. The whole cast did a photo shoot for *YM* magazine, and I was on the cover of *Sassy* and *Teen* magazines. I had just finished high school—it hadn't been long since I'd been reading these magazines, and now there I was in them. In fact, when my dad was casting *90210,* I grabbed my teen magazines and recommended Jason Priestley (whom I'd seen in the sitcom *Sister Kate*) and Shannen Doherty (whom I knew from *Heathers* and *Our House*). When my dad saw the photo of Jason, he said, "He's really good-looking." Next thing I knew, he was cast as Brandon.

Not only was the show doing well, but it seemed like as soon as I finished high school, the cast started accepting me. I could tell because they'd talk about my dad as a producer in front of me without being afraid that I'd go tattle. They were comfortable and knew we were all in it together. Oh, but of course it wasn't always that simple. I was on *90210* for ten years, from when I was sixteen to when I was twenty-six, so for better and for worse I grew up on the show.

My life was on the set, which meant I had a full-time job while everyone I knew was starting college. It kind of sucked that I didn't get to go to college. Instead of walking into a dorm room, meeting my roommate, and signing up for classes, I got to hear about it from my friends and then act it out on TV. At least I didn't have to gain the freshman fifteen, puke up grain punch every night, or write papers. But the flip side was that all my flirtations and friendships were on the job. There I was, trying to grow my character, develop as an actor, and generally conduct myself in a professional manner, and at the same time I was completely caught up in the drama of who was flirting with whom and who was sleeping with whom.

And there was plenty of drama. In fact, sometimes instead of going to college, it felt as if I was reliving high school. And not just because of the topic of the show. The whole cast was young: Brian and I were the same age. Jennie was a year older than we were, Shannen three years older, Jason four years older, Luke and Ian ten years older, and Gabrielle Carteris (who played Andrea) was twelve years older. For a while these people were my whole social world. When someone knocked on my dressing room door, there was always a flutter of *Who's it going to be—Luke Perry or Brian Green?* Or Jason would pop into my dressing room to say hi and I'd be psyched.

The split center of this high school clique was definitely Shannen and Jennie. The press about Shannen was harsh. She'd been famous since she was young, starring in *Little House on the Prairie, Our House,* and the movie *Heathers.* Shannen had everything, but she could be arrogant and carefree. Meanwhile, Jennie worked hard. She started at the bottom and appreciated what she had. And Jennie was outspoken when she thought Shannen was out of line. Shannen didn't appreciate that. She liked to be in control. Sometimes they got along, but there were explosions. Once, walking back to their cars, they actually got into a fistfight. Ian and Brian had to break it up.

I always felt like I was in the middle. If I wanted to have lunch with Jennie, I'd sneak into her dressing room so Shannen didn't come looking for me. And there were times Shannen would say, "Let's ignore Jennie. When she talks to us, pretend you don't hear her." Then other days Shannen would say, "Let's do something nice. Let's go out for drinks and invite Jennie." When Shannen reached out, Jennie always responded—who wants that kind of friction?—but Shannen, for no apparent reason, might change her tune again the next day. It was all so unnecessary.

Shannen took me under her wing, and because I didn't know any better, I gratefully accepted my new perch. A night with Shannen meant going to the hottest club and drinking until the early hours. I knew she was a "bad influence," but I liked her anyway. She made the rules, and I never said no. She'd say, "We're having lunch in my dressing room today," and we would. I just followed her around obediently, but we had fun together. I heard later that Shannen used me to get her way on set. If Wardrobe gave her a dress she didn't want to wear, she'd say, "Tori said it doesn't look good, and she's going to tell her dad if you don't change it." The producers, wardrobe, makeup, and hair people believed her. Only later, when they knew me better, did they realize that I didn't pull that stuff. I didn't go all diva for myself, so why in the world would I do it for her?

There were different cliques at different times, but for the most part the cast and crew functioned as a close, hardworking family. We saw people get married and divorced. Friends left the show, came back, and left again. We took trips together—to Big Bear and Palm Springs—and in the course of the ten years the show was on the air, everyone in the cast pretty much slept with everyone else, and no serious relationships ever developed. We all would laugh about it years later. At the end of the day we were always together and always there for one another.

During my time on *90210*, I had my first serious boyfriend and my worst serious boyfriend. I met Ryan right before we both graduated from high school. I was just turning eighteen. He was friends with four of my best friends: Jenny, Mehran, Jennifer, and Kevin— lifelong friends I'd met a couple years earlier, just before I started on *90210,* when they were all still in high school together in the Valley. Ryan had a summer job working at his dad's tire shop, but he'd take me out to dinner, which none of my high school boyfriends ever did (unless you count our chef, but cooking for my whole family isn't exactly "going out"). On our first date he took me to Benihana in the Valley. And as the summer went on, Ryan would pick me up and take me to Islands for burgers and fries. It was my first real relationship—the kind where you see each other or talk on the phone every day. One afternoon, after his cousin's bar mitzvah, we ended up in his room, and I had sex for the first time. It's funny, the details you remember about the important moments in your life. I remember that I was wearing a Betsey Johnson tank dress. It was stretchy black cotton with peach flowers. It was an unplanned milestone—it just happened. Then I went home and got in bed and cried. I was eighteen—I definitely thought I loved him. But I'd done something irreversible. I'd shut the door on my childhood. If that doesn't deserve a good cry, I don't know what does.

After Ryan and I shared a romantic summer together, he went away to college for his freshman year. The next year he transferred to USC to be close to me. But suddenly I was busy, working on *90210,* going to parties and clubs—my life was changing rapidly.

The MTV Video Music Awards, a hip awards ceremony, was really my first big event. Ryan wanted to go with me as my date. I admit that this is a reasonable notion for a boyfriend to have. I didn't want to say no, but I didn't want to hang out with him at the show. I wanted to flit around and try out my new stardom. So I told him he couldn't go with me, but I did get him and my brother tickets to the show. That's right, I set him up with my fourteen-year-old brother.

That year Shannen was presenting an award. It was also the year that Howard Stern did his famous—or rather infamous—"Fartman" bit onstage with Luke Perry. That's how hot *90210* was. My hair was in an updo, my makeup was professionally done, and I was wearing a short, tight, cream Vivienne Westwood bustier dress. Shannen was in black, with big red lips. When she saw me, Shannen said, "I'm so glad you're finally here." Then she kissed me right on the middle of my cheek, leaving a mark with her red lips as if to say, *You look good. Remember who's boss.* I'd been tagged. When I tried to wipe off that lipstick, along came half of my painstakingly applied makeup. (Also, for the record, my bra was completely stuffed with toilet paper. Now they have real contraptions for that. For years I just used toilet paper. I was so lucky it never fell out.)

Aside from the lipstick smudge on my cheek, I was feeling glamorous and important at the afterparty. I said a quick hi to Ryan and my brother, then left with my friends. Nice, huh? So much for stardom not changing a person. We went out for two years, but the relationship had lost its footing. *90210* was my career *and* my social life. Meanwhile, Ryan would stay at my parents' house and just hang out with my little brother when I was busy. It seemed pathetic, and I lost respect for him. In retrospect I know that wasn't totally fair. I'd gotten swept up in my brand-new world of success and fame. Um, can I get away with "It happens to the best of us"?

I had a thing for bad boys, and Ryan was a good boy, so of course I ended up cheating on him and leaving him. Just to be completely unoriginal, I cheated on Ryan by hooking up with my costar Brian for the first time. It was a no-brainer. Brian was the only guy on the show my age. We were having the experience of becoming famous together—in a way we were the only people who understood what the other was going through. Plus, I'd had my eyes on him from the moment we did the pilot.

Brian and I had something going (or not going) over the years we worked together. We dated on the show, but it wasn't just on TV where we connected. We were always getting into fights, but it was the same kind of crush-teasing as when a boy pulls your pig-tail. During one summer hiatus we made a personal appearance at Disneyland (Donna and David do Disneyland). Brian was being mean to me, and we had a huge fight in the middle of a crowd of fans. Finally I said, "I hate you and I'm never speaking to you ever again." He grabbed my arms and said, "Did you ever consider that I start fights with you because I'm in love with you?" Whoa. This was news. I said, "Really? I love you too!" Then we realized that we were surrounded by people. He led me behind a concession stand and kissed me.

There was some puppy love there, but I don't think Brian was quite comfortable being himself—in the years we knew each other, he went from white rapper to spiritual to cool. With his shifting interests, sometimes I fit in and sometimes I didn't. He'd flirt with me, then blow me off. One summer we kind of dated, in that unde-fined, group date, hookup kind of way. When we were involved, being together on the show made real life feel like more than it was, and it was nice to have an excuse to kiss. But other times we'd go out together, then he'd call me the next night and ask for my friend's number. *Then* it was harder to be his loving girlfriend on the show. The next week he'd say, "But I like *you*." We were always fighting, and making up, and having fun together, and hating each other. We were just young.

All that back-and-forth was pretty much over by the time our characters got married. The series finale of the show was our wedding: "David and Donna get married," and afterward I had a surge of wondering if I was still in love with him. It seemed so real on camera. I told Jennie Garth I still felt a connection with him, but she said it was probably a normal side effect of the plot. As we played out that fairy-tale wedding, I was swept up in the romance of it all. (And it wouldn't be the last time a perfect wedding seemed like all I could ever want.) Afterward it faded away and I realized Jennie was right—it was just filming. Strangely, Brian is the only fellow cast member I haven't seen since the day the show ended. There's no real reason that I know of. Our characters may still be happily married somewhere, but whatever we had just faded away.

Ryan was my first real boyfriend, and after him came the worst boyfriend: Nick. I met Nick out at a club with my friend Jennifer. They'd gone to elementary school together. I'd just come off dating Ryan, and if Ryan was a pushover, Nick was the opposite. He was charming and cool. He smoked cigarettes, drank, had a tattoo, and took me to clubs. Everywhere we went, he knew actors and club promoters. Ryan and I had walked side by side holding hands. If Nick took my hand, he led the way. Even though we were the same age, he seemed like such a man.

Shannen's boyfriend and Nick became best friends, so the four of us would go out to clubs and even take vacations together. We all went to Hawaii for an unforgettable vacation. We stayed at the Westin on Maui, and the first surprise was that the paparazzi had actually sent crews to photograph us. It was my first taste of being followed. In the beginning we had the standard Maui vacation: lying out on the beach, snorkeling, hiking, going to a luau. But then Shannen and her boyfriend did the drive to Hana, which is supposed to be the most beautiful road in the world. On a beach in Hana he asked her to marry him and gave her a huge five-carat ring. The next day I heard screaming and crashing coming from their room. Her boyfriend stormed out, and Nick followed him. I heard Shannen yelling at the top of her lungs and crying. I gathered something about him threatening to go home the next day and the engage-ment being in jeopardy. I stepped out in the hallway to see if I could help. The corridor was strewn with shattered glass, and maids were hurrying this way and that. Shannen informed me that she'd "gotten him back." She told me that she'd gone down to the gift shop and asked for their most expensive item. It was a two-thousand-dollar crystal dolphin. She'd said, "Charge it to his room," then had come upstairs and smashed it down the hallway. Hence the glass. Crystal dolphin? Two thousand dollars. That never-taken paparazzi shot of an enraged Shannen hurling it down the hallway? Priceless.

Back in L.A., I'd been living with my parents in their house. Well, "house" is an understatement. My parents had purchased Bing Crosby's old estate in Holmby Hills, a pricey, exclusive neighborhood in western L.A. I had my twelfth birthday party in Bing Crosby's old house, but soon afterward they demolished it and started from scratch. My mother named it "The Manor" and had pens made that said STOLEN FROM THE MANOR. The Manor is supposedly the largest single-family residence in California—about forty-six thousand square feet (slightly over an acre) and 123 rooms. I mean, I can't say I ever counted the rooms—that's just what I read in the papers.

Anyway, we didn't move in until I was seventeen so, big as it is, it wasn't exactly a huge part of my youth. And now my mother was encouraging me to move out. This was the woman who had insomnia and sat up every night, watching horror movies and waiting for me to come home. Now the inconsistency of my schedule was tough on her. I was out late clubbing. Or I'd sleep over at Nick's house without calling home. It was too much. I was planning to move in with a friend, but Nick talked me out of it at the last minute. He said, "We're always together anyway. Let's just live together." So just before I turned twenty, Nick and I moved into our own apartment.

We rented an apartment in The Dorchester, a full-service building in the Wilshire Corridor, a two-block stretch of desirable condo buildings between Westwood and Beverly Hills. For dinner the night we moved in, I boiled pasta and served it with Ragú sauce from a jar. We ate it on two stools in the kitchen—we didn't have all our furniture yet—but I felt so grown up. I was on my own for the first time. I was cooking my own meal, and soon I'd be doing my first load of laundry and ironing clothes, folding them and putting them away. I was only nineteen years old and I'd barely had time to fantasize about this life: shacking up with the man I loved. Now here we were. Alone.

The show was doing well, and Donna was one of the main characters, but I was still one of an ensemble. Then something happened that put me in a different category. I got offered a TV movie. I was sent a script and an offer for one hundred thousand dollars. This was huge. Not only was that a lot of money—my dad still had me on a relatively low salary at *90210*—but it was the first time in my life I'd been offered a job without having to audition. I took it.

The script was called *Death of a Cheerleader*, though by the time the movie came out (in 1994), it had been changed to *A Friend to Die For*. It starred me and Kellie Martin, who was then on the family drama *Life Goes On* and was a big TV name. It actually wasn't the first time Kellie Martin and I had been in a movie together. Years earlier we'd both been in *Troop Beverly Hills*, but she'd had a starring role and I'd only had a small part and felt excluded by her and the other child stars. But now that we were in a movie together and on the same level, she was perfectly sweet and seemed to have no memory of the early teen on-set cliqueyness.

Ironically, in *A Friend to Die For* I'm a popular cheerleader and Kellie Martin's character wants to be in my group—to be me—and winds up killing me. My character was a snotty bitch, which was a nice change for me since on *90210* I was "sweet Donna Martin," the girl next door. In fact, I was so shy and sweet that it was a little scary to do that role. But I thought it might be the turning point for a career in which I'd prove my diverse range. . . . Well, not so much. To date, that's essentially the only bitch role I've gotten to play.

Years later, when I went to NBC to pitch my sitcom *So NoTORIous*, one of the executives said that he was working on TV movies for NBC when *A Friend to Die For* aired. He remembered its premiere as a milestone. He explained that TV movies come and go in popularity, and they hadn't been doing well at the time. Only an older generation was tuning in. As I mentioned, before *90210* there weren't really any teen dramas. Teens only appeared as the youngest players in family shows. The same thing was going on with TV movies. They all starred Valerie Bertinelli, who was in her mid-thirties. She wasn't over-the-hill by any means, but definitely not a teen. According to this executive, *A Friend to Die For* was NBC's attempt to test the market for TV movies with younger stars. They didn't know what audience would watch, if any.

At that time TV movies were on Monday nights up against football. The night it aired, *A Friend to Die For* took away more than half of the football game's male viewers. I guess men who like football also like to watch blond cheerleaders die. It was the highest-rated TV movie of the year, and it would be years before another surpassed its numbers. In doing that single movie, I went overnight from being Aaron Spelling's overprivileged daughter to being an in-demand actress who had scripts pouring in every day. It was a huge milestone in my career.

Suddenly I was NBC's golden girl. They wanted me to star in every single TV movie. Before and after work I was at home reading script after script. I did three movies in a row for NBC, but I also did them for the other networks. And no matter which network it was—CBS, ABC, NBC, et cetera—it was one woman-in-peril movie after another. How did they want me stalked? Let me count the ways. Stalked in high school. Stalked on campus. Stalked while skiing. Stalked while stripping. Stalked while skiing and stripping. Stalked while whistling Dixie on the White Cliffs of Dover.

Because I was the key star, I had some power. Now I had some say in casting and production. I wasn't smart enough to ask for producing credit, but I should have. There I was, nineteen years old, and I'd be sitting there with the producers, writers, and executives, giving notes like, "This line doesn't make sense here because we already revealed this in the story." I loved being a part of the process—guess all those years giving unofficial help to my dad had gotten into my system. (And I don't mean helping him get rid of dog poo, though sometimes there were similarities.)

I was crazy busy. On top of *90210,* I did TV movies constantly— three a year for two years. The minute *90210* broke for Christmas I'd start shooting a movie, finishing right before we were due back on the set. And during summer break I'd do two more, back-to-back.

The press started calling me the "TV movie queen," saying that I was taking over where Valerie Bertinelli had left off. We (meaning my management) started worrying that I'd be pigeonholed, that all this TV queendom would interfere with my ability to get feature films. All I really cared about was playing a great role, no matter what medium. But a young actor's management always steers her toward features because they're what make you a big star. Hindsight likes to admonish me that I never should have stopped doing those stalker flicks. They were so lucrative, and at the time that I pulled back from them, I had the highest salary for a female actor in a TV movie.

The first time I realized that people recognized me was in a mall in L.A. when I heard a group of girls screaming, "Donna!" I looked around for the other Donna, the person who had the same name as my character. Then I realized they were talking to me. To this day I'm still kind of oblivious when people come up and wave. I always think I must know them from somewhere and am about to get in trouble for not knowing their names. I've never gotten to the point where I just assume they know me from TV—in a way I hope I never do.

Before my Monday-night stardom I'd been one of a bunch of young stars in a hit drama. Suddenly I was much more widely known. I'll never forget being at the register of a store in the Beverly Center—my favorite mall at the time—waiting to pay for something and hearing two nearby girls talk about me. One of them said, "Oh my God! That's Tori Spelling."

The other one said, "No, it's not."

"Yes, it is." They went back and forth like this pretty loudly until finally one of them said with absolute certainty, "No, it's not. That girl's much prettier than Tori Spelling." Thanks . . . I think.

## CHAPTER FIVE

# America's Virgin

My relationship with Nick changed slowly, but drastically. In the beginning it seemed a result of my increasingly hectic schedule. When we first started dating, we'd go out together. Now as I was arriving home from work, he was leaving to go out. I guess he missed having me with him, so he took my bank card to keep him company. And he must have missed me a whole lot, because to deal with the loneliness, he withdrew the maximum—five hundred dollars—*every day*. Nick was losing lots of money gambling. One year my whole season's salary went to the gambling debts. He would play big-stakes poker games, lose twenty-five thousand dollars, and then I would write him a check.

The concept of managing my money was completely foreign to me, but not to Nick. What better accessory for a high roller than a slick ride? When Nick and I started going out, I still had the same car my parents had given me when I was sixteen—a BMW convertible. Yes, I got a BMW convertible as soon as I could drive. Every teenager's fantasy, right? Not me. What I really wanted was a red Volkswagen Rabbit convertible. I didn't want some showy, expensive car that people would notice and hate me for. I was insecure enough as it was. The Rabbit was cute, cool, and, above all, normal. It was my dream car. My mom thought they were too unsafe. She said, "Well, if you *were* to get a BMW, what color would you want?" I said that I wanted a white or red Rabbit, but on the BMW lot, which my mother insisted we visit, she pointed to a BMW and said it was "great for blondes—that shimmery champagne color," but I held my ground. Why should they spend three times as much money on a car I didn't even want?

At my sweet sixteen party, an all-girls' luncheon, my parents presented me with . . . a champagne convertible BMW, with a big bow around it. Surprise! Far be it from me to complain about getting a luxury car for my birthday as a teenager. I'm fully aware that this story is unlikely to make the average reader go, "She wanted one car, but her parents gave her a different, more expensive car? The poor thing!" But, again, it was never about what I wanted. And for some reason, when Donna got a car on *90210,* my father made sure it was the same champagne convertible BMW. I have no idea why. Maybe he agreed with my mother that it was the best color for my hair?

Now, three years later, Nick convinced me we should get rid of the champagne mobile and have two cars for the two of us: a Jeep Cherokee and a black Porsche Carrera. A Porsche! Had I turned into a Porsche kind of girl? I didn't think about it. I just followed his lead.

The Porsche cost nearly half my annual salary. One week after we brought it home, Nick totaled it. To add insult to injury, someone told me that he'd left a club with a girl and was driving her home in our car. When I confronted him, he said, "You're pathetic. What's wrong with you? I was in a car accident, and *this* is what you care about?"

Nobody had ever spoken to me like that before. But with the money drain came other changes. Suddenly Nick and I had a volatile relationship with crazy fights. He'd tell me I was ugly and, again, pathetic. I'd find notes in his pockets from girls. I'd break up with him, have all the locks changed, then he'd call and I'd take him back. I kept hoping that the guy I'd fallen in love with would come back. I knew he was in there somewhere, and I blamed myself for losing him.

I didn't really talk to anyone about Nick and our problems. He'd drawn me away from my family and friends to the point where I was either with him or home alone. It was hard to gain perspective. Part of me was scared of him, and partly I must have liked the drama, but eventually his name-calling came true: I *was* just pathetic and terrified. I'd give him money and beg him not to leave me.

My dysfunctional home life eventually started to creep into my work. One time I did a cover shoot and interview for *Sassy,* the now-defunct kick-ass teen magazine edited by Jane Pratt before she did *Jane.* The article was supposed to feature me as a young, popular, rich, successful actress. The writer came to the photo shoot to do what writers normally do at photo shoots—write down stuff like, *Tori arrives fifteen minutes late with her lapdog in tow. She's cheerful and apologetic, wearing a babydoll dress, leggings, and Guess mule boots.*

You know the drill (early-nineties style—now every actress is always wearing jeans and a T-shirt).

Nick was supposed to come with me to the shoot, but he'd gone out all the night before and was too hungover to join me. We got into some fight about him being out so late. I left. I cried on the way, then Nick showed up and the fight continued while I got ready in the dressing room. He accused me of telling people at the photo shoot that he wasn't being nice. "They're all looking at me funny. I'm sure you said something."

The writer overheard us arguing. What was she supposed to do, ignore it? *Sassy* wasn't a fluff magazine.

I was so excited for the magazine to come out. It was my first solo cover. But I was in for a surprise. There I was on the cover, looking sweet and angelic in a white flowing peasant top, with natural-looking hair and makeup. The photo was captioned *America's Virgin,* but the headline read POOR PITTLE RICH GIRL. The article talked about how I had so much in my life but wasn't exactly living the dream. It said I looked sad, like I'd been up all night crying. I'm sure I did, after my teary drive to the photo shoot. That article could have been a wake-up call, but it wasn't. Instead, when it came out, all I could think about was how when Nick saw it, I'd get in trouble, and indeed I did. He blamed me, saying, "You provoked me, and now people think I'm a bad guy."

*Sassy* wasn't the only bad press my relationship with Nick got. In part this was because we'd have fights in public, and he was no stranger to the barroom brawl. But also in the beginning I was young and suddenly in a difficult relationship. I trusted the journalists—I was open with them about what I was going through and how it felt.

Turns out that wasn't such a good idea. I talked too much and I was too honest. I had to learn the hard way that the press is not your friend (but not exactly the enemy either).

For one of my movies I did an interview with *Playboy*. Plenty of major actors do it. As part of the interview *Playboy* likes to pose semi-risqué questions such as "What's your favorite body part?" or "Where have you had sex in public?" I was as candid and irreverant as usual. One of the questions was "If you could have a threesome with a famous Hollywood couple, who would it be?" I said Tom Cruise and Nicole Kidman. Next thing you know, it was all over the *National Enquirer* and other tabloids: "Tori Spelling is looking for a ménage à trois." Hello? They *asked*.

The day that *Playboy* interview came out, Army Archerd, a *Variety* columnist who was an old friend of my father's, called him at the office. My dad had no idea about the interview, and Archer took him off guard, asking, "How do you feel about her article in *Playboy*? Did you know she says her butt is her favorite body part?" My dad didn't know that it was a respectable interview to give. I mean come on, Jimmy Carter did it. Regrettably, my dad replied, "It certainly doesn't sound like Tori. It's certainly not the Tori I know." The next day *Variety's* gossip column announced that my father was ashamed of my candid "sex article," and every other magazine followed suit.

At the time I was new to being tabloid fodder, and this seemed like a big deal. Since we never talked directly about feelings in my family, when difficult issues arose, we often wrote letters back and forth—even when we were all in L.A. and/or reachable by phone. Now I wrote my father a letter saying, *Don't you know when you're talking to press you can't say things like that? It always gets misconstrued.*

*I did nothing wrong and now look what I'm dealing with.* My being in the public eye had triggered an in-print family conflict. This time it was short-lived—my father quickly apologized. But in the not-too-distant future the tabloids would be the primary medium in which my family drama played out.

Some of the snark I faced had nothing to do with my inexperience dealing with the press. It was just the nature of the beast. There was a story in the *Globe* when I was seventeen or eighteen. I saw myself on the cover and bought the tabloid for the first time. I thought it was cool that I was now considered a big enough star to be tabloid fodder. I waited only until the first red light on my drive home to flip to the page where I appeared. There I found a photo of me when I was maybe twelve next to a current photo. Circles and arrows pointed out all the plastic surgery I'd supposedly had done. It was no secret that I'd had my "gigantic" self-image-demolishing nose done when I was sixteen. But the article went on to say I'd had my chin reshaped, cheek implants added, and some ribs removed. There were quotes from people saying, "I went to grade school with her and she looks totally different now." Um, it's called *puberty*. Idling at the now-green stoplight, I started to cry. And that was *before* I knew that the plastic surgery myth would shadow me for years, effective immediately.

The next time I learned about my own plastic surgery in the press came after I'd gone to Hawaii with Nick, Shannen, and her boyfriend. In Hawaii, Nick and I had been seduced into buying a parrot as a pet. It was an eclectus parrot we named Charlie even though it was a girl. She was gorgeous: bright red with a rainbow tail. When we were home, we'd let her out of her cage, and she'd fly around the apartment imitating me, saying, "Hi, Charlie bird. Charlie's a pretty girl." But I was working long hours, and Charlie wasn't getting enough attention. Not only that, I suspect that Nick was mean to her. I heard him screaming at her, and one time I saw him blow cigarette smoke in her face. Poor Charlie started to rebel. Out of her cage, she'd sneak up behind you very quietly, then lunge and bite your Achilles tendon. One time she literally chased me and my friend Jenny down the hallway, squawking and flapping. We hid in the bathroom as she hurled herself at the door for forty-five minutes. It was scary and heartbreaking.

Despite the bad behavior, I still loved Charlie. Every night when I came home, I'd go up to her cage, say, "Hi, Charlie bird," and kiss her through the cage. But one night when I walked in, she didn't say hello. When I put my face up to the cage, instead of tapping me gently with her beak, she grabbed my nose and wouldn't let go. When she finally released me, I thought, *God, that really hurt.*

I walked into the bathroom to assess the damage, and all I could see was blood pouring onto my shirt. In a panic, I called Nick. "Charlie just attacked me. Can you take me to the emergency room?" He said, "I can't do it. I'm on the freeway on my way to the casino. Call your mother." Then he hung up. Far be it from me to stand in the way of him spending thousands more of my hard-earned dollars.

My mother came to pick me up. On the way to the hospital she had the presence of mind to call a plastic surgeon. When he examined me, he said that if the bite had been any deeper, my nose would have come off.

Back at *90210* they temporarily wrote me out of the scenes, but after a couple days I had to go in and be on camera with a Band-Aid on my nose. The story on the show was that Donna's foster dog had nipped her. But the story in the tabloids was that I'd had another nose job. VENGEFUL PARROT BITES TORI SPELLING! As if I'd make that up.

A few years later I had almost the opposite experience. Instead of being mauled by an animal and requiring plastic surgery, I . . . well . . . it really starts with me lying flat on my back at my parents' house. Right after you have your boobs done, your whole chest is tightly bound. You're immobile, eating ice chips and pain- killers, unable to sit up on your own. There I was, watching TV, when a light went on in the hallway. The door opened, and my mother was standing there, holding Gracie by the collar. Gracie was a dog I rescued off the street when I was filming *House of Yes*. She was a sixty-pound wheaten terrier mix, and now she was panting and lunging toward me, eager to jump on my compro- mised chest. I still see it now: my mother in the doorway, the dog anxiously lunging and pawing the air in my direction. My mother said, "Gracie's here!" and, as if in slow motion, I saw her hand release Gracie's collar.

Gracie leaped. I screamed. Help arrived. I was convinced that my mother had done it on purpose. My mother was outraged, saying, "Here I am taking care of you. I can't believe you'd think I would try to hurt you." We didn't speak for two days. And then it went away, but I still always wonder whether, consciously or not, she brought that dog up and let her go on purpose. (And, by the way, I never tried to claim that my boob job was the result of a dog attack.)

* * * *

Back in TV land, Donna was still a pure vestal virgin. In this case, rumors are true. My dad couldn't stand the thought of making my character sexually active. All the other characters were coupling and uncoupling, so the writers figured they'd make something of Donna's innocence. She'd be a popular high school girl who was proud to be a virgin and didn't care if people thought it was uncool. Her friends would support her. All those chaste viewers could relate to her.

As a teenager when all of this went down, I initially worried that I'd be the only character who didn't get to have a cute boyfriend on screen. But the writers were onto something. As soon as Donna's commitment to virginity was revealed, there were some amazing reactions. People my age would come up to me on the street and thank me for being a role model. Girls and guys alike. And this was L.A., not Utah. Suddenly I felt like I was doing something important.

But at home things weren't so inspirational. After a night of partying Nick wound up in the emergency room. While I waited for him to be released from the hospital, a girl called to find out if he was okay—she'd dropped him off at six a.m.

Nick was seeing other women rampantly, flagrantly, and a bunch of other adverbs I never imagined I'd have to use to describe my boyfriend's behavior. It was to the point where a few days into a press tour in New York, I got a call from my friend Melissa. She told me that she'd called our apartment (where I paid all the rent and bills and bought all the furnishings and food) and some girl who answered the phone identified herself as Nick's girlfriend. As insane as it sounds, the next day I hurried out to buy him a Rolex watch. I was so worried that he'd leave. You may find this hard to believe, but giving him a gift when he cheated on me didn't seem to stop the cheating. Crazy, I know.

Meanwhile, Nick was aggressively jealous of me. When Casper Van Dien, who went on to star in *Starship Troopers,* came onto *90210* to play my boyfriend for a few episodes, he flirted with me. Casper was a heartthrob, sweet and absolutely gorgeous. One time he called me at home and Nick picked up the phone. When Casper asked for me, Nick freaked out, threw the phone at me, and pushed me into the kitchen counter. I picked up the phone and shut myself in the bathroom. On the other end of the line Casper was distraught, insisting that I call the police, but I told him it was nothing, that I was fine. Still, back on set, he made me take pictures of the huge purple bruise on my thigh in case I decided to press charges.

Casper wasn't the only cast member expressing concern. The cast of *90210* cared about me and was never pro-Nick. Jennie regularly got into fights with him in front of me, all of which started with her saying she couldn't let him speak that way to me. Luke and Jason were also protective. Jason was always pleasant to Nick's face, but Luke made no effort to hide his hatred. I'd get in trouble for that: Nick would yell at me, saying, "What lies are you telling them? Why do you make people hate me?" Even Shannen would say, "Nick is bad news," but never to his face, since we always socialized with her and her boyfriend. That's right, the notorious Shannen Doherty was telling me my boyfriend was bad news. You'd think it would have sunk in. But it didn't.

Nick and Luke finally came to blows at my parents' annual

Christmas Eve party. It was an extravagant event, of course, but on a more intimate scale. The guests were a mixture of my parents' friends, my father's business associates, cast members, and my brother and my friends. There was caviar and shrimp cocktail, but also sandwiches from Nate 'n Al's, an old-school Hollywood delicatessan. The bartender refilled your glass between sips of champagne, so everyone got wasted. The same piano player played every year, and carolers would make an appearance to sing Christmas songs. I loved those parties. They were relaxed and, despite the extravagant touches, normal. It was the most normal thing my family did.

So on this particular Christmas Eve, when Luke and Jason arrived, I went over to say hi, and I asked them to say hello to Nick. I knew he'd make a big deal out of it if they didn't. Jason dutifully went over and shook his hand. Luke started to make his way toward Nick, but didn't make it there. I don't know if he got distracted or changed his mind. Regardless, Nick went up to him and said, "What's your problem?" Luke said, "You're my problem. I love her and you should not be in her life." Then Luke pushed Nick, and suddenly they were having a full-on brawl. At the Manor. In our living room. In front of the eighteen-foot Christmas tree. (Did I say "normal"? It took days to decorate that enormous tree. Crews of workers came in. It was practically a union job.) At any rate, before the tree could topple, Jason pulled Luke off and sent him outside to cool down. Nick stormed out of the party. I cried and told Luke I hated him. Then, surreally, it was over and the party went on as if nothing had happened. My parents never mentioned anything.

Not long after the Christmas Eve fiasco, the cast called me into a dressing room. When I came in, I saw that everyone was there. Then they went around the room, each saying how he or she felt about Nick and me. Luke led the effort. The upshot was that they loved me, they thought I deserved better, and enough was enough. They didn't want him on the set anymore. It was amazing and touching that they all cared about me enough to do this, but at the time I was still so young and naive. I'd never known anyone who had such problems and had no idea how to deal with it. All I could think was, *Don't they know this is just making it worse on me?* When he heard that he wasn't welcome on set, Nick would certainly take it out on me. He'd said it a million times: "What have you been telling them, what lies?" I pleaded with my friends, "Don't do this. You don't understand. You're just going to make this harder on me." But they stood their ground. They said they wouldn't condone the relationship. Still I didn't break up with him. After that Luke and I didn't speak for months.

My parents were beyond distraught. My relationship with Nick totally separated me from my family. I went from living at home with them to sporadic phone calls. They had no idea how to help me, so they went to a therapist to figure out how to get me out of the relationship. But they never said anything to me. Years later my mother told me that she wanted to maintain our relationship instead of judging me. Ironically, she was the one person who might've gotten through to me.

I knew what my friends were saying, but like the women in peril I was playing on TV, I didn't have the strength to leave. (A couple years later Donna would struggle with similar issues when her boyfriend Ray Pruit, played by Jamie Walters, turned abusive. But I didn't make the connection back then—probably because Ray was physically abusive and I never thought of Nick that way. Now I've got to wonder if the *90210* writers were making art imitate life.) The way I dealt with the Nick situation was to put up a front of being fine and say that my friends were the ones acting badly and making the wrong judgments. The longer I did that, the harder it got to admit that they were right.

## CHAPTER SIX

# Confrontation Is Inevitable

When I was little, I learned quickly that trying to take control of my own life never got me very far. As a kid I was dying to grow out my hair. My mother's hairstylist would come to the house to cut her hair, and she'd have him do mine at the same time. For a while, when he sat me in the chair, I'd tell him what I wanted. Although he seemed to listen attentively, he would proceed to cut my hair into bangs and a bob. The same bangs-and-bob cut that I loathed every single time. Once he bent down and whispered into my ear, "Sorry, your mom told me to cut it short." I didn't choose my own Halloween costumes. I got my mother's favorite dolls as birthday presents. I drove the car my parents thought looked best on me.

So why bother trying to argue my case? By the time I was an adult, nonconfrontation was a way of life. Even now, if it's been a while and I should call a friend, I worry that there'll be some kind of direct discussion of thoughts and feelings, and I can't bring myself to pick up the phone. Thank God for my BlackBerry, without which I would lead a very lonely life.

This nonconfrontational approach to life was in full swing when I met Shannen Doherty on the set of *90210*. I was younger than most of the cast and grateful for her friendship. For a long time I saw her treating people in ways that made me uncomfortable. She was constantly coming in late to work with crazy excuses. She'd say someone broke into her house the night before, and I'd sit there getting my makeup done, knowing it wasn't true. *I'd* been at her house the night before—and I was an invited guest. It was one grand story after another. Shannen never just admitted, *I fucked up. I overslept.* And when a pretty brunette extra appeared on the set, Shannen had her fired. I never had the gumption to say what I thought.

I cared about Shannen, but I feared she was on a downward spiral, and I wanted no part of it. After a couple years I was pretty much over wanting to go to clubs all the time. I'd been club-curious, but the fast life wasn't exactly my style. I was more of a TV-watching, takeout-scarfing couch potato. So Shannen and I were hanging out less and less. But we were still friends until one day on set when I finally took a stand. Shannen was doing off-camera for a guest star, meaning they had a scene together, and the guest star was shooting a close-up while Shannen said her lines off-camera. Shannen was throwing away her lines, making a joke of them. I took her aside and said she shouldn't be acting that way. It was the first and only time I'd ever dared say something about her behavior. She shot me a terrible look, a *How dare you?* look. Given that look, I think I was right to think twice before speaking my mind for all those years. It was pretty scary.

Later I was in my dressing room getting ready to go to lunch. Shannen came in and closed the door behind her, blocking my way. She let me have it, saying I'd better watch my back. I totally believed that she'd have someone kick my ass! When I came home that night, I was so clearly terrified that my fourteen-year-old brother demanded to take the next day off from school so he could come to the set and protect me. My sweet little brother, Randy—he hadn't even had his growth spurt yet. But, indeed, in the morning he came to work with me and followed me around like a 250-pound bodyguard. After every scene he'd give me a professional nod, as if to say, *You're okay.*

Not long after that Shannen came in late for the gazillionth time. You know what they say: A gazillion strikes and you're out. Being late to set is a big deal. Everyone is waiting for you: the crew, the cast, the producers, loads of people. And time is money. On this particular day she was about four hours late. Four hours! It's pretty much unheard of unless tragedy strikes your family. This was the last straw. Everyone was saying they'd had enough. Shannen started to make up one of her excuses. Ian turned to her and said, "You're a C-U-N-T." Ian was the sweetest guy. He never said a harsh word to anyone. There was a long, awful silence before he tapped his forehead and added, "Can't Understand Normal Thinking." Shannen made some retort, then stormed into her dressing room and slammed the door.

Everyone wanted Shannen gone. The rest of the cast—Jennie,

Ian, Brian, Jason, Gabrielle, and Luke—told me they had decided to go into the producer's office to call my father and say that she had to go. But they needed a consensus. They wanted me to come with them. It was a hard moment. She'd been my friend, and I didn't want to betray her. And I definitely didn't want anyone to ever say that it had happened because I was part of the group phoning my father. I said I wouldn't go into the office. They said, "But we have to all agree. Do you agree?" Finally I said that yes, I agreed, but that I wouldn't be part of the call.

When Shannen left, I felt the same as everyone else, like I could breathe again. As soon as she was gone, we could all hang out comfortably, without anyone feeling left out or talking about each other behind our backs. High school had ended.

I know being nonconfrontational seems harmlessly passive, but my case is extreme and it's gotten me in plenty of trouble over the years. When it came to my relationship with Nick, although we fought, I couldn't see the reality of the situation. I didn't have a boyfriend; I had a money-sapping verbal abuser making a fool out of me on a daily basis. I acted as though I were trapped, but I learned that even I have a breaking point. The final straw came during one fight that wasn't much different from all the other fights. Nick was screaming at me. He'd always let loose about how ugly and untalented I was. He said the same stuff now: "You'll never get another acting job because they don't hire people as ugly as you." And then: "You know why I don't stay home with you? Because you're ugly." This time something clicked. His words were familiar, and not just because he'd said them before. He sounded like the tabloids, the tabloids that were forever mocking my acting and appearance. I'd learned how to throw away those weeklies, and I was finally ready to toss him out too.

He railed on, but I just shut up and waited for him to storm out the door. Then I called my girlfriends—Jenny, Jennifer, Melissa, and Jodi—and told them I was breaking up with him. They'd heard that from me before, but I swore this time it was for good. I told them all to drive to my house in separate cars. When they arrived, I was ready with a plan. I called a locksmith. We packed up everything he owned into garbage bags and threw them into their cars. The locksmith arrived and I had all the locks changed.

Nick's half sister happens to be Nicollette Sheridan. We drove to her house. It was eleven o'clock at night, and my friends started dumping all his stuff out on her front lawn while I sat in my car, numb. (I said I had a plan. I didn't say it was a *good* plan.) In the middle of this pandemonium Nicollette came out of her house. She very calmly asked what was going on, and my friends told her that this was Nick's stuff. She asked where I was, and they pointed to my car. By the time she knocked on the window, I was shaking and hiding on the floor of the backseat. I was such a chicken. I looked up at her and said, "I'm so sorry. Are you mad?" She said, "Mad? I told you to break up with him a year ago. Now come inside and have some tea." So that's what we did. We went inside. We drank tea. It was so civilized that I forgot all about her clothes-strewn lawn until we opened the door to leave. "What should we do about this stuff?" we asked. Nicollette said, "Don't worry about it. I'll get it to him," and smiled warmly.

I pretty much never saw Nick again after that. I ran into him once, and he showed me how he'd changed the tattoo of my nickname that he once had on his upper arm. It had said *Toto,* which is what my dad used to call me. Someone had suggested that Nick change it to *In Toto,* Latin for "in all." Was I supposed to congratulate him?

I never really thanked Luke Perry properly—for hating Nick enough to throw a few punches and for staging a bad-boyfriend intervention on the set of *90210.* So thank you, Luke, for being a real friend.

Not long after I evicted Nick, I myself got evicted. I was away filming a TV movie, and my landlord sold the apartments out from under me. My mother saved the day, putting all my stuff in storage. When I came back, I camped out with my parents temporarily. As it happened, my mother and I had recently, mostly out of curiosity, toured an apartment in a beautiful building, the most expensive building in the Wilshire Corridor. The Wilshire was over-the-top amazing. Each apartment had a private elevator entry, all the fanciest fixtures, and fabulous views. There was a twenty-four-hour concierge and parking valet, a gym, and a pool. In spite of my reassurances, my mother was nervous that I'd continue to see Nick. She offered me a deal. She said, "You know that apartment we loved? If you promise me that you'll never see Nick again and that you and Jenny will live there together, I'll buy that condo for you." She always loved my best friend Jenny, and she wanted us to be roommates.

It wasn't a bad offer. I had no desire to see Nick. And Jenny and I wanted to live together anyway. And (did I mention?) the apartment was beyond luxe. But my first instinct was to say no. I didn't want her to buy me anything. I was earning a living and didn't depend on my parents, and why should I? Besides, I knew people would ask me if I owned it, and I didn't want to have to say, *Yes, Daddy bought it for me.* I'd spent so much time fighting the assumption that everything was handed to me. . . . On the other hand, I was working my butt off, and there was still no way I'd ever be able to afford that condo.

I told my mother that I felt weird just taking such an enormous gift. She was very understanding and asked what would make me feel better. I said, "I'd like to pay rent." She said I didn't have to do that, but I insisted. I asked her to come up with a number, and she suggested a thousand dollars per month. Jenny would pay eight hundred for a slightly smaller room. It was way under market, of course, but fine. We had a deal.

The apartment was new construction, so although the floor plan was in place, the floors were still concrete and the final details were left for the owner to customize. We put in wood floors, moldings, and light fixtures. We picked out furniture with my mother's interior designer. I'd never really decorated a place from scratch like that, but I knew what I wanted—I was into shabby chic at the time. It wasn't my mother's style. She was buying me everything, and I soon realized that all went smoothly if I picked a piece she liked, but if she didn't approve, it was a no go.

Furniture-hunting for my grown-up apartment, I tried to show a little spine. I couldn't afford that red Rabbit convertible when I was young, but now I had the means to assert my own taste, and I finally did. There was some piece I wanted—I think it was a dining room table. When my mother said she didn't like it, I said that I'd pay for it with my own money. She said, "If you want to pay for it, you should pay for the rest. I was just trying to help." The message was loud and clear: If you want to control what's in your apartment, you buy it. And so, from then on, that's what I did.

When Jenny and I moved in, we soon discovered that our neighbors were an eclectic group of Hollywood types: Rodney Dangerfield, Charlie Sheen, Carol Burnett, former congressman Michael Huffington, and later Farrah Fawcett. I don't remember a whole lot about the time I lived in The Wilshire with Jenny. I just know I didn't leave the couch. Jenny was working for my dad as a casting director. I was on *90210*. We both worked all day long. Every night when I came home, Jenny would be in flannel pj's on the couch, TV on, delivery menus spread out on the coffee table. It was the height of *Friends*' popularity, and every Thursday night we watched it faithfully. Eventually we'd fall asleep in front of the TV, and around ten p.m. we'd wake up and go to our rooms.

Even though our rent had been established to make me feel better about living in my parents' apartment, my mother raised our rent every year. I'd get an e-mail from our mutual business manager notifying me of the increase. When I asked why, I was told that she had to raise the rent for tax purposes. In the ten years I lived there, my rent went from one thousand to forty-three hundred dollars per month, which was probably still under market value. But in all that time my mother and I never said another word about it.

After two years in that apartment Jenny met a guy in New York. She up and decided to join him there. I was away filming a TV movie when she called to let me know that she was moving out in a week. Luckily, my friend Pete, who's also part of the Valley group with Mehran, Jenny, and Jennifer, was living with his parents at the time, and the minute he heard what was going on with Jenny, he said, "I'll move in with you." I didn't think hard about it. Problem emerged; problem solved. Pete moved in.

Pete was just out of college and in the middle of medical school. He was one of my best friends, but he loved to party. And he loved the ladies. A group of us would go out to a club, and we'd be ushered into the VIP section. There was always a certain kind of girl who was thrilled to be able to join us there, and Pete knew it. These were skanky, bottom-of-the-barrel girls. Low-end strippers with boob jobs and seven-inch stiletto heels, one after another. Some of them were hanger-on girls who paid attention to him because he lived with Tori Spelling. Pete would buy them drinks and, often, bring them home.

Pete was all about maximizing his potential score. We'd go to lingerie parties at the Playboy Mansion. We'd dress up—not in skimpy slutwear—I'd go to the store Trashy Lingerie and pick out a matching nightgown and robe, and wear them with nine-inch stripper heels. Or I'd put together a cute outfit, but never a G-string and thong like some of the guests. It was a huge, great place for a party. There would be about a thousand guests, everyone in young Hollywood, with bars everywhere and tables of food. (I was obsessed with the little lamb chops served in frilly panties.) There was a huge swimming pool and the infamous stone grotto. I remember standing next to Leonardo DiCaprio and seeing Martin Landau and Scott Baio in a ten-foot radius. Anyone and everyone was at those parties.

Thanks to Pete, there was no end of female visitors to my apartment. I never knew who would be there when I got home or woke up. One time I came out in the morning to find an unfamiliar girl sitting at the counter, eating a bowl of cereal. She looked at me as if I were a masked intruder and said, "Who are *you*?" I stammered, "I'm Tori. Pete's roommate." She said, "Oh. Well, you're out of milk." I thought, *I am now,* slunk back into my bedroom, and hid there until she was gone.

Some girls would appear overnight and . . . stay. I wasn't exactly thrilled to have a revolving door of unsavory roommates. Pete would say, "Oh, yeah, she was evicted. She's just staying a couple days." I'd peer through his doorway and see all of her clothes and shoes in his closet. Weeks later she'd disappear without a good-bye. Which I guess makes sense since there usually wasn't much of a hello.

My least favorite of Pete's girlfriends had to be the one named Tori. (No, sharing first names did not bring us closer, but thanks for asking.) I saw a simple diamond pavé band at Fred Segal that I thought I'd like to wear as a pinkie ring. I have small fingers so I had it custom-made (I guess the old habits of my custom-made childhood died hard). One Saturday I came home to find this other Tori, who identified herself as Pete's "girlfriend" (there were so many), sitting in my living room on my couch watching my TV. Pete was nowhere to be found. I joined her on the couch. After I while I glanced over at her. She was wearing a diamond pavé ring. On her pinkie. My ring.

Far be it from me to actually confront her, but it was my ring and I wanted it back. So what did I do? I said, "I really like your ring. I have one just like it." She was nonresponsive, seemingly riveted by a *Who's the Boss?* rerun. I tried again. "Did you get that at Fred Segal?" I asked. She said, "Yeah, my mom got it at Fred Segal." Then I knew beyond a doubt that it was mine. No way did her mom buy it. It was a special order! That's kind of the point of special orders—nobody else has the same thing.

When Pete came home, I immediately pulled him into his bedroom. "Your girlfriend stole my ring," I said. He was furious. He started screaming at me, saying I had no proof and that I always hated his girlfriends. He had a point—I did hate them. But it's not like it was worth liking them—they were so short-lived. And that's the most flattering thing I can think of to say about them. Pete stormed out of the room, and I retreated into my bedroom to check my jewelry box for the ring. Indeed, it was gone.

The next morning Pete handed me the ring. He said, "I owe you an apology, but it's not what you think. She was just embarrassed to tell you the truth because you were freaking out. What really happened is that she found it on the carpet in the hallway. She claimed she didn't know whose it was." Let's see. It's not like she found it on the street or in the hall of a hotel. She found it in the hallway of my apartment. I was the only woman who lived there! Not exactly the circumstances under which the finders-keepers rule was established.

For Pete's birthday that year a big group of us went out to dinner. I'd baked him a cake and decorated it. Afterward I was going to watch movies at my friend Mehran's. Pete asked if I minded if he had some people back to our place. Um, yeah, I kind of did. More of Pete's randoms in my apartment? I hadn't even hidden my valuables. But it was his birthday—I couldn't say no.

The next day I came home to find the place trashed. All the liquor had been emptied from the bar. The toilet was overflowing, and the soles of my shoes stuck to the floor. But what really devastated me was the state of my Sea-Monkeys. You know, those little shrimp they sell in comic books as novelty pets. I'd kept mine alive in a container on the bar for a year and a half, possibly a world record. But now the tank was completely empty. The counter was a dried, sticky mass. My Sea-Monkeys! Someone had spilled them and just left them there. Not to be insensitive, but that counter was the Jonestown of Sea-Monkeys. Poor little guys.

Maybe it was that night, maybe it was one of the other nights that were regrettably similar, but one of Pete's guests made off with some of my personal photos. And, of course, subsequently sold them to the tabloids. There's a picture of me that has appeared in all of the magazines, time after time. I'm standing behind a couch with one leg kicked up, holding my teacup white poodle, Greta. I'm wearing a tank top and a G-string and have a cigarette in my mouth. According to the *Enquirer,* the photo was taken when I was at a house party and spontaneously started doing a striptease. The truth is that Pete and Jenny were visiting me on the set of a TV movie. It was my twenty-second birthday, and we were listening to the *Grease* album and dancing around. Just the three of us. In a hotel room. And so my raucous lifestyle goes down in history.

I was always kicking Pete out. Or saying I was going to kick Pete out. Or planning to say I was going to kick Pete out. Or thinking about planning to say I was going to kick Pete out. But there were three problems: (a) Kicking him out would have meant I had to be alone, and I'd never lived alone; (b) Kicking him out meant I had to stand up for myself, and I'd never done much of that either. Oh, and let's not forget: (c) He was my best friend. I loved him despite his faults. I couldn't just kick him out. So Pete stayed.

* * * *

For all the chaos at home, when it came to work, life was uncompli-
cated for a long time. *Beverly Hills, 90210* ran for ten solid seasons.
At the beginning I had no idea it would go on so long. I'd always
wanted to go to college at Northwestern because they were supposed
to have a great drama department. It seemed like a reasonable plan.
But remember how my parents didn't like me to go to my friends'
houses for sleepovers? The idea that I would go somewhere requiring regular plane flights to visit was unfathomable, particularly for
my father the nonflyer. They nixed any notion of me considering an
out-of-state college. So I applied to USC, and let's face it, my dad
probably donated a bunch of money. I was accepted during the first
year of *90210,* and my father suggested that I defer for a year to keep
doing the show. We didn't know if it would stay on the air. There
was plenty of time for me to go to college. Ten years later . . . there I
was. Still working on *90210.*

Poor Donna was a virgin for most of that time. As the years went
by, I started to say, "This is getting ridiculous. Donna's the oldest living virgin." And as I developed a fashion sense, I added, "And P.S.,
Donna's the sluttiest virgin in the history of time." But my father
stuck to his guns. He wanted Donna to stay a virgin. He claimed
that the fans loved it. To some extent they did, but my father bla-
tantly wanted me to stay a little girl, to be innocent forever. Finally,
when the show was starting its seventh season, I went to the writers
and begged them to unlock Donna's chastity belt. They talked and
agreed. This was the year that Donna would lose her virginity. I was
twenty-four. Sorry, Dad, but it was about time.

When *90210* started, I was just a sixteen-year-old producer's daughter with a token part on a hot new show. At the beginning of the eighth season I remember thinking how amazing it was that I'd been playing the same character year after year, week after week, and I was still excited to come to work. But things started to go downhill. By the tenth year the writers didn't seem to care much about the series. They were banging out scripts, and nobody gave a whit about the quality. Even my dad's studio (Spelling Entertainment/Torand) and Fox viewed it as a finely oiled machine that didn't need tinkering with. They'd moved on to other projects. But the actors were still invested in the show. We didn't want the fans to see us performing horribly written scenes. We'd been so proud of it. Why would we want it to go on the air and suck? Brian and I started rewriting our scenes. Jennie would come to me and say, "Can you look at this scene? It doesn't work. What should I do?" I'd rewrite it for her. I actually liked the work. It's rare that an actor has that kind of freedom. Nobody seemed to notice or care.

We tried our best to make the show better, but it still wasn't up to par. The scripts were full of stilted lines like "I'm extending an olive branch to you and you're not accepting it." Who talks like that? Donna had a career in fashion, and the writers were pressed to come up with a serious issue for her every week. One week she'd single-handedly take down a sweatshop. The next she'd discover her assistant was a cutter. These were "meaty" topics, but come on. After ten years it felt like the writers had finally run out of subject matter and were scrambling to find issues they hadn't dealt with on the show. Anyone care to defend those final episodes? Nah, didn't think so. People were already talking about how old all the actors were.

Brian and I were only twenty-six, but everyone else was older. The end was near, and everybody knew it.

Every year we renegotiated our contracts. When the time came to renew my contract for an eleventh season, I couldn't summon much enthusiasm. Donna was one of the most popular characters on the show. But I was more than ready to take my career in another direction. I'd done the independent movie *Trick,* which was nominated for the Grand Jury Prize at Sundance, and Fox had made an overall deal with me to develop my own sitcom. My manager told Fox that I wasn't coming back to *90210.*

To my surprise this caused a huge fuss. The year before, Jason Priestley had done the same thing, but the show went on, and I figured the same would be true in my case. First my father had the VP of his company and the guy under him take a meeting with me to encourage me to stay. Needless to say, he never mentioned the first word about my departure to me in person. Not a phone call. Not a single word. Yes, nonconfrontation was a family issue.

When my father's efforts failed, the then-chairman of Fox Entertainment, Sandy Grushow, took me out to lunch at the Polo Lounge with my manager to convince me to stay. He said, "If you don't come back, the show's not coming back. There's no show without you." Hearing those words, I felt pressure to return, but I also couldn't help but feel proud. No show without me, huh? I was the girl nobody thought deserved the part. I was a side character. I was, as *Variety* had once decided, "attractive, if somewhat limited in the talent department." I only had the part because of who my father was. Okay, we all know my dad's name got me in the door, but hadn't I made the most of the opportunity? Wasn't it ironic that a decade later the head of Fox was telling us that the life of the show hinged on me? My manager and I didn't really buy that they'd cancel the whole show if I left. We figured it was just a negotiating tactic. *90210* was an institution. It wasn't going anywhere. So for once I stood my ground. I knew what I wanted.

The next day Fox made the announcement. The tenth season would be *90210*'s last.

## CHAPTER SEVEN

# Build Me Up, Buttercup

A pattern has emerged in my life. It goes something like this: Just when I've given up all hope (in my career, my love life, my hair—you choose), I get an amazing opportunity. This amazing opportunity gives me new hope. I'm determined to make the most of it. I throw myself into it. I try really hard. My efforts seem to pay off: *Looks like this will really lead to something!* And then . . . nothing. It all goes to pot. Like I told you about getting the lead part in the third-grade play: The parents mutinied and the play was canceled. Or when I was so excited to do my bit part on *90210* and got terrible press even though I barely had any lines.

The movie *Trick*, an independent gay romantic comedy, was released in 1999 when *90210* was coming to a close. A couple years earlier I'd been in another indie, *The House of Yes*, which was also nominated for Sundance's Grand Jury Prize. There was one scene in

*Trick* where I did a rambling monologue of which I was particularly proud. And the critics took notice. They went from calling me "TV movie queen" to "indie movie queen." And then . . . you guessed it. Nothing. It just went away. Interviewers would ask me, "So why didn't you do more movies like *Trick*?" and I'd say, "I don't know. You tell me. Why didn't I do more movies like *Trick*?" But that's what being an actor is about. No matter how much success you've had, you're always jockeying for work. I'd had great fortune with *90210* going on so long. I wasn't daunted. I was determined to put in whatever time and effort it took to keep my career going.

Not long after *90210* wrapped, I went in to audition for *Scary Movie 2*. *Scary Movie,* a parody of teen slasher flicks, had made $150 million the summer before. The sequel was bound to be huge. The whole thing was so hyped and top secret that they wouldn't release the script for auditions. I was dying to do comedy—in this case, a very out-there comedy. Like any actor on a long-running series, I was typecast from doing *90210*. With a movie like this, I could escape Donna Martin in a big way. So I went in to audition in front of Keenen Ivory Wayans, the director. They handed me a monologue on the spot, and I loved it. That night I found out that I'd been called back. They gave me another scene that I was expected to perform the next day. I thought it went well, but then . . . nothing.

I kept pestering my manager about *Scary Movie 2*. I was so hungry for that part. Finally the feedback came in: I wasn't in the running anymore. They thought I was over the top in the second scene I'd performed. Um, yes, I was over the top. The character I was playing, Alex, has sex with a ghost and then stalks him. The ghost is scared of this nutso stalker lady. In the audition scene I was supposed to be anticipating sex with my ghost-lover. The stage direction was *Alex on all fours getting herself primed for sex.* It was all physical comedy. I'm not exactly sure how you can go over the top with a scene like that.

Disappointed, I was in New York with my mother for Fashion Week when I got a call. It was about *Scary Movie 2.* The movie was to start shooting in two days, and they now wanted me for the part. I don't know why they decided at the last minute. My guess is that the studio was initially reluctant to cast Tori Spelling. At any rate, they said, "We need her to show up at rehearsal tomorrow." Rehearsal was in Los Angeles. I was in New York. This was my post-*90210* big break. Of course we cut our trip short. But I have to hand it to my mother. She had all sorts of shows and parties planned, and she abandoned it all because I was too scared to fly home alone (a fear I inherited from my father).

The next day when I landed in L.A., there was a car waiting to take me to rehearsal. The driver handed me a script. I had no idea what to expect—to that point all I knew about my character was what I'd seen in the two scenes I read in auditions. As we drove, I flipped through the script. I couldn't believe what I saw. Page after page, there was my character's name, over and over again. The part was huge. I was one of the six main characters in the movie. I was doing a major movie, and my dad's name wasn't on it. This was it. I was going to be a big star.

The first day we filmed, I shot the big monologue that was my audition scene. Afterward I was sitting in my director's chair, and Keenen came up to me. He said, "I had no idea you were this funny." I said, "I love doing comedy, but nobody knows because I was on a drama for ten years." Then Keenen said something I didn't anticipate: "You need your own series about what your life is like. Like Roseanne. Then they can't say, 'I can't picture Tori Spelling being a waitress.' You need to give them what they expect from you, but at the same time give them yourself and show them who you really are. That's what's going to make you." It was great advice. Years later I would remember it when I came up with the show *So NoTORIous*.

I was thrilled to work with the three Wayans brothers. Shawn and Marlon wrote and starred in the movie, and, as I said, Keenen was directing. A week after we started filming, Keenen called me over and said, "I'm going to let the camera roll. Just improv." *Just improv?* Those are two of the most frightening words an actor can hear. But this was part of the Wayans brothers' method—Shawn and Marlon improvised half of their scenes. They knew what they wanted but left things up in the air and changed scenes daily. I was terrified I'd be a disaster—either I'd stand there frozen and silent, or I'd take the scene in some direction they hated. Keenen said, "Trust me. If I didn't think you could do it, I wouldn't ask."

When you first see her, my character, Alex, seems sweet but a little out there, then as the film progresses, you realize how crazy she is. The Wayanses liked the idea that I was this little white girl in pigtails with a filthy mouth. Keenen asked me to improvise a scene when the ghost rapes me. There was absolutely no script, so I went with it. I'm slapping my ass as he rapes me across the ceiling and saying things like, "Who's your daddy?" and "Say my name, bitch!" When Keenen finally called "Cut!" he had a huge smile on his face. "How hard was that?" I went home that night feeling really proud. They thought I was funny!

That day was a turning point. From then on the filming took a completely different route. I'd have a day off, but I'd get a call in the morning and they'd ask me to come in as soon as I could. When I arrived, they'd say, "Keenen wants you in this scene. Just play it how you think it should go." One scene took place at a dinner table. We all had our lines, but twenty minutes before we started shooting, they told me to say grace. They said, "You're a nutjob. You stalk everyone. You have a beef with God. Go with that and start to say grace." Another time Marlon said, "Just try to say 'raw dog style.' *You* saying that will be funny." So I said to the ghost, "Remember when you were all up in me, raw dog style?" This turned into our regular process. They kept adding me to scenes. None of it was scripted. They'd say, "You're a natural-born writer. Just do your own stuff."

I started calling my manager to report how well things were going. I said, "I'm getting even more scenes. They keep adding me to scenes!" The first movie was such a big hit that the Wayanses had the money to work on their own time line. *Scary Movie 2* was supposed to take two and a half months to film but ended up taking five. It was an amazing experience, but there was one glitch.

When my deal was made, the studio, Dimension, said there wouldn't be any nudity. One of the horror movies that *Scary Movie 2* spoofed was *Entity*. There's a scene in that movie where Barbara Hershey is raped by a phantom. She's lying in bed when he pulls her shirt up and grabs her boobs. The entity is invisible, but you see the indentation of his grabby hands on her chest. When I first got the script, I saw that I was supposed to play that scene. One of the stage directions was *He pulls her top up*. I brought it up, but a producer at Dimension told my manager not to worry. I wouldn't have to do nudity. They promised the scene would be cut.

Near the end of shooting I heard talk about getting a prosthetic build of my chest so they could show the indentations when the ghost grabbed my boobs. This wasn't exactly cutting the scene. It didn't matter that they planned to use a body double. I knew perfectly well that nobody watching the movie would know or care that it was a body double. And no matter how amazing that body double's boobs were, I knew I'd never hear the end of it. It wasn't worth it—maybe for an intense scene that was a critical dramatic moment in a serious movie, but I wasn't into doing it for a spoof comedy. Dimension kept assuring my agency, Creative Artists Agency (CAA), that the scene would be cut, and CAA kept saying that I wasn't going to shoot it. It went back and forth like that for a while until it escalated to the point where the head of the agency—I believe Kevin Huvane—had to call Miramax, the company that owned Dimension. Miramax was run by the Weinstein brothers. Huvane made it clear to them that they couldn't use a body double without my consent.

At some point during all this back-and-forth my manager suggested that I ask my father whether he thought I should do the scene. It wasn't like, *Oh, you're at a tough point in your career, ask old Dad what he thinks.* It was more in the vein of *He knows this business as well as anyone else. He'll know what to do.* Still, this was the man who'd kept my character a virgin for seven long years. I called, assuming he was going to say, *Oh my God, no! Not my baby Tori!* But my father must have had his producer hat on that day. I can't remember his wording, but he said for a big movie like this he thought I should do it. He said, "If I know the Weinsteins, they'll cut you out of the whole film if you refuse to do it." I should have marked his words, but by that time we were too deep in battle to back out. My representatives fought tooth and nail, and in the end the scene was cut out of the movie.

All that negotiation happened behind the scenes. Meanwhile, everything on the set was still going smoothly. When the movie wrapped, I couldn't wait for its release. My part, which started out bigger than I could have dreamed, had only grown. I hadn't seen the finished product, but a friend of mine saw Keenen's cut of the movie in a private screening and reported back that I was in every scene. He said, "You have a filthy mouth, but it's funny." The movie was opening wide, and it was going to change my career path.

The publicity tour was two to three weeks away. The lead girl, Anna Faris, was still relatively unknown. So for the publicity I had several solo appearances since I was the biggest name and one of the leads. The itinerary was set and it was impressive. I was scheduled to go on the *Late Show with David Letterman*—I'd never been on *Letterman*. Then, out of the blue, my publicist and manager called. They said, "Apparently, they don't want you on the publicity tour anymore. You're not one of the leads in the movie." Then they told me that the Miramax publicists were pitching my role as a cameo! I couldn't believe it. There had to be some mistake. I said, "What are you talking about? I'm a lead in the movie. I'm in every scene!" And my publicist said, "Well, they're willing to do a screening for you. They want you to see the movie so you aren't surprised when it comes out—your part was cut considerably."

I went to the screening at the Miramax offices. It was a small audience—just my team. They'd cut my scenes, all right. They'd cut so much of me from the movie that there were places where it didn't even make sense. There is a scene where five of us are in a room. We're standing in a line. I'm standing at the end of the line. Originally, I freaked out, held a gun on them, delivered a monologue, then ran out of the room. But they cut my freak-out, my monologue, and my exit, so all you see is that one moment I'm standing in the line, the next I've disappeared. Maybe I was also supposed to be a ghost? Whatever the case, they were right. I was no longer one of the main six characters. I'd spent five months improvising a cameo.

My manager at the time was kind of conservative and over-protective. She was always trying to sell me as young and innocent, the girl next door. She even had me dye my hair brown to fit that image. When I was cut from the movie, all she really said was, "It sounds like good news in disguise. It's an R-rated movie, and the Miramax publicist said that your part was very dirty. You wouldn't want that image on screen anyway." What?! The whole movie was dirty. Of course I wanted that image on the screen. I was proud of my work. I'd been so close to that brass ring, and now it was gone. (And I've still never been on *Letterman*. Dave? Are you reading this?)

I was embarrassed to go to the premiere, but when I recovered from the initial shock, I thought, *Well, who do I think I am? It's better to have a cameo in a big movie than to have nothing at all.* But to this day I still don't know why my part disappeared. Keenen's cut—the director's cut—supposedly had me in it. I wish I'd had the balls to call Marlon or Shawn to find out what happened. I wish when I'd seen Keenen at the premiere I'd had the courage to ask, *What went wrong? Why is my entire part gone?* When I saw him, that conversation went through my head. But instead, I just said, "Hi, it's so good to see you." I gave him a hug and walked away.

After all that excitement when I'd seen the script, after all the compliments I'd received on the set . . . I'd even dared to hope that *90210* and being Daddy's girl were forever in the past. What could I do? I wasn't about to sit around and mope. I had to focus on what was next. I was back at square one.

One thing I'd gotten out of *Scary Movie 2,* besides the feeling that my life was just a recurring lesson in disappointment, was the chance to exercise my comedy chops. I was still trying to focus on comedy after a decade of being on a drama. Every year after *90210,* I auditioned for the new comedy pilots. Before a network decides to put a show on the air, they cast and produce the first episode—the pilot. Then, based on how those pilots turn out, they decide which pilots they want to order as series. When you're a new actor in L.A., just getting an audition for a pilot is a big deal. But when you're a "name" (even if it's a name like Tori Spelling), you can find yourself running all over town auditioning for two or three pilots every day during pilot season. A few years after *90210,* I went in for a comedy for UPN called *Me Me Me,* which was supposed to be a modern-day *Laverne & Shirley.* It was about two young girls living on their own, broke, trying to make their lives work. After my audition my agent called, as she always did, with the feedback from the casting director. I wasn't right for the part.

But then, a couple weeks later, the producers of *Me Me Me* called me back in. Later one of the writers would tell me that they auditioned four hundred girls and kept coming back to me. This time after the audition word came back that they liked me. To land a role, you generally have to leap through three hoops. I'd just made it through the first. Now they were sending the tape of my audition on to the studio in New York: hoop number two. Again, the news was good. The studio liked me. Now they asked me to audition for a third time to make a tape for the network (hoop number three)—this time with some direction and notes from the producers. But after that audition my agent called with feedback worse than anything I could imagine. They didn't say I was wrong for the part, or that I didn't take notes well, or that I just didn't nail the character. No, the producer—yes, we were back at hoop number one—said, "I'm watching this tape, and I can't get past the fact that she's Tori Spelling." He didn't want to send the tape to the network. I can change a lot. If you don't like my delivery, I can change how I say a joke. If you don't like my tone, I can work on my character's attitude. If you don't like my nose—just kidding. Mostly. But what I can't change is the fact that I'm Tori Spelling. That's the story of my life: My name opens doors for me, but before I can cross the threshold, it slams those same doors right in my face.

I wasn't about to let that one slide. I asked my agent to tell the producer I wanted to come in again to audition in person. He agreed, so I went in for a fourth time. By now the other girl (the Shirley one—obviously, I was destined for Laverne: blond and spacey) had already been cast, so I read with her. And, I swear, I saw it happen in the room. At some point the producer raised his head and started watching me intently. When I was done, he walked me to the door and shook my hand. He said with surprise, "You're fantastic." I got the role. The pilot didn't get picked up, but that's how it goes in TV. Unless you're Aaron Spelling. From what I witnessed growing up, all pilots went to series, and all series stayed on the air for at least a decade. It was a harsh awakening.

Another year I auditioned for a pilot called *Way Downtown*. It was another modern-day *Laverne & Shirley*. (Apparently, Hollywood really, really wants a modern-day *Laverne & Shirley*. Every year dozens of writers must walk into networks and say, *Okay, imagine this: We open on two young women skipping down the street singing a Yiddish-American hopscotch chant!*) Anyway, I auditioned, they loved me, and the callback was smooth sailing. I went in for the test deal, and the studio approved me. So all that was left was to win over the network, The WB. There were eight of us there—four potential young women for each part. They started pairing us up with the other people to figure out which two had the best chemistry. I was the only "name" there, and every time I met one of the other girls, they were surprised to see me. They couldn't believe I had to audition—usually "names" don't. Little did they know I was going to a million auditions (sometimes, it seemed, a million auditions for a single job) just trying to do whatever it took.

After that audition The WB signed off on me. But now the executive producer started to have doubts. Word came back to me that she'd said, "I'm not sure. It's *Tori Spelling*." This was starting to be old hat. So I dutifully went back in to read yet another time to convince yet another doubter to give me yet another part on yet another pilot that, it turned out, would never make it on the air.

If only we lived in a world where hard work and dedication always got their due. There are always mitigating circumstances. For some it's not having connections. For some it's not having money. For some it's not having talent. For some it's not having the right look. I had, I'd been told, more or less all of the above. I just never expected my name to be my primary hurdle.

But once or twice I felt like justice was served. Like when *90210* was canceled because I'd left the show. I finally had proof that my hard work had paid off. Even though my father had gotten me the part, I'd made myself a critical part of the show. Another time when I felt like the world was surprisingly fair came while I was still on *90210*. The parody slasher film *Scream* came out, starring Neve Campbell. In it there's a moment when Neve Campbell's character says something like, "If they make a movie about me one day, with my luck, Tori Spelling will play me." I knew that line was in the movie—I'd even auditioned for it knowing that line was in the movie. So what? They make fun of me. It's funny. I get it. Wes Craven, the director, had heard I had a sense of humor about it. So for *Scream 2,* in which they actually *are* making a movie about Neve Campbell's character's life, he asked me to do a cameo playing myself, playing her. Finally—a chance to be in on the joke. I loved it. (I guess there's just something about me that appeals to the directors of tongue-in-cheek horror movie sequels.)

So where does the justice come in? Well, when the movie came out, *Rolling Stone* did a photo shoot for their cover with the headline THE GIRLS OF *SCREAM 2*. I was happy and surprised that they wanted to include me. I'd appear with Neve Campbell, Sarah Michelle Gellar, Jada Pinkett (pre-Smith), and Heather Graham—very fine company for me. I only had a cameo, as did some of the others, but I had the very smallest part.

The cover was to be a group shot—the contract didn't say so specifically, but it was understood that we'd all share the cover. And after that each of the "Girls of *Scream 2*" would pose individually for the inside of the magazine. As I was getting my makeup done, I heard some kind of ruckus. Apparently, a couple of the stars were making a fuss over who would be first to have her solo shots done so she could go home earliest. Me, I didn't care when they did my solo shot. I was loving every minute.

Then, when we went to get our clothes for the group shot, another star was bitching about her options. And, mysteriously, one of the women insisted on having her makeup done in a separate room. I was listening to all this, feeling lucky and thinking that these women had forgotten how rare and great it was for them to have gotten as far as they had.

Mark Seliger, an award-winning photographer, was shooting the cover and layout. By the time I went in for my solo shot, it was the end of a long day. He seemed annoyed. He'd had a hard time, one diva after another. In a tired voice he asked for my requirements for the shot. I had no idea what requirements I might have. The only thing I told him was, "I'm so excited to be here." He thanked me for being so compliant and seemed to relax.

That was all there was to it—until I got a call from my publicist. *Rolling Stone* had called to say that the magazine was going to be released the next day, and . . . I was going to be the cover—alone! The cover of *Rolling Stone*. It was unbelievable. The message they gave my publicist was that I was such a surprise and a pleasure to work with that they wanted to do it for me. Just imagine! What if the whole world worked on the principle of nice girls finish first?

The next morning the concierge at my building showed me his

copy of the magazine. There I was on the cover, looking as if I were naked in the shower, à la *Psycho,* but turned to just the right angle for modesty's sake. The cover folded out and the rest of the group—Neve, Sarah, Jada, and Heather—were all together on the inside. I'm sure they all took it very well. It's funny to me to think that for *Scary Movie 2,* I went from a major role to a cameo, while for *Scream 2,* I went from a cameo to the publicity of a major role.

For the most part after *90210* my name seemed to work for and against me in everything I did. I had a stigma that in the business they like to call "too TV-recognizable." Then an opportunity came along that could have been the high point of my life, if not my career. It almost was. "Almost" being the operative word.

*Maybe Baby, It's You* was a play that Charlie Shanian and his writing partner, Shari Simpson, wrote to showcase their writing and acting talents. It started as an off-Broadway play that ran in New York. They both starred in it there and when it came to L.A., but after a while the Coronet Theatre in L.A. wanted to extend its run while Shari wanted to go back to New York. The producers decided to cast a celebrity across from Charlie in order to give the show a publicity boost.

It was a great play, but a tough one to act. There were eleven different comedic vignettes on love and finding a soul mate, and the female star had to play eleven different characters—everything from an eighth-grade know-it-all nerd in science class to the Greek queen Medea to an eighty-year-old Bostonian grandmother watching a soccer game. She had to dance in some bits and to sing nervously in another. It was the kind of show that many actors didn't want to risk.

It took forever, and a specially staged showing, to get me to see the show, and when I saw it, all my fears came true. It was a dream role for a comedian. I knew I'd be an idiot to pass up the opportunity, but I'd only done "true" theater in high school (*Tom Sawyer* in second grade didn't count), and I remembered being scared every night. And that was just a high school play. People weren't paying to see it. If I screwed up at a reputable theater, I'd be screwing up big-time.

But I was offered the role, and I couldn't say no. We rehearsed for months, and by the time the show opened, I was still nervous but felt good about the show. Then the reviews started coming in, and it was one amazing article after another. The *LA Times* said, "Yes, Tori Spelling belongs on a stage. She brings solid comic instinct, a nice flair for characterization and a lot of exuberance to her limited engagement." I'd barely gotten a good review in my life! True, there was something funny about the wording: They were full of compliments like "*Surprisingly,* Tori Spelling is a great comedic actress." Or "*We hate to admit it,* but Tori Spelling was born to be on the stage." (My italics, thank you very much.) Nonetheless, the show ran for four months and was a huge success for the Coronet.

I finally thought, *I'm good. I'm hilarious. I've turned the critics around.* I was sure it would lead to something huge. But nothing happened. Except that I met Charlie, my costar and one of the play's writers. Charlie was a good person, a real person, a trustworthy person, and a welcome change from the bad boys of my past. Throughout my career I'd always wondered why I climbed mountains only to have them disappear. I started believing that the reason *Maybe Baby, It's You* had happened was so that I could meet Charlie. We would soon get married, and had we lived happily ever after, then, yes, that would have meant that something amazing came out of the play. But I'm getting ahead of myself again.

## CHAPTER EIGHT

## No More Mr. Not-Nice Guy

Before I tell you about Charlie, I should tell you about Vince. Between Nick and Charlie—for almost three years—there was Vince, and it was while I was dating Vince that I decided I needed to change my destiny. Vince, my *90210* costar and love interest, was a model-turned-actor, a James Dean type with spiky hair, a beat-up black leather jacket, jeans, and motorcycle boots. Okay, he was just plain hot. The first time I saw him, he was sitting in a corner by himself reading Hemingway. (In retrospect I can't guarantee that he ever turned a page.) Vince was a classic bad boy: good-looking, mysterious, and interested in me—but not really. And we both liked independent films, art, and eclectic designer fashion. Otherwise, there didn't seem to be much going on in that pretty head of his.

Vince was raised in a family with three boys and a stay-at-home mom. He expected me to prepare dinner and to otherwise be stereotypically wifelike. I practically lived at his house—shopping, walking the dog, cooking him dinner every night, and cleaning up afterward. He'd watch TV, and I'd bring him his drink. It was so 1950s, but I kind of liked feeling domestic and self-sufficient. My whole life everything had been done for me. This was some version of "normal," and I wanted to try it out.

But Vince's fifties vibe wasn't so cool with me when it came to our weekend plans. He'd go to bars and clubs with guys and wouldn't bring me. If you ask me, his newfound fame was going to his head. He wanted to go out and bask in girls' attention. I was no stranger to this phenomenon. It was exactly what I'd done to my first real boyfriend, Ryan. Even if Vince and I were invited to the same party, we wouldn't go together. Then, starting Sunday night, we'd be as good as married all week.

The beginning of the end with Vince came one night when I went to my former costar Brian Green's house for a small Christmas party of maybe thirty people. Vince was off with his guy friends. I was in Brian's kitchen with Ian Ziering's then-wife Nikki. I'd just smoked pot and was scarfing Christmas cookies when a debonair black man appeared out of nowhere.

The man walked directly up to me and said, "I need to speak with you." He had a commanding presence and was very serious. For some reason I was feeling a little paranoid—probably it was all those Christmas cookies—so I said, "I'm sorry, can we do it later?" He didn't push it. He just said, "How about in a few minutes?" I agreed and went back to ravaging the food table. Moments later (or so it seemed) there he was again. He said, "I really need to speak with you." His tone was pleasant enough, but intense. He made it clear that he wanted to go someplace private. Warning bell. What woman isn't wary of an intense stranger claiming he has to talk to you alone? Plus, did I mention I was stoned? I just said, "Listen, would you mind if my friend comes along?"

So the three of us went into Brian's study. We sat down on the couch. He looked into my eyes and said, "I don't want to scare you, but I have psychic ability. It runs in my family. I was born with it. I'm not a card-reader or a palm-reader." Nikki jumped in: "Tell me! Tell me what's going to happen to me!" But he kept focused on me. "It's not the type of thing where I look at you and know things about you. It just comes to me that I have to find a specific person because there's something I have to tell them." I was high, and the whole thing was way too heavy. Nikki and I cracked up. I felt rude—this man was so earnest. So I apologized and confessed that I was stoned and I didn't smoke pot very often and I was uncomfortable. But he was unruffled. He said, "Don't worry. It's human to laugh."

Then the man got down to business. He said, "I sought you out because I was given a message for you. You're on the wrong path in life, and I'm hoping to change that path. You're making a mistake, the same mistake that you've repeated for many a lifetime. I've been sent to help you change your path." Yikes. I tried to make a joke. "Um, thanks anyway, but I really don't smoke pot very often." But he went on. "You don't think enough of yourself. You choose relationships that aren't worthy of you. If you don't stop, that's going to be your life. In past lives you had great wealth. You were a queen or princess. Every lifetime you were given great opportunity, and you threw it all away for relationships that changed your life for the worse. You keep missing opportunities to take the right path."

At this point in the conversation my brother poked his head in the door, scanned the scene, and raised his eyebrows at me as if to ask, *Are you okay?* I sort of shrugged. I found out later that Randy went to get Brian to find out who this guy was. Good ol' Randy.

My new personal psychic finished his message. He said, "I'm simply here to tell you that you can change your course of life. I'm not saying this to scare you. I'm just passing on information." He said, "I'm going to leave now," and sailed out the door.

I stood up, feeling shaky. He'd gotten to me. I knew my relationship wasn't good for me. Why did I keep making bad choices? And why had I stayed with Vince for over two years?

Suddenly Brian appeared in the room. He said, "This is crazy. I can't find him. He's gone." I asked Brian who the guy was—figuring he'd say it was some friend of a friend or a hired party fortune-teller or possibly some dude who'd died in this apartment ten years ago to this very day. But no, Brian said it was his next-door neighbor, Terence Trent D'Arby, the Grammy Award–winning musician now known as Sananda Maitreya and actually reputed to be something of a psychic. Brian was a big fan of his and had invited him over. So my psychic was actually a respected member of society. That was a bit of a surprise. But Brian was still talking about how weird it was. He said, "He came in. I took his coat. He talked to you. And then he disappeared."

I'd never given much thought to whether people can have real psychic abilities. But Terence Trent D'Arby caught my attention. Here was a successful, talented musician who wanted nothing from me and had absolutely nothing to gain from giving me his message. He just came, delivered it, and left. That gave him credibility, and I considered chasing him down for his lotto picks, but that seemed a little disrespectful. At any rate, his voice stuck in my head. I knew I was going to break up with Vince. It was just a matter of when.

The moment came on Valentine's Day. I was in New York for Fashion Week with my mother—this is the same New York trip when I got the news about *Scary Movie 2*. While I was gone, Vince planned to go to a party at the Playboy Mansion. I wasn't into it. I'd been to plenty of parties there myself and knew that it was pretty much a pickup scene. I thought it was inappropriate for him to go without me, especially on Valentine's Day. Nonetheless, he insisted it was no big deal. Ultimately, I accepted that he was going to the party whether I liked it or not, but I asked him to call me when he got home. It would be three hours later in New York, but I told him to wake me up no matter how late it was.

During the night I woke up a few times realizing he hadn't called, but whenever I subtracted the three-hour time change, I figured he was probably still at the party. I wasn't about to call his cell—I'd been demanding enough. To chase him down at the party would make me feel like a total loser. But finally, when I got up to go to the bathroom at around six in the morning, he still hadn't called and I knew he wouldn't.

I was done. That was it. Terence Trent D'Arby had spoken, and I was finally ready to listen. I called Vince and told him it was over.

Although he took me for granted, Vince didn't go easily. He kept asking to see me. He called me crying. He brought me flowers, toys, necklaces. It didn't matter. I was so done that I couldn't believe I'd ever been with him. Finally he said, "I know every year for my birth-day I go out with the guys to have drinks, but all I want this year is to go to Santa Barbara with you and have a nice birthday by the pool." He'd been a distant guy who sometimes wouldn't give me the time of day, but now he was a sobbing mess. I felt bad and agreed to go.

That night we were in bed. I was wearing full flannel pajamas, the last word in unsexy, just to make it clear that nothing was going to happen. Still, he presented me with an engagement ring and asked me to marry him. There was nothing magical about it, and it wasn't hard to refuse. Some time after the fact, Pete told me that according to Vince, he'd spent all his money on the ring, but my guilt only goes so far. I wasn't about to marry him because he'd made a lousy investment. I was ready to break the chain of bad boys that Terence Trent D'Arby said had been my mistake over many a lifetime. Vince was it. I had to find a different type of guy. From then on every time my friend Mehran and I heard the song "Wishing Well," he'd say, "Terence Trent D'Arby changed your life!"

For better or worse that's when Charlie appeared. Things with Charlie started about the same way they did in my bad-boy relation-ships. We were doing the play together, and I wanted to see if I could get his attention. I always did that with my costars—probably because I started *90210* so young that for most of my dating life I'd only met guys when I was working. Charlie had dark hair and looked intellectual. Well, he wore glasses, anyway. My friend Jenny always says that I was overly impressed by the glasses, and I have to confess that they did give him some level of credibility. I thought for sure he was Jewish, which I knew would make my parents very happy. Turned out he was Greek Armenian. Oops.

Charlie was different from every guy I'd ever dated before. Not just in appearance—I'd always gone for somewhat fashion-conscious pretty boys with twenty-twenty vision, and look where that had gotten me. But we also had pretty different personalities. If we'd gone to the same high school, we wouldn't have been in the same group of friends. If I'd been in the social, "in" crowd (I know, not necessarily something to be proud of), he'd have been part of the geeky theater group.

On the set of *Maybe Baby, It's You*, I'd flirt with Charlie. Nothing over the top—I'd try to dress cute for rehearsal, and I'd smile and talk to him. He didn't respond at all. That seemed odd. I never had great self-esteem, but I did feel pretty confident that I could get a response from a man if I wanted one.

Then one day after rehearsal a bunch of people from the theater went across the street for a wine and cheese party. Charlie and I were sipping wine and chatting. I had this habit—which came to play in many of my relationships—where I'd be talking to a guy and, within a few minutes, I'd sense what personality he wanted me to have and transform myself into that. If he wanted low-key, I was low-key. If he wanted to go deep, I went deep. If he wanted witty repartee, I gave witty repartee. If he wanted vampire fetishist, I was . . . outta there. Girl's gotta draw the line somewhere. Anyway, it was my own fault that most guys I was with thought we had everything in common when we didn't. I followed his lead and entered the relationship as a skewed version of myself that leaned heavily toward who I thought the guy wanted me to be. It happened partially because I had a case of Why Would They Want the Real Me Syndrome, but I certainly didn't do it on purpose. And nobody was more deceived than I was.

I'd think we were having this amazing conversation even though it wasn't remotely a conversation I'd have with friends. I'd just convince myself that it was: "Yeah, yeah, I *do* find the world of custom motorcycle paint jobs fascinating—*finally* someone's talking to me about it!" That night Charlie and I lingered over our wine while I subconsciously tried to make myself into his dream woman.

The next week we went out for drinks. I still wasn't sure if he liked me when he grabbed my hand under the table. I looked at him and he smiled. After dinner he walked me to my car and kissed me good night. The feeling wasn't so much fireworks as it was like playing a game booth at a fair. You fire your water gun, hear a balloon pop, and realize you've won the competition of the moment: *Ding ding ding! He thought I was funny, took my hand, walked me to my car, and kissed me. Ding ding ding! I win the prize! Score one for my womanly wiles.* (But the metaphor ends there. No jokes about taking home the cheap stuffed animal, please.)

From the moment Charlie and I got involved, it was hush-hush because of the play. *Maybe Baby, It's You* was Charlie's big break, and I was the high-profile actress starring in it. He didn't want anything like romance or gossip to interfere with this opportunity. And— though I had for the first time in a long time picked a genuinely nice person—taking second place to his work only made me want to be with him more.

As the play ran, we'd rehearse during the week, then the show would play on Wednesday, Thursday, Friday, and Saturday nights. The reviews talked about the electrifying chemistry onstage. Maybe I should have given more credit to my acting, but I figured what everyone was seeing onstage had to be true in life. We must be good together. Sure. And that ghost in *Scary Movie 2* really loved me too.

After the Friday-night shows my best gay friend, Mehran, and his boyfriend, Jeremy, would pick me up and we'd go out for drinks. Jeremy was skeptical of Charlie. "I don't see him with you," I remember him saying. "He's not your type. I mean, look how he dresses. He looks like a massage therapist. You can't date a massage therapist." It was true that Charlie's typical getup seemed to be tennis shoes and sweats, T-shirt, jean jacket, and a fanny pack, but I wasn't about to cop to being so shallow. The more my friends told me he was wrong for me, the more I'd push back. "No. That's how I've gotten into trouble." I was done with cool, handsome, and well dressed, and the more I said it, the more I convinced myself it was true. Even when it came to (wince) the cutoff jean vest. I let it go. Besides, Mehran and Jeremy weren't the final word. When Jenny met Charlie, she gushed. "We love him. He's amazing. He's the nicest guy. He so adores you." Jenny is tall, thin, and gorgeous, with long blond hair and a turned-up nose, but she's the biggest Jew you've ever met. She declared Charlie a "mensch," and she was right.

The first time I went to Charlie's apartment, I noticed that there was a Bible on the nightstand next to his bed. That should have been a red flag. Not that I'm hard-core Jewish. I'm not religious so much as spiritual, but—because of that—it was extreme for me to see a Bible sitting out on a nightstand. What's on your nightstand says a lot about who you are as a person. It's the last thing you read before going to sleep. He had a Bible. I had a stack of *Us Weekly*s. He was obviously serious about religion and I wasn't. Then, I think it was that same night, he told me that he was afraid of commitment. I remember telling my manager about the Bible and the commitment phobia. She said, "Forget the Bible. The commitment phobia is the real red flag. You can't go out with this guy. He just gave you the biggest gift he can give you: telling you you should get out now." She sent me the book *Men Who Can't Love* with key passages highlighted and a note that said, *Read this book. Get out now.* But the idea that I couldn't have him only made me want him more. Are you with me, girls? Wanting to "get" him made me stay. (Now, reflecting on that conversation with Charlie about commitment, I think the reality was that he'd never had a serious relationship. Ever. He was thirty-five or thirty-six at the time. Once he'd dated a girl for six months who'd broken his heart. It might have spared us both a lot of trouble if he actually *had* been hard to get.)

Soon after we started dating, I went to meet Charlie to see his friend's play. The show was in a small theater in a seedy area of Hollywood. His friend was starring in it, and Charlie had gotten there early to help her sell tickets. As I pulled up to the theater I saw him out on the corner, waiting for me, looking up and down the street for my car. My stomach turned in an *Ew, that is pathetic* way. I parked, and then I sat in my car and thought about it. He was out there waiting for me. Why did I find that pitiful? What the hell was wrong with me? I thought to myself, *For the first time in your life here's a guy who cares. He's being a gentleman, looking out for your car, making sure you're safe.* If I found that unattractive, the problem wasn't with him. It was with me.

I'd turned thirty. Ever since I was a child, I'd felt unworthy of being loved. I picked men who weren't available. They were present, somewhat, but they never took care of me the way people who love each other take care of each other: listening, helping, understanding. I never felt like I had a true companion. A person who was by my side, looking out for me as I would for him. For a long time I never thought I deserved more. Now I wanted to break that pattern. I wanted to enjoy being doted on. I wanted to be married. I wanted to have kids. I wanted to rent movies and eat takeout and tell my husband not to leave the toilet seat up. I wanted that whole life. I was ready to change my path.

So I changed it in my head. I told myself I was a good person. I deserved devotion. I deserved a man who would dote and care as much or more than I did. My mother liked to tell me, "Always remember: A man should love his woman a little bit more than she loves him." Charlie was different from anyone I'd ever dated. He cared about me the way a man should. So if my reaction to him was wrong and unhealthy, I would simply correct it. It was kind of an inward struggle—having a negative reaction to the man I was supposed to love and making a mental adjustment to correct it—but eventually it became such a habit that I forgot I was doing it. I thought it was a huge step.

Charlie's family was a major part of the attraction. After we'd been dating for six months, he took me to his mother's house in Peabody, Massachusetts. It was total suburbia, something I'd only experienced on TV (specifically, *Leave It to Beaver*), and I loved it. The house was a pale yellow gingerbread clapboard row house with white trim. Inside it was decorated in purple and yellow with floral fabrics every-where. And wreaths.

His mother had little knickknacks that said things like GARDENS GROW WITH LOVE. (My mother's version of that knickknack would say GARDENS GROW WITH A LARGE, FULL-TIME STAFF OF HORTICULTURISTS.)

I even thought it was adorable that Charlie's mom wouldn't let us sleep in the same room unless we were married. So quaint.

Charlie's parents were divorced, but they still did everything together for the sake of the family. He had two older sisters, both married with kids, within a ten-mile radius. When I first came into the house, his mother gave me a big hug. She asked me questions about my life. She was clearly proud of me, and she didn't even know me yet. My family never showed that kind of affection.

Dinner that night was served family-style. At the Manor a butler used tongs to deposit homemade dinner rolls on bread plates garnished with frozen balls of butter that the chef had carefully rolled in the kitchen. Here we passed around store-bought rolls and a stick of butter on a plate. At the Manor the wine, which dated from before I was born, was stored in a categorized, temperature-regulated wine cellar and recorked on a regular basis. When I couldn't find the red wine in the kitchen, his mother said, "Oh, but it's right there in the refrigerator!" I looked around at the house, his sisters, his parents, the meal. These people were everything my family wasn't. Close. Loving. Accepting. Interested. I wanted Charlie's family. I wanted to want him, but I didn't. I wanted the idea of him. I was completely in love with the idea of him. He was a nice guy, we were great friends, and I enjoyed his company on some level. I knew I wanted a nice guy, but I had too little experience with nice guys to know that one could actually be selective while staying in the nice-guy category.

Charlie doted on me, and in return I set out to be the best girlfriend I could. I tried to embrace everything he was and to become everything he wanted me to be. Sort of like my manager, he liked the sweet, funny, girl-next-door side of me. When he moved into my place, we didn't do it cavalierly. It was a big deal for both of us, and we knew it meant we were serious.

When Charlie moved in with me, the biggest change was that I became a churchgoing lady. Early in our relationship, soon after I'd caught a glimpse of that bedside Bible, he told me, "Religion is very important to me. It's a huge part of my life. I need a partner who understands that and participates in it with me. If you're not open to that, I don't know where this can go." After he moved in, we started going to church every Sunday. To me church was a foreign concept. I didn't have any friends who went to church other than with their families on Christmas Eve. Charlie never pushed it on me, he never forced it. He just said, "If you're interested in coming, I'd love that." I wanted to be his ideal mate. I decided to go with him every single Sunday.

I did it because it meant so much to Charlie, but I can't say I enjoyed church. The organization and structure of it weren't how I connected to God. For me spirituality is abstract and very individual. I believe in God and past lives and afterlife and angels, but not in a defined, "Here's how it all works" way. Honestly, in church with Charlie, I just wore the right clothes, sat politely, stood up when everyone else stood up, sat back down when everyone else sat back down, and got nothing out of it. It was like an acting exercise. Or a giant game of Simon Says. And even though I was doing it faithfully (so to speak), I didn't quite think of it as a life commitment. Then Charlie told me that when we had kids, they would go to church every Sunday. I said nonchalantly, "I don't know about that." But he said very certainly, "No, they will. My children will go to church every Sunday, and they'll go to Sunday school. You don't have to go if you don't want to. That's your choice." Yikes. Red flag number one was at full mast and waving heartily, but (surprise, surprise) I put off pledging allegiance.

Inevitably, the longer we were together, the more I let down my guard. I figured, *I'm with this person, he likes me, I can relax*. I'd tailored my overcoat of a personality to fit him, but little holes began to appear. One Sunday afternoon we were having drinks with a group of his friends in someone's backyard. I was talking with a few of the girls, and we started talking about sex. I said something raunchy, who knows what. Raunchy comes naturally to me—I don't log my raunch. It may have been something as relatively tame (for me) as using the f-word or talking about poo.

At home that night it came out that Charlie was totally offended. He said, "The way you behaved was not acceptable for someone I'm with." I was surprised. It seemed so old-fashioned for him to think I was unladylike. I was telling a story! The girls were laughing. I was being dirty, normal-dirty, the way I am with my friends. He said, "A girl I'm with isn't going to say the f-word and talk about sex in a joking manner." He'd caught a glimpse of the real me and didn't like it. How could I not be myself?

This old-fashioned side of Charlie wasn't completely unfamiliar. One day the two of us got into a car that a guy friend of ours was driving. I climbed into the passenger seat, leaving Charlie to slide into the back. Later he said it was inappropriate—that if there were two men and one lady in a car, the lady should always sit in the backseat. "Lady"? Hello, ginormous red flag number two.

Did I confront the issue head-on? Who, me? No, not even close. I just divided up my worlds. We'd go out with his friends. We'd go out with my friends. And then I'd go out alone with my friends so I could be silly, gross, dirty, or whatever, without worrying what he thought. There'd be a Marc Jacobs party and I'd say, "It's a fashion party, and you're not into that, so I'm going to go with Mehran." True, he didn't like that kind of party, but it was also my excuse to ditch him so I could feel comfortable being myself. It was the opposite of my life with the bad boys: Now I was the one who went out with friends and came home to find him waiting.

That's not to say we didn't have fun together; we did. For example, we'd gone to look at engagement rings. I loved doing that. Wait a minute. Why were we talking about marriage? I had to have known by now that I didn't want to be with this guy forever, right? Well, maybe I did, but I kept going. I wanted my life to fall into place. I wanted to get married. I desperately wanted Charlie to be the right guy. We lived together. We got along well. I cared deeply about him and liked his family. Everything was falling into place.

It was fall, almost Thanksgiving of 2003, when Charlie surprised me with a ring. He concocted an elaborate scheme involving his friends from New York, Bret and Dina. They were staying at Shutters, a top-end beachfront hotel on the beach in Santa Monica, and we were allegedly going to meet their baby in the hotel room and then go out to dinner. As we drove there, Bret called and said that something had come up—they'd be late but we should get a key from the front desk and just meet them in their room, or so the story went. I didn't think twice about it.

When Charlie opened the door to Bret and Dina's alleged hotel room, there were candles lit everywhere and music playing softly. In the first moment I thought, *Wow, this is awkward. Is this really safe with a baby around?* But a second later it was like a bunch of Polaroids assembling in my head. Flash: candles. Flash: rose petals everywhere. Flash: chilled champagne on the table. *Oh my God!* And just as I was putting it together, I turned to see Charlie on one knee. It was really happening. The moment every girl dreams about. I was a five-year-old girl dressed in a pink party dress realizing that her prince was coming. I was breathless. The ring was classic: a jaunty two-carat princess-cut diamond with filigree on a platinum band. It was from Philip Press. I'd spent years of my life repulsed by the showy diamonds my mother wore. I'd never wanted a classic big diamond. But for some reason, as I thought about getting married, I forgot who I was and turned to some image of what I thought a perfect wedding was supposed to be.

And Charlie was living up to that image. The whole moment was "perfect." I couldn't wait to call all of my friends. In hindsight I confused excitement with love, but hindsight and I have had lots of conversations about what happened with Charlie, most of which end in me saying to hindsight, *Thanks for all the information, but you're a little late.*

Charlie and I were debriefing on how it had all gone down when all of a sudden I said, "Did you ask my dad for my hand?" I was so caught up in the idea of our fairy-tale relationship that now I was making sure everything matched the illusion. I didn't stop to think about who I was or what was meaningful to me. All I knew was that in the movies the guy asked the dad for his daughter's hand. Charlie said, "Yes, actually, I did. I asked both your parents." I was impressed. What a great guy. He did everything right. And there was a reason I was doubly impressed. At the time my mother and I weren't speaking.

It all started with dinner at the Four Seasons. It was a big Thanksgiving-like dinner with our family and some other couples who were friends of my parents. Nanny was coming, as she always did to family gatherings. Her birthday was around that time, and I called my mother to see if she'd ordered a cake for Nanny. She said no, she hadn't. I said, "Well, we should call the Four Seasons. We have to get a cake." My mother said, "No. I have friends coming. We're not going to be celebrating her birthday." I started to get upset. "But it's her birthday! We have to acknowledge it." My mother was short and dismissive.

My next move was to get my dad on the phone. (Yeah, the old standard of parent manipulation. If Mom says no, call Dad.) I assumed my father would be horrified. But this time my mother had gotten to him first. When he got on the phone, he dismissed me, saying, "No. It's not happening." I called my mother back, and by the time the conversation ended I was so angry that I said, "Fuck you," and hung up. I may sometimes be foulmouthed, but never in my life had I said anything remotely like that to my mother. She's my parent. I was raised (by Nanny) to respect my elders. But I felt justified. I couldn't believe she'd refuse to do this for Nanny.

It was a lovely dinner at the Four Seasons. There were about ten of us seated at a long table in the restaurant. Dinner was a huge buffet with everything from a prime rib carving station to a sushi spread. My mother and I were civil to each other, but I hadn't forgotten Nanny's birthday. I brought a big purse with a small cake in it. When the right moment came, I pulled it out, lit candles, and led the singing. Nanny blew out the candles with a big smile on her face. I was satisfied. It was worth whatever family strife I'd caused to give one minute of pleasure to the woman who gave her life to my parents and raised their kids.

It was only a week or so later when Charlie took it upon himself to ask my parents for my hand in marriage. My mom and I hadn't spoken since the Cake Incident. Charlie called my parents' assistant one evening and made an appointment to see them the next day. Soon after he hung up the phone, the assistant called back. My parents would see him. Right now. Charlie wasn't prepared. As he told me that night at Shutters, he went to the freezer, grabbed two airplane mini-bottles of vodka, and downed them for courage. I don't blame him. He was going straight into the lion's den, and he knew it.

When Charlie arrived at the Manor, my parents were waiting for him in the office, which sounds weird, but it is the most comfortable room in the house (and *that* is the weird part). My father offered Charlie a drink, which he declined. Then my mother said, "We know why you've come." Charlie relaxed a little—maybe this wouldn't be so bad—but then my father said, "I can't believe Tori spoke that way to her mother." It suddenly dawned on Charlie: They thought he was there to patch up the fight over Nanny's cake. Charlie stopped them. He said, "I'm actually here because I respect and love your daughter. I will always take care of her, and I would like to ask for your blessing to marry her." There was a long pause. My mother and father sat there silently, if politely.

Finally my father said, "How 'bout that drink?" My mother added, "I'm sure Charlie could use a drink." The butler was called, and he brought three drinks. But there was no toasting or well-wishing. In fact, there was no response at all to Charlie's question. Instead, my father said something about football. I know nothing about football, so as to what he might have said about the 2003 football season on the occasion of being asked for his blessing in his daughter's marriage, your guess is as good as mine.

Charlie, bless his heart, stuck to his guns. He said, "I just asked for your blessing in marrying your daughter." They said something like, "Yeah, of course, yes." Again, Charlie pressed on. "I just asked for your daughter's hand in marriage. Don't you have any questions for me?" Once again, there was a long, reactionless pause. Then my mother said, "Tori spoke to me that way. How could she do that? I'm so hurt." My father said, "Her mom's really upset." My mother said, "Tori needs help. She needs major help. That's a very angry girl." The engagement was never mentioned again.

Although this was clearly . . . odd, it wasn't so unusual for my family. My whole life we didn't talk about anything emotional. I'd say, "I'm dating a guy," and they'd say, "Oh, great." No questions asked. When I'd have lunch with my dad, he'd never say, *Are you happy? What's going on? How's life?* He'd talk about my career and ask about the dogs. He sure cared deeply about those dogs.

We got engaged on a Saturday night. On Sunday, I called my parents. It was a tough call to make. I had so many mixed feelings: I still thought my anger about Nanny's cake was justified, but I knew my behavior was bad. Anyway, I ended up apologizing. I half hoped that the response might be, *I'm sorry too. I'm sorry I didn't listen.* No such luck. She said, "It's okay." And that was that. When I told her Charlie and I were engaged, she invited us over for dinner that night.

Dinner at the Manor was pleasant, even cordial. My mom asked a few questions about what we had in mind for the wedding. My dad didn't participate in the conversation. I doubt he had anything against Charlie. The best I can figure is that personal level of my life didn't exist for him, and he wanted to keep it that way. Nobody said, *We're so happy for you guys.* Nobody asked to see my ring. There were no hugs. There was no "Oh my God!" excitement. That was reserved for when my father had a show picked up. It was just a nice dinner together. So we sat there at the long table for twenty in the big dining room of that vast mansion where the hollowness of their response had plenty of room to echo.

The next day we flew east to Charlie's family. What a difference a day and a family made. It was radical. Charlie's family went crazy. There were hugs and good wishes all around. They welcomed me to the family, told me they loved me, asked questions about the engagement night and the wedding, and there was an abundance of love and warmth all around. *Yes*, I thought. *This is the way it's supposed to be. This is what I was missing.*

That night at his parents' house, Charlie went to bed in his separate room (yep, engaged still doesn't mean married). But I stayed up late looking for wedding venues on his mother's computer. The minute we were engaged, I became obsessed with the big party I was going to throw, the party of a lifetime. I didn't stop to think, *This is so nice. I'm engaged. I'm happy. I'm in love.* It was all wedding all the time.

## CHAPTER NINE

# Strings Attached (or Why I Didn't Notice That I Shouldn't Be Getting Married)

Charlie and I never fought. But less than two months before our wedding we went out to celebrate my birthday with a bunch of our friends. After dinner we were barhopping a little (if you can call it that when you're over thirty). At some point Charlie decided the night was over and he wanted to go home. I wasn't done, and I definitely didn't want to be told when to go home on my own birthday. Charlie grew increasingly pouty and agitated, and consequently, the party dwindled. It must have been around midnight when we ended up at Trader Vic's with my friends Mehran, Suzanne, Scout, and Bill. By then Charlie wasn't talking to me. I was annoyed and dismissive. He was a buzzkill.

When we got home, we talked about what had happened. I started saying things like, "Maybe we're too different. Maybe we're not meant to be together." And he was saying, "Why, because you want to stay out and drink more with your friends?" I'm sure he couldn't see why staying out a few hours later was a big deal to me. And it shouldn't have been. Except it was.

The next morning I woke up and heard him in the kitchen making coffee. I realized we hadn't resolved our argument—as far as I was concerned, we'd left it at: *Maybe this isn't right.* I walked into the kitchen not knowing what I would face. Charlie said cheerily, "Morning, honey. What do you want to do today? Maybe take the dogs on a hike?" And there it went, under the rug with all the other red flags. (Not to mix metaphors.)

Planning a wedding is notoriously a time when a bride and groom negotiate some of the issues—finances, family, friends, taste, religion, china patterns—that they'll have to navigate for the rest of their lives together. But planning our wedding wasn't about me and Charlie. It was about me and my mother.

As soon as Charlie and I announced our engagement, we started planning a party. A magazine was going to chip in for the cost. Meanwhile, my mother was recovering from back surgery at a Beverly Hills hotel called Le Meridien with a special floor for guests who want to recover Four Seasons–style. Before the surgery I'd e-mailed my mother asking for the names of the friends she wanted to invite to our engagement party. When I went to visit, I asked her if she'd been able to put together a list. She gestured toward copies of the Neiman Marcus and Horchow catalogs on her bed and said, "Please, Tori. I haven't even had a chance to read my magazines yet. How would I have a chance to put together a list for the engagement party?" Tears welled in my eyes. I didn't know what I'd done wrong. I think now that she didn't like that we were pulling the party together ourselves. She wanted to be more involved. I was her daughter. She wanted me to need her.

Then, a few weeks later, something fell through with the magazine. They backed out of sponsoring the engagement party. I was fretting about it, trying to figure out what we could afford, and of course all my friends were saying, "What's the big deal? Why don't you just ask your parents to help out?" It wasn't that simple, but I managed to ask my mother, who was home from her recovery retreat by now, if she wanted to be a part of the party, to help me plan it. She said, "Barbara Davis says she's never even heard of an engagement party." Barbara Davis is the high-society wife of the late Marvin Davis, the billionaire former owner of Twentieth Century Fox and the Denver Broncos, among other famous properties. The Carrington family on *Dynasty* was based on the Davises. And that was my mother's whole response: "Well, I talked to Barbara Davis, and she says she's never even heard of an engagement party." As if I were being self-indulgent and excessive for even having the idea.

I mean, I know an engagement party is not a mandatory milestone without which life can't be lived. But it wasn't something I invented. I'd been to plenty of engagement parties. All my friends had had them. It seemed likely that my mother had attended a fair share too. And Barbara Davis, for that matter. (In fact, not long after we were married, one of Barbara Davis's daughters would have one of the biggest engagement parties the world had ever seen. Barbara must have thought she invented the idea.) But I didn't want to argue with her. The next time we saw each other, I brought along an etiquette book. I said, "Look, Mom. Engagement parties exist. People have engagement parties." Ultimately, she decided to help me plan it and to pay for it.

As we planned the party, there were some differences of opinion, but we managed to compromise. She agreed to my florist. I agreed to her photographer. She wanted formal invitations that looked like wedding invitations. I agreed. Mostly, I let her do her thing, and the result was a wonderful party that Charlie and I wouldn't have been able to afford ourselves. But as we turned our attentions to the wedding itself, there were some danger signs. When it's someone else's purse, there are often strings attached. I call it the Champagne Beamer Syndrome. Growing up, my mother and I would go shopping together. I'd find a dress that I liked and call her attention to it. She'd walk away and select what she wanted to buy for me. Her wallet, her taste.

My mother liked to be involved, but her involvement came at a cost. I wanted a fairy-tale wedding. I'd always dreamed of a four-tiered wedding cake, the big white dress, my father walking me down the aisle, and the romantic first dance with my Prince Charming. And yes, I pretty much expected that my parents would pay for it. It was going to be expensive, but in context of what my parents had (and how much they spent on, say, my mother's jewelry), it wasn't exactly going to cramp their style. It was only when we started planning the wedding that it became clear just how big a price *I* was going to pay. In small, painful increments.

Charlie and I had our hearts set on getting married that summer at a vineyard. Okay, *I* had *my* heart set on getting married that summer at a vineyard, but it was the first thing we decided about the wedding. We wanted it outdoors. We were at my parents having dinner when we told my mother. We mentioned looking for venues in Santa Barbara, which is a couple hours from L.A., or in Napa Valley. My mother was against it. The reason she gave was that she didn't think my father should drive so far. True, my dad had been through throat cancer. But he'd been in remission for a couple of years. He wasn't his old self, but there was nothing physically wrong with him. He was still going to work, though on a modified schedule. I loved my father and cared just as much about his well-being as she did, but I didn't see why he couldn't step out of a chauffeured car and walk to a hotel room.

But maybe she was right. I wanted to accommodate him. (When I asked him how he felt about traveling, all he'd say was, "Oh, they don't want me to leave town.") We said that maybe we could find a vineyard in Malibu. My parents had a beach house in Malibu that they still went to all the time. They regularly drove to events in Pasadena, which is about the same distance away. But again my mother said it was too far. She said, "It needs to be within ten minutes of this house." I said, "Like at a hotel?" She said yes, but that was exactly what I didn't want. I knew I wanted an outdoor wedding. There was nothing gentle in the conversation, no *I'm sorry if you had your heart set, honey, but you have to consider* . . . She simply said, "It's not happening that way. You will not be getting married out of town."

I was too timid to stand up to my mother, but Charlie and I didn't let go of our idea. We finally found a vineyard in Malibu. It was the absolute closest vineyard I could find. I mean, you try Googling "Los Angeles vineyard." The heart of the city isn't exactly fertile wine country. Charlie and I went to look at it with Jenny and her husband, Norm. As we walked the grounds, I could picture the whole wedding: the cocktail area, an area where we could put lights in the trees and set up a dance floor, the exact place under a huge weeping willow tree where we'd get married.

I begged my mother to let us get married there. I reminded her that she and my dad could sleep at the beach house. There was some hope of convincing her—she said she wanted to see the place.

My mother had recently been spending a lot of time with my "Uncle Mark." Mark was an old friend of my father's who'd introduced my parents. He was always around while I was growing up, the fun, crazy uncle who would take us out for ice cream and start an ice-cream fight. We loved him, and he brought out a good side of my mother. He'd say, "Oh, Candy, warm up," and she'd laugh and soften. He somehow managed to make my family less uptight. Then he got convicted of racketeering and my parents cut their ties.

Then my mother ran into Mark at a charity event when my father was recovering from throat cancer. He asked how my dad was doing, and Mom broke down. She came home and said she had invited him over to a movie that weekend. It seemed silly to her that they hadn't talked for years. She thought he deserved a second chance.

Within five years it seemed like he'd taken over the family. What do I mean when I say that? He cultivated separate relationships with all four of us, winning our trust, and planting seeds against each other. He'd show up at my apartment and invite me out for lunch. At lunch he'd say, "Your dad's really hard on your mom. He's always putting her down," or "Your dad's losing it a little." Meanwhile, he cultivated my father's dependence on him, so if something went wrong in the house, instead of calling his assistant, Dad would call Mark. He'd say, "Mark gets things done around here." He made himself the glue of the family until both of my parents believed they needed him. Eventually the assistants had to go through Mark. Some of the house staff quit. My mom's two assistants who had been there for twenty years: gone apparently because they couldn't deal with Mark. Before he quit, one of the guards told me that Mark had asked security to keep logs of my father's behavior.

Uncle Mark put himself to me and Randy as the go-to guy. He'd say, "I can get your mother to agree to anything. Whatever you need, tell me." I know, the whole man-worming-his-way-into-an-unsuspecting-wealthy-family sounds like some TV movie cliché—which means if anyone should have recognized what he was doing, I should have. Oh well. Instead, when it came to selling my mother on the vineyard wedding, when Mark said, "We'll come with you and check out the place," I thought, *This is a little weird, but maybe he can convince my mom.*

At the vineyard Mom was skeptical. She was worried about the bug factor, and the sloping lawn, and the difficulty of wearing heels in the grass. But Mark told me she was going to agree. The place was pretty popular for weddings, so we booked the only weekend date that was still available: July 4. We sent out "save the date" cards. It was really happening!

On April 22 we went out to dinner to celebrate my father's birthday. Things were going along fine until, out of the blue, my mother dropped bomb number one. She said that she wanted to have the wedding at the Manor. To me family is closeness—at least that's what I craved from my family. It had been impossible for us to be close in a house that big. It was literally hard to find each other. The Manor, with its oversize, formal rooms, extensive live-in staff, unused party rooms, and odd indulgences like the doll museum displaying the Madame Alexander dolls, just seemed to further separate an already alienated family. She wanted to have my wedding in the ostentatious, impersonal, I-hated-everything-it-represented Manor? My stomach sank. And what was her great reason for changing the wedding location so late? Her friends didn't really want to drive all the way out to Malibu on a holiday weekend. The traffic could be so terrible . . . and that brought her to bomb number two. She wanted to move the wedding to July 3. Now my stomach turned. It was an amusement park ride in there, but I was anything but amused. And what was her great reason for changing the wedding date so late? Her friends had other parties and events on July 4. And besides, the wedding planner had told her that they would have to pay overtime for the valet parking at the Manor on the holiday so it would save money if we had it on July 3.

Let me remind you, this was April 22, and the wedding was set for July 4. Charlie and I looked at each other. Most of my guests lived in L.A., but Charlie's family was coming from Massachusetts and a number of his guests had already booked their flights to get early-bird rates and had made reservations at Malibu hotels. It wasn't so simple to change the date by a night. My mother said, "Don't worry. I'll pay the difference for anyone who changes their ticket." She said her travel agent would make the arrangements and pass the bill for the flight change on to my parents. It didn't make sense to me—surely the flight changes would cost as much or more than the parking valet's holiday rate. Still, Charlie and I said we would talk about it.

The next day Charlie and I went to the Manor with Mark and the wedding planner, who started showing us how it could work if we did the wedding on the grounds. Mark told me, "Think about this carefully. She wants it at the Manor. Think about how much you're going to get on other things if you give in on this. She won't cheap out at a party held at her own house." It might have occurred to me that Mark was feeding my mother the same line he fed me: *I can convince Tori to do anything.* Nonetheless, Charlie and I consented. We knew we could do worse than to get married on the manicured grounds of the biggest house in Los Angeles.

Unfortunately, as suspected, most of the people who had to change their tickets were on Charlie's side. He called my mother's travel agent to deal with his sisters' tickets. But the travel agent said, "There's a problem. I'm afraid I won't be able to make this change." It turned out that the new tickets were going to cost an extra thousand dollars each. The travel agent said that my mother had only authorized her to pay a maximum difference of *fifty dollars per ticket.*

This was exactly the situation my mother had promised she would smooth over. Charlie called her and said, "There must be some misunderstanding. I thought you said that you would pay for the difference." My mother said, "I don't understand why it's a thousand dollars. I talked to people, and they said it never costs more than fifty dollars to change a ticket." Charlie was flabbergasted. Did she think he or his sisters were trying to cheat her? He tried to clear things up. "Mrs. Spelling, I want to assure you I love your daughter, I want to make her happy, I would never take advantage of you." She said, "I don't know you, Charlie. I don't know your family." End of conversation. Charlie gave up. He was done. Charlie and I ended up paying for the many people who had to change stuff. She got her way.

Now that we'd "agreed" on the time and place, it was time to do the invitations. We didn't have much time. According to our wedding planner, they were supposed to go out two months before the wedding. We quickly ordered them up. Then my mother told us that she wanted us to sign a prenup. She offered to pay for Charlie's lawyer. I talked to Charlie about it. He wasn't thrilled with the idea. He thought prenups put a bad spin on things, a lack of faith in our love. But he said, "I love you. I don't believe in prenups, but if it makes your mother happy, I'll do it." That was part of what I loved about Charlie. He believed in us. He wanted me to be happy. His heart was in the right place.

We started the process. The lawyers were going back and forth. One or the other of them was always on vacation. It started to take a while. Meanwhile, the invitations were all printed and ready to go out. But my mother said, "Well, I'm not sending out the invitations until the prenup is signed." Er, okay, but if we'd known that, we would have started working on the prenup as soon as we got engaged. Two months to the wedding. Invitations sealed, stamped, and imprisoned on my mother's desk. The countdown was on.

That's about when it all started falling apart. Everything became a problem. My mother told me to reduce the guest list by fifty people—we were exceeding our budget. I'd never asked for anything in terms of catering or booze. But now she wanted me to call people who'd gotten "save the date" cards and tell friends they couldn't bring dates and wives they couldn't bring their husbands. It wasn't until a few days before the wedding that I finally laid eyes on her own guest list. It was a Who's Who of celebrities I didn't even know my parents had met, people like Jay Leno (who didn't come) and Anjelica

Huston (who did). She said that they were "frequently at parties together," but we were at a party three weeks before the wedding, and I remember seeing Anjelica Huston walk right past us without stopping. But she and her husband came to the wedding. Less than two months to the wedding. Fifty of my people uninvited.

The tension between me and my mother was too much for Charlie, so my friend Mehran stepped in to play husband at the cake tasting, the food tasting, the wine tasting, and the florist's. He's pretty much my gay husband anyway, and he was a good middleman. My mother was nicer to him than she was to me. She was completely over me, no matter how hard I tried to appease her. If I said I loved gardenias, she suddenly hated gardenias. The smell gave her a headache.

The third (yes, the third) flower meeting was supposed to be at two thirty. With a day's notice I called the wedding planner to tell her I had an audition. The wedding planner agreed to change the appointment to three o'clock and promised she'd let my mother know. When I arrived at three, my mother was there and she was fuming. She let me have it, shouting, "This is the last time you're doing this. You're late to everything. I won't take it anymore." I said, "I wasn't even late." She stormed out of the room. I wasn't even late. The wedding planner (brave woman) called her and admitted her mistake, but my mother said it didn't matter. She was angry at how I had spoken to her.

Time passed. Nothing was going right. The prenup still hadn't been finalized. The invitations still hadn't gone out. Three weeks before the wedding, a Thursday evening, I turned on my computer to find a businesslike e-mail from my mother. It read: *Tori: If the prenup is not signed by the end of business day tomorrow I will have no choice but to cancel the wedding.* Period. Then the wedding planner called me in a panic. My mother had told her to put everything on hold. The wedding might not happen. At least this panic virus seemed to wake the sleeping lawyers from their endless vacations and comma changes. We finally got a prenup and signed it. Great. Now the invitations could go out.

Ah, the invitations. The invitations that said to please respond by a certain date, a date that had long since passed. These now very late invitations finally got mailed. Then word started to filter back to us that people thought they were on the B-list of invitees because they'd received the invitations so late. What an achievement! We'd managed to alienate all our closest friends and family right before they came to bear witness to the biggest moment of our lives. I couldn't let them go on thinking they were second tier, so I sent out an e-mail saying that this was a problem that had to do with my family. At least that shifted the blame back in the right general direction.

Cut to a week before the wedding. Charlie's parents were hosting the rehearsal dinner on Friday, and my parents were hosting the wedding and the Sunday brunch, as the etiquette book dictated. Brunch was at the Hotel Bel-Air, a legendarily luxurious five-star hotel which happens to be the closest hotel to my parents' house. Even though it was just going to be July 4 hot dogs and hamburgers, and I'd paid for and made centerpieces with flags and sand and seashells myself, it was going to cost nine thousand dollars for about seventy people. That's the Bel-Air for you.

Then, one week before the wedding, my mother's chauffeur hand-delivered a letter to me. In it my mother said that she'd had so much stress planning the wedding that she couldn't deal with the brunch as well. I didn't know what to make of it. The brunch was already planned. The only "planning" that remained was paying the bill on the day of the brunch. Ah, that's what my mother must have meant. She didn't want to pay for the brunch. But why? Your guess is as good as mine. All I know is we didn't have nine thousand dollars to spend.

It's not like I'd insisted on the Bel-Air! Far from it. As my maid of honor, Jenny, pointed out, she would have been happy for me to have a post-wedding barbecue in her backyard. But how could I change everything now? The Bel-Air was also where I was to get ready for the wedding, and where Charlie and I were to spend our wedding night. Plus, our guests had already RSVP'd. Charlie's mother cried when we told her what was going on. She was so upset for us that she generously volunteered to pay for it, but she was already paying for the rehearsal dinner. Nine thousand dollars was nothing to my parents, but it would certainly have been a real expense for her, as it was for us. We agreed to split it.

My beloved dogs had long-planned roles in the wedding. Mimi La Rue was our flower girl, and my other dog, Ferris, would be the ring bearer. Mimi had a special dress designed for the occasion to match the bridesmaids' dresses, and she was to be transported in a floral, rose-decorated wagon. Ferris had a custom-made tux with a matching bow tie. But the day before the wedding rehearsal Charlie got a call from Uncle Mark. The message from my mother and father was that dogs would not be allowed at the wedding. When Charlie spoke to my father, he said, "Well, this is just silly. She's not an eighteen-year-old girl. She's an adult. All our friends are going to be there. It's going to be embarrassing." We compromised: The dogs were allowed up the aisle, but then someone had to take them home right away. They were not permitted to remain anywhere on the property, not even in the guards' room with all my parents' dogs.

The rehearsal for the wedding was at the Manor. Charlie and I showed up fully dressed for the rehearsal dinner. Like the wedding, it had a twenties theme—well, maybe "theme" is too strong and cheesy a word—it was a twenties "feel." I was wearing a dusty rose Yves Saint Laurent dress with long loopy fake diamonds by the yard. (I had asked my mother if she had any such diamonds in her collection that I could borrow, but she said, "No, I have nothing like that," so I bought them at XIV Karats in Beverly Hills, where they had crystal costume ones.) My mother came to the rehearsal in a jogging suit. She'd have plenty of time to get dressed before the dinner.

The rehearsal dinner was at a Mediterranean restaurant called Byblos in Westwood. When my mother came in, I was shocked to see what she was wearing. She had on a dusty rose top—the exact color I was wearing. She knew I planned to wear that dress—it was the same color as my bridesmaids' dresses. And she'd just seen me in it at the rehearsal. Interesting choice. But to top it off, she was wearing diamonds by the yard. The real ones. The ones she'd definitely said did not exist.

No matter. There were belly dancers, music, dancing, food, and toasts to refocus my attention on more important things. I had given Charlie a watch, but that night he gave me a much more personal present. He had two best friends who were songwriters, and he worked with them to write a song for me called "I Love You, Crazy" about how he loved me in spite of the many fears and compulsions

I had. With his friends accompanying on the piano, he sang it to me that night. My friends thought it was cheesy and showy, but I thought it was cute and it made me cry.

After I'd had a bit to drink and been softened by all the warm toasts and spirit of the night, I decided to mend bridges with my mother. I hugged her and told her I loved her. She said she loved me too, and we both cried. These moments happen in our relationship. We have periods of stress and tension, then we go out, have a few drinks, and end up hugging and teary-eyed, promising to make an effort. I knew this wasn't "happily ever after," but after all the planning stress, the wedding was finally happening. We'd made it. It had to be smooth sailing from here, right? *Right?*

*CHAPTER TEN*

# Last-Minute Changes

The morning of the wedding I woke up with a migraine. In a full panic Jenny called the hotel desk for help. Ah, the Bel-Air. They sent over a guy with a massage chair to rub my shoulders. Amazingly, it worked. (Note to self: Always have a guy with a massage chair handy.) My bridesmaids and I ordered eggs Benedict and mimosas and watched Lindsay Lohan in *Confessions of a Teenage Drama Queen*. In the early afternoon we all had hair and makeup done. Meanwhile, it had been organized that trays of food were sent over to my apartment, where Charlie and the guys were getting ready.

We arrived at the Manor early, so we could have our photos taken before the guests arrived. I found out later that before I appeared with my party, Charlie and his groomsmen were led to a room and instructed to stay there. Security was posted outside the door. They literally weren't allowed to leave the room! Maybe my parents were afraid they'd steal something. I was wearing a Badgley Mischka dress that I'd designed. My hair was down, parted on the side with soft, old-fashioned curls. I wore an antique diamond headband, earrings, and bracelets, all of which were borrowed from Neil Lane. Attached to the headband was a veil that matched my dress and didn't cover my face. My makeup was light and glowing. I turned to my mother and said, "Mom, you look so beautiful." She thanked me but said nothing in return. I was standing there in my wedding dress. I'd had my nose done fifteen years earlier, but I still didn't get to feel pretty in her eyes. With Mark, I was more direct. He was bustling around, in organizational mode as always: checking on security, making sure no guests entered the forbidden zone that happened to be the entire house. Again, no reaction to me as bride. I said, "Well? Do I look okay?" He said something canned like, "Oh, yeah, you look beautiful," and then went back to directing the caterers.

My "bridesmaids" were Jenny, Jennifer, Amy, Sara, and Kate, and two guys: Mehran and Pete. Charlie's two nieces were my junior bridesmaids. Charlie had five groomsmen, I think, including my brother, and three women in his wedding party. One of his friends, Mary, went up to my mother to introduce herself and say thank you. She reached out to shake hands. My mother said, "Mary, can't you see I'm holding my bouquet?"

I wanted the wedding to look like the movie *The Great Gatsby*, with old-school twenties glamour. Not like a costume ball—nothing gaudy, just a tone. After the guests left their cars with the valet (July 3!—discount rates!), they entered the service parking entrance and garage for a prewedding cocktail hour. That's right, cocktails in the parking lot, but you never would have known. They put down carpet, lattices, and flowers. Twenties music was playing. Waiters in white dinner jackets with black bow ties and black pants served mint juleps and hors d'oeuvres. Or so I'm told. Charlie and I weren't there—we were still having pictures taken.

The wedding took place in the big front courtyard of the Manor— the grand entrance that I never used when visiting my parents. There was a huge circular driveway with a fountain in the middle of it. For the wedding the fountain had been covered with a platform. Now, on top of the covered fountain, below a chuppah of white roses and flowers, a rabbi, a minister, and Charlie stood waiting for me to arrive. The wedding party was below, surrounding the fountain, and the guests were spread out on what was ordinarily the vast driveway. Although we had the rabbi, I didn't want to offer yarmulkes to the guests. My mother thought we had to give guests the option, but I disagreed. On the wedding video, as Charlie waits for me to approach, you see a sea of white disks on the male guests' heads and you can hear him say, "Oh, God, Tori's going to be furious. There's yarmulkes." The wedding planner later told him that my mother insisted. (And, apparently, instructed that it be kept secret from me.)

There was one moment in the entire wedding that really moved me. I was standing inside. I had picked a song to accompany my wedding party as they walked down the aisle. It was the theme song from *Ice Castles*—surely you remember? "Through the Eyes of Love"? I know it's beyond cheesy, but the song had such a huge effect on my life. I loved the movie. I wanted to be an ice skater because of that movie. When I took piano lessons, "Ice Castles" was the first song I learned to play. When I took singing lessons, "Ice Castles" was the first song I wanted to sing. When I lost my virginity, "Ice Castles" was . . . not on the stereo. Geez, give me a little credit. Anyway, it was always a big song for me. A string quartet played the processional and somehow managed to make it sound exactly right. Watching my old, beloved friends walk down the aisle toward the fountain, I cried so hard that my nose was running when my turn came.

My father walked me down the aisle. Because my father was older, I always had a fear that he'd die before I got married. That walk down the aisle was something that I desperately wanted to share with him. It wasn't the moment itself so much as knowing that no matter how young I was when he died, I'd always have that memory. No matter what happened, it wouldn't be something I'd missed. That was worth the whole wedding right there. He was eighty-one and pretty frail. It took everything he had to walk with me.

Maybe every bride feels a little removed from the wedding itself, but as I walked, I felt like I was onstage. I was trying to have the exact right amount of emotion and grace, trying to make sure my face showed what a bride should feel. I found out later that my friends weren't staring overwhelmed at my perfect balance of modest beauty. No, they were too busy trying not to laugh at Charlie. According to Jenny, when he saw me appear, he gasped and clutched his heart with passion. Jenny said, "I almost pissed in my pants."

Wait. Let's leave me walking down the aisle for a bit. What about my friends? What did they think of this whole wedding train that was barreling toward marital collapse? (Oops—did I give away the unhappy ending? Nah, didn't think so.)

Suzanne, one of Charlie's best friends (and now mine—I won her in the divorce), had an inkling this wasn't a perfect match. Suzanne helped me register since she knew what china and what crystal and what silver I should like and (in spite of the fact that I would later discover that my mother has an entire room devoted to silver) I knew nothing. After going to Gearys in Beverly Hills to choose a china pattern, we went out for cocktails. Suzanne, in her Southern accent, said, "You sure about this? Because you know he's very Christian and doesn't believe in divorce." Imitating her accent, I joked, "But momma does." Though I believed in marriage, some part of me knew that divorce was an escape hatch if I needed it.

Mehran, to his credit, kept asking, "Are you sure? Are you sure you want to marry him?" Mehran often told me Charlie wasn't right for me. He'd say, "I just feel like he only knows ten percent of you. How can you be with someone like that?" I didn't want to hear any of it. I'd say, "I've already planned the wedding! Why are you doing this to me?" Even as I brushed him off, Mehran's concerns stayed with me. He was right. Charlie only wanted the sweet, perfect-wife part of me. I haven't done all the math on my various personalities, but I'm pretty sure Mehran was right: sweet, perfect wife is only about 10 percent of the whole package

Mehran was remarkably persistent. He, his boyfriend Jeremy, and I all had the same therapist. I don't know why the two of them had the same therapist—that doesn't seem ideal—but I know why I did. Because one year for Christmas, Jeremy gave me two presents: a tank top that said DONNA MARTIN IS DEAD and a gift certificate to their therapist. If that isn't true friendship, I don't know what is. Anyway, even our therapist was telling Mehran he had to shut up and let me go through it. But Mehran wouldn't stop. He kept saying, "Who cares about the wedding? If you're not sure, don't do it."

He was so fixated on this whole he-isn't-right-for-you thing that it became kind of a joke. Mehran and I started envisioning grand scenarios of how I would escape the wedding if I changed my mind. Mehran would say, "Just look over at me and give the cue. I'll pull out my walkie-talkie, a helicopter will appear out of nowhere, and a ladder will unfurl. Halfway down the ladder will be a butler with two glasses of Veuve. We'll climb up and escape to the south of France, where we'll lounge on the beach until the scandal dies down." (Later, for my show *So NoTORIous,* I came up with a whole episode where each of the main characters envisions a great escape out of the wedding. You see each escape through a different character's eyes. The last character is Mimi. In her fantasy she's a Great Dane. The camera runs and pants toward me and my ill-chosen groom. Great Dane Mimi knocks him down and swoops me away. But *So NoTORIous* wasn't on the air long enough to get to any wedding episode.)

My maid of honor, Jenny, took things a little more seriously than Mehran. Jenny is always very practical and down-to-earth. A week before the wedding she (unbeknownst to me) called Mehran and said, "Stop it. You know Tori. She's not going to cancel the wedding. It's too late. At this point she's going to have to figure out for herself that he's not right for her."

Mehran and I joked about the great wedding escape, but in a way what happened with his boyfriend—my dearest friend Jeremy—had something to do with why I went through with it. A year earlier, when I was almost thirty and Jeremy was twenty-eight, he died of sudden heart failure.

One night he and Mehran went to pick up food from Chin Chin at Sunset Plaza. They drove over a bump. Jeremy grabbed his heart, said, "That was a big one," and started having a seizure. Mehran called 911. While all this was happening, I was coming home from watching a friend's music performance. I'm not a phone person. I never answer my cell phone or check my voice mail—the mailbox is almost always full and not accepting new messages. Sometimes I just clear it all without listening to the ninety or so messages that have accumulated. But that night for some reason I checked my voice mail. The most recent message was Mehran, and he was crying. He said, "Jeremy's been rushed to Cedars. He had a heart attack."

I went straight to Cedars Sinai (a big hospital in West Hollywood). Mehran pulled up at the same time. They put us in a waiting room. Eventually a doctor came in and started asking us questions in a dispassionate tone. Finally Mehran interrupted to ask, "Is he going to be okay?" The doctor said matter-of-factly, "No, he's passed."

My first instinct was to care for Mehran, to pull myself together for him. That night Mehran came to my apartment. Charlie moved into the guest room, and Mehran stayed with me. Every morning when I woke up, the first thing I heard was Mehran sobbing. We did a shiva even though Mehran and Jeremy weren't Jewish, having people over throughout the day and night for seven days.

Charlie was wonderful during that time. He was so gentle and caring. Not only did he sacrifice his place in our bed to Mehran, but he gave us time together, picked up food for us, and tried as best he could to be quietly helpful and supportive. I knew he'd take care of me like that forever. It made a huge impact. I was in this for keeps. And today was the day I said so to the world.

Okay, now back to the walk down the aisle. As I walked out of the Manor, I realized that there were helicopters buzzing constantly overhead. Wow, maybe Mehran really did have an escape plan for me. Later I'd find out that there were helicopters filming and news crews trying to interview people as they walked into the wedding as if it were a red-carpet event. Throughout the ceremony you could barely hear anything over the helicopters. The rabbi and the minister did their bit. Bride and groom kissed. I still felt like I was in a play. Not a dream, a play, where I was the bride and the vows made me shaky and excited and the kiss made my heart flutter. Did my heart flutter? No. But I was so in the character of the bride that I almost believed it did.

The string quartet played a funky, upbeat version of "I Got You Babe" as we recessed up the aisle. I know it sounds cold, but it was Charlie's choice. It meant nothing to me.

After the ceremony was a second cocktail hour, this one poolside. In the center of the pool was a topiary shaped into an intertwined *C* and *V* (for Charles and Victoria—our real names). It was the same intertwined symbol that appeared on our wedding invitation. Candles floated in the pool and adorned the patio. Under the gazebo there was an old-fashioned champagne fountain. The champagne wasn't served in traditional flutes. Instead, we had it in champagne saucers. There were more hors d'oeuvres and a bar with a sushi chef making rolls and sushi. (It was practically my wedding to Mehran—he and I planned the whole thing.)

Charlie and I didn't go to this cocktail party either. Instead, they took us up to one of my parents' rooms. It was supposed to be an intimate time where we could have some hors d'oeuvres and champagne while looking out the windows at all our wedding guests below. There was a makeup station—a mirror surrounded by lightbulbs—

and people touched up my makeup and hair. Then one of the two photographers decided that the light was absolutely perfect for some black-and-white movie-star photos of me. So he started shooting me in various retro poses, alone, while Charlie waited. So much for our moment of intimacy and reflection. Not that I was dying to stare into his eyes. Nor did the nonconfrontational part of me want to go down and talk to strangers—half of the guests below. (Did I mention that Ed McMahon was at my wedding? Ed McMahon was at my wedding. I have no idea why, except that he once gave my father a tacky fish-themed windmill that was my father's pride and joy.) Also in attendance: Jackie Collins, Paul Anka, Bob Newhart, and Don Rickles.

After cocktails the guests walked to a big white tent in the middle of the back lawn for dinner and dancing. The tent took up nearly the entire lawn. It had chandeliers and huge floral arrangements. Wolfgang Puck catered the wedding—the Spago Wolfgang Puck, not the airport chain Wolfgang Puck. Mehran and I had handpicked everything for the tables: the napkins, the napkin holders, the glasses, the silverware, the chair cushions. There was antique lace draped over the tables. Outside the tent was a lounge area with a martini bar and all-white furniture—couches and armchairs—and white rugs. We had those fancy port-a-potties you can get for weddings, and guests could also use the pool house bathroom. There was a big band—maybe twelve people?—that started by playing jazz. Then, as the night went on, it progressed to fun karaoke rock that people could dance to.

Charlie and I were introduced and came onto the white dance floor for our first dance. We'd taken six dance lessons to choreograph and perfect our performance. The band kicked in with our song, Harry Connick Jr. singing "More" by Andy Williams, and we started. Charlie was totally screwing it up from the very beginning. I started whispering into his ear, telling him he was doing it wrong and trying to get him back on track. Charlie whispered back, "Relax, who cares?" But I cared. It was a big show. I was trying to impress everyone there. It wasn't about me. It was about them. Did they like the party I planned? Was this a beautiful, memorable, moving wedding? Was I a perfect bride? I don't know who that bride was: Ordinarily, I don't care about appearances. At any rate, our dance went down the tubes. We were so out of rhythm that we stopped and I said, "Oops, take two!" Everyone laughed and we tried again.

During dinner there was a guy we'd flown in from Vegas to sing Sinatra crooner songs. He sounded just like him. Then, when he finished up, my mother took the microphone to announce for all the guests to hear that she had a big surprise for me and Charlie. She'd hired Michael Feinstein, the famous singer and pianist of *Great American Songbook* fame, to fly in from New York to sing for us. I have no idea how much people like that cost, but my best guess would be a hundred thousand dollars. After all the cuts and budgeting, after telling friends they couldn't bring their husbands, here was Michael Feinstein, who anyone in *my* generation would agree is very appealing to *her* generation. That was our big gift. For him to play for her friends.

As it turned out, Charlie's dad was a real Michael Feinstein fan (like I said: *her* generation). He was so blown away that during the performance he came up to my mother to say thank you. She said, "Well, if you love him so much, why don't you go and listen to him." Charlie's poor, harmless dad.

During dinner there were toasts. At one point my parents came up to the microphone. My father, who was sort of out of it, said something like, "And I don't care what people always say, my dear wife does nothing wrong." I had no idea what he was talking about.

My mother grabbed the mike away from my father and commenced her own speech. Teary-eyed, she called me her "princess," something she'd never called me before. She welcomed Charlie's family to ours. It was hard to believe that what came out of her mouth was sincere. From the moment Charlie asked her and my father for their blessing, there hadn't been a single moment where I felt like she cared about my life with this man, about my happiness, about who I was or what this night might mean. There had been no hugs and kisses. Yes, we'd had our moment the night before, but it had been booze-lubricated. As she spoke, I realized that I couldn't forget everything that had gone on between us throughout the six months of planning the wedding and on the day of the wedding itself. Whatever hope I'd had that this celebration and the process leading up to it could bring us closer was completely gone. The damage was irreversible. I felt hollow. There was no question in my mind that my mother's wedding toast was for the benefit of the friends (and celebrities I'd never met) she'd invited to my wedding.

We didn't go around to tables the way some brides and grooms do (and the way my mom and Mark did together). I honestly didn't know half the people there. What was I going to say? *Hi, Ed McMahon. Nice to meet you. Thanks for coming to my wedding. It means so much to me that you could bear witness. Oh, and would you mind going up to the mike and saying, "Heeeeeeeere's Tori"?* I don't think so. Afterward my mom said people were disappointed that I hadn't made the rounds. Even so, plenty of the people I'd never met came up to me. Some told me about their wedding experiences. Some said they were happy for me. It was all so stilted and formal. There was no way I could enjoy myself talking to strangers like that. But then at some point Jenny, excellent maid of honor that she was, grabbed me, sat me down, and started feeding me and handing me drinks. Then I started to loosen up.

Dinner finished, and the party kicked in. The photographer was hired until midnight, but the party went until one a.m. When they asked if it was okay to work overtime, I said yes. It cost an extra nine hundred dollars. (My mother sent me the bill.) And in spite of, or because of, the two cocktail parties and the martini bar, we ran out of alcohol, so they had to dig into my parents' wine cellar. (My mother didn't charge me for that.) When people come to Aaron Spelling's daughter's wedding, they apparently expect to booze it up.

I spent the last part of the wedding talking to my friends—Jennie, Tiffani, Jason, and Ian from my *90210* days were there—and on the dance floor. While I danced, Charlie was with his family and friends. He was my new husband, but we didn't have a single real moment together, no chance to look at each other and connect. We were both so busy the whole wedding. Or so I thought. Now I think it was me, that I didn't make room for that connection and didn't want to notice that it was missing. When the time came to go home, I didn't want to leave my friends. Charlie had to pull me off the dance floor.

As our guests waited for their cars at the valet, they were served cookies and shot glasses of milk. But Charlie and I were driven to the Bel-Air. On the way Charlie said he was sorry he'd pulled me away but it was our wedding night and he refused to be one of those couples who stayed too long, got drunk, and didn't have sex on their wedding night. Our suite back at the Bel-Air had been cleaned up after all the bridesmaid prep. Now it was rigged out with chocolate, champagne, and music playing. There were rose petals everywhere. I was really excited to discover that there were gardenias floating in the tub (since my mother didn't want them at the wedding), so I took a bath and luxuriated there, drinking champagne by myself, delaying consummation as long as I could.

The next day was the Fourth of July brunch at the Bel-Air. As planned, it was a casual barbecue. My mom showed up with Mark. She seemed perfectly fine, pleased with how the wedding had gone and happy to be there. Eye of the storm—I should have known.

The wedding planner called my cell phone right before the brunch. She said the hotel didn't take credit cards over the phone. They needed to see my mother's credit card in person to charge us for the two-bedroom bungalow that I'd stayed in. It was an expensive bungalow. I shared it on Friday with all the bridesmaids and Mehran. Plus, my wedding party had food and champagne as we were getting ready. Then I stayed there Saturday and Sunday nights with Charlie. The suite was thirty-five hundred dollars per night, and the total bill came to over ten thousand dollars. (I know: gasp. It's a really expensive hotel.) The wedding planner told me to ask my mother to stop by the hotel office with the card. Uh-oh. I knew how this was going to go. The wedding planner wouldn't have booked the suite without my mother's approval, but based on her financial withdrawal from the brunch, that approval wasn't exactly reliable. Now the wedding planner was having me do her dirty work. She was probably just as scared as I was.

It was the day after my wedding. I didn't want to deal. So I asked my brother to do it. In short order Randy came back and said, "She says she wasn't told about this." She knew. Of course she knew. We'd talked about it. She'd had catered food delivered to Charlie's wedding party but not mine because she knew we were charging it to the room where she knew we were staying and which she knew we couldn't afford.

My brother didn't want to get in the middle. I was forced to go over to her. I was shaking, but I walked up to her calmly and drew her aside. I kept my voice low. The brunch was in full swing now, and I didn't want anyone to know there were money conflicts. At Aaron Spelling's daughter's wedding! Again, my mother said, "Well, I wasn't told about this." I told her it was in the budget, but she claimed not to know about it. I was so frustrated, I started to cry. I said, "Fine, Mom. I will pay for it. But I can't afford it right now. Can you pay for it and I will pay you back?" "No," she said, "and you're embarrassing me. Keep your voice down." Then she said, "I can't believe you're doing this to me right now." I didn't know how to respond to that.

Then Mark swooped in as he did so well. He handed me his credit card and said, "Take this to the front desk. I'll sort it out with your mother." Apparently, after I left, she burst into tears. She turned to Mark and said, "I have to leave. I can't be here any longer. Take me out of here."

I retreated to the bathroom crying hysterically. The night before had been wonderful. It seemed worth all the months of struggle with my mother. But this erased all of it. Our relationship was in pieces. I thought she'd treated me horribly. She probably thought she'd given me an expensive wedding and I didn't appreciate it. What had gone so terribly wrong?

It was over. I was married. To Charlie. There was no wedding drama left to distract me from the reality of my relationship. The next day we left on our honeymoon. I called home once but my mother wouldn't come to the phone. My father said, "She's busy packing for a trip to Vegas, but you have a great honeymoon."

Right when I came back from the honeymoon is when I decided to do *So NoTORIous*.

CHAPTER ELEVEN

## The Joke's on Me

*Beverly Hills, 90210* was long past. I'd pitched shows where I was meant to star as a publicist or a radio host or a dolphin-trainer. I'd done several pilots that hadn't gone anywhere. I was always playing someone poor: a poor waitress, a poor shoe saleswoman, or a poor dogwalker. In one of the pilots I pull a quarter out of the couch and say, "Now maybe I can afford to pay rent!" It got a big laugh from the studio audience, and I'm pretty sure it wasn't my delivery of the line so much as the notion of Tori Spelling hunting for spare change.

I still hadn't lived down my own name. When I did talk shows, they'd always ask about my parents' mansion and being Aaron Spelling's daughter before they asked about whatever project I was there to promote. My heart would sink. I'd walk out as an actress, and in a moment I'd be back to everything I was trying to escape.

At first I tried to answer their questions accurately. I'd say, "Well, technically, I didn't grow up in the mansion. We didn't move there until . . ." But as I became more seasoned, I just laughed it off, saying, "I still haven't seen every room" or "Once I was lost for three weeks before they found me." Then I'd move on to talking about my project.

One night I was at dinner with my agent, and she said, "You have amazing stories. You should just do a TV show based on your life. *That's* what people want to see." It reminded me of the advice Keenen Ivory Wayans had given me on *Scary Movie 2*—to give people what they expected of me at the same time that I showed them who I really was. I'd been in *Scream 2* making fun of myself. I was finally ready to go whole hog. I was tired of trying to get away from being Tori Spelling. I figured, if that's what everyone wants, they can have it. Forget that dream of being Meryl Streep. I was ready to give them me. Tori Spelling. I started to pitch a scripted comedy loosely based on my life after *90210*. It was called *So NoTORIous.*

I put together a whole binder of the horrible tabloid articles about me. I had a T-shirt made that said NO, I DON'T LIVE AT THE MANSION. NO, I DON'T HATE SHANNEN DOHERTY. NO, I HAVEN'T HAD RIBS REMOVED. BUT YES, I DO DRESS UP MY PUG. I went to the networks, saying, "Here are the things that have been written about me, and here's the truth. Please laugh at it. Laugh at my life. I do."

Even though most of my pitch was about what it was like for me growing up, the executives ate up the bizarre celebrity stories. I told them about how Farrah Fawcett moved into my building, right next door on the fourteenth floor. My friends assumed I knew her

because my dad produced *Charlie's Angels,* but the truth was that I
hadn't seen her since I was four or five years old.

Soon after Farrah moved in, I had a Halloween party. It was
maybe thirty to forty people, with a mix of catered food and stuff
my friends and I had made. The music was on, not very loud, and it
was still pretty early. Then the phone rang. It was the concierge calling from the lobby. He said, "Hi, we have Miss Fawcett on the line
for you." I panicked. What did she want? Was the music bothering
her? It was only nine o'clock. I wasn't about to take this one on. I
said, "Can you take a message?"

When I got off the phone, my friends were very excited to hear
that Farrah Fawcett had called. They didn't seem to care that she
was probably furious with me for causing a public nuisance and was
calling to chew me out for being such a terrible neighbor. No, my
friends were into her, and they wanted me to call her back right
away. My friend Amy, tipsy, took it upon herself to call down to
the concierge. She came back all proud of herself. She said, "I spoke
to the front desk. Farrah explained the situation. She would like to
borrow a potato. That's the message she left. And she left her phone
number so we can call her back directly."

I was confused. I hadn't had any contact with Farrah Fawcett since
I was a kid. Why would she want to borrow a *potato*? Why would
she want to borrow a potato in the middle of a Halloween party?
Amy said, "Don't you get it? 'Potato' means 'pot.' She didn't want
to tell the front desk that she wants to know if you have any pot.
It's a code." So Amy, with very enthusiastic support from the other
assembled guests, called Farrah back.

A few minutes later a somewhat less enthusiastic Amy came to find me. "Well, it turns out she really does want a potato." Farrah and her boyfriend were making dinner, and they had steaks but they didn't have potatoes. She thought maybe we had potatoes. Amy said, "I told her there's plenty of food here and invited her over."

Farrah and her boyfriend were coming to my Halloween party! I looked around—luckily, there was nobody in a Farrah Fawcett costume. Everyone was psyched. Then the doorbell rang, and Farrah and her boyfriend came in. Since she didn't know anyone, I put aside my other hostess duties and focused on Farrah. They got some food and sat down on the couch. I smiled and nodded at her. She smiled and nodded back. Everyone sat there, smiling and nodding at each other. Soon all the friends who'd been so enthusiastic about her attendance slowly moved away, leaving an empty circle around her spot on the couch. Twenty minutes later everyone was gone. What happened? All she'd done was sit pleasantly on the couch and have a few bites to eat. From then on we joked that if we ever wanted to clear out a party, we'd just invite Farrah back over.

My pitch wasn't just a bunch of novelty celebrity anecdotes. All the characters were based on real people in my life. My roommate on the show was based on Pete. Pete is respectable now, married with a family, and he hates to be reminded of his sordid past, but when he saw that he was being played by a very handsome actor, James Carpinello, all was forgiven. The gay best friend character, Sasan, was based on Mehran and played by Zach Quinto, who became a real friend. His portrayal of Mehran was pretty much dead-on. There were some differences: Sasan lived with his parents and didn't really have a job. Mehran has a business degree and is a serious professional. The character Janey started off based on Jenny, but Janey's overtly sexual, and that's not Jenny at all. In the show Janey was my girlfriend from before I was famous and my fame didn't mean anything to her. She just called it like it was. Jenny's very much like that—honest and protective.

*So NoTORIous* had other familiar characters in it: a nanny, and a controlling mother, and my father appearing only by speaker phone à la Charlie in *Charlie's Angels*. There were flashbacks to some of the more unusual moments in my childhood, some real, some fiction, and some in between. In the episode called "Whole," there's a scene that takes place in a cult. A bunch of people are sitting around a circle confessing what's keeping them from being "relevant." One says, "I'm a crystal meth addict." The next says, "I'm a sexual compulsive." When my turn comes around, stymied for any better description of my lifelong struggle, I pause, then, flustered, burst out, "I'm a . . . Tori Spelling." That's what *So NoTORIous* was meant to mock. Tori Spelling was my personal affliction (custom-made like all my Halloween costumes). It was the punch line to the joke of my life. Tori Spelling wasn't me so much as it was a name I'd spent most of my life trying to live down. *So NoTORIous* was exactly what Keenen Ivory Wayans had been getting at—a place where the perception and the reality of who I was would intersect. My life was already being documented by paparazzi. Now I would document it myself and show what it was like from my perspective.

The response to the pitch was better than I could have hoped. There was a bidding war between NBC, The WB, and UPN. Then The WB dropped out, and it was between UPN and NBC. I didn't know which one to go with. The show could be a small fish in a big pond (NBC) or a big fish in a small pond (UPN). Ultimately, I chose NBC. I figured if I was going to put a version of my life out there, and I was going to play myself, then I wanted to really go for it and play with the big guys. At the time NBC was *the* place for sitcoms. I didn't want to have any regrets.

Just because the network hires you to write a pilot doesn't mean it's going to be filmed. And just because it's shot doesn't mean they'll put it on the air. I'd been involved with enough failed pilots to know the risks and hurdles.

My writers, cocreators, and I finished the first script, and it was picked up, which meant that we'd get to make our pilot. That's a huge triumph. As we worked on the pilot, I'd talk to my dad about it as a producer. I was so proud and excited to be in the editing room. My dad would say things like, "Oh, you mentioned NBC. Well, I know everyone there. I can put a good word in for you." He wanted me to use his writers ("I have the best writers"). He offered me his editors ("I have the best editors"). My dad really wanted to help the only way he knew how, which was by doing it for me. He couldn't quite grasp that I was accomplishing something all on my own.

My mother knew at least a little about the show. Soon after the script got picked up for a pilot, my mother e-mailed me saying, *Congratulations on your script being picked up. We have some concerns about it being about the family. Before you go ahead and film this we request to see a script.* Word was that the actress Susan Blakely (who played my TV mother in *Co-ed Call Girl*) had run into my mother at a luncheon and said, "I just auditioned for your role yesterday." I didn't respond to the e-mail. She had nothing to hold over me at this point (except her apartment where Charlie and I lived). Nothing was going to stop me now.

As the networks figure out what shows they're picking up for the new season, the agents and managers start to hear rumblings about what's going to get green-lit. Some shows went away, but word was that ours was still in the running. Then NBC called one of our producers who was on vacation in Hawaii. They asked him to change his ticket and come back from Hawaii right away because they wanted him to start hiring staff for the show. That was a very good sign. It was pretty much unheard of that they'd make a call like that and then kill the show. They screened *So NoTORIous* for a test audience, and people seemed to love it. I was on a high. A career high point, where everything seemed to be going my way and the future looked too good to be true. Had I learned nothing from my past?

I went with Charlie, two of my best girlfriends—Amy and Sara— and their significant others to the Kentucky Derby. I was in a full ball gown at a pre-Derby evening party when I got an urgent text message from my agent: *Call ASAP.* I knew. I just knew. This call wasn't going to be *Oh my God, we got the pickup!* I went into the bathroom to call back in private. My agent confirmed what I already anticipated: NBC hadn't picked up the pilot to go to series. My heart fell. I was calm on the phone, saying, "It's okay, it's okay. I'm okay." Then I got off the phone and cried. Randomly, Tara Reid was in a nearby stall to console me.

We'd come so far, and this time I wasn't ready to give up. The next day, during the actual Kentucky Derby, I was hunched over my BlackBerry, e-mailing with my producers and agent and manager to figure out our next steps. The show was so much more to me than a job opportunity. It was personal. It let me look at my life in a way I never had before. It seemed like everything, all the rises and falls, silver spoons and custom costumes, had brought me to a place where I was finally able to laugh at myself. I was going to make a success out of it. And then that chance was taken away. I know network TV isn't all about my personal revelations, but it felt like my whole life led to this. This is why I went through all that craziness. If *So NoTORIous* happened, my life up till now made sense. So when the show didn't get picked up, I couldn't bear to just let it disappear.

NBC agreed to release the pilot, which meant we were free to try to find another place for it. We started sending it out to every network. UPN and The WB said, essentially, "You should've gone with us to begin with." Networks don't love sloppy seconds. But a week later we got a call from VH1. They'd been tracking this project since the very beginning but didn't think they could compete for it. Now they were very interested in buying it.

VH1's pitch to us was that they were a small network. They'd never done a scripted show before—this would be an experiment for them—but they felt it was right for their audience. They said, "We're not like NBC. We won't cancel you after three episodes if the ratings aren't there. We don't expect huge numbers at first. We stick behind our shows and grow with them." I thought it was great that they weren't a prime-time network. We'd tried being a small fish at NBC, and that hadn't worked out. With VH1, they needed us more than we needed them. It all fell into place. They ordered ten episodes.

*CHAPTER TWELVE*

# The Evil Eye

The summer of 2004 was a crazy time. *So NoTORIous* was picked up by VH1 in June. Charlie and I celebrated our first wedding anniversary in July. And I'd been offered a TV movie called *Mind over Murder* that started shooting in August. The *So NoTORIous* producers weren't wild about this whole TV movie thing just as we were going into preproduction. They wanted to brainstorm more story ideas. But we worked out a schedule where I'd keep working with them throughout the movie shoot.

Just two days after I accepted the part in *Mind over Murder*, Charlie and I went to New York for two weeks. From there I'd go straight to Ottawa, Canada, to start shooting the TV movie. On this particular trip to New York, I was busier than ever. Not only was I working with the *So NoTORIous* writers, but Mehran was also in town so we could meet with buyers for a line of jewelry we developed together called Maven. Ever since we were teenagers sketching my future Emmy gowns, Mehran and I have always wanted to go into fashion together. We eventually hope to design clothes, but we decided to start with jewelry. My agent Ruthanne ran an animal rescue organization called Much Love Animal Rescue. I'd been working with them for several years. The first piece I designed was a diamond dog-bone necklace as a gift for Ruthanne's birthday (eventually raising over twenty-five thousand dollars for Much Love by selling the dog-bone necklaces). Then I had an idea for charm necklaces, and soon thereafter Mehran and I sat on my bed stringing them furiously in order to deliver them to stores on time. After that we sat down to develop a complete line of hip-chic fashion jewelry. We have bold necklaces, bracelets, cuffs, and earrings with some semiprecious stones. Aside from the diamond dog bone, which was just for Much Love, there are no diamonds. It's all stuff I would actually wear myself. When people ask me why I designed the line, I half-jokingly say, "Because my mother said only diamonds mattered, and I want to prove her wrong."

My New York trip was busy enough, but I had one more task to accomplish: see a voodoo priestess named Mama Lola. Every time something went wrong in my life, I'd joke, "Oh, another pilot didn't get picked up? I guess it's because my mother has that evil eye on me." Once I said it in front of Charlie's best friend, Kelley, and she looked at me, dead serious, and said, "You *have* to go see Mama Lola." Kelley had just returned from New Orleans, where she'd met Mama Lola, and told me next time I was in New York, where Mama Lola lived, I absolutely had to see her. It's not often in one's life that one has a chance to meet an honest-to-God voodoo priestess. (Mama Lola doesn't have a storefront or anything. She's a devout practitioner of Haitian voodoo. The real thing.) But for a long time it stayed stuck on that list of things I always meant to do when I was in New York: tour Ellis Island, walk across the Brooklyn Bridge, get a colonic, visit that voodoo priestess. I never did any of them.

This time, for some reason, I was determined. If there was an evil eye on me, I wanted it off before I went any further with *So NoTORIous*. So I called Mama Lola to make an appointment for me and Mehran. (What, you think I wanted to visit a voodoo priestess by myself?) It was set for the next day.

But when I called Mehran the next morning, he was hungover and refused to go. Charlie had gone to Boston to see his family. I couldn't go alone! Mama Lola lived in Brooklyn. I'd have to cross a bridge! (On the plus side, I could cross another item off my to-do list.) The normal me would have canceled, but this was my only chance, so I decided to go. By myself. To Brooklyn. Radical.

I knocked on the door of a tired-looking house. A young girl in a dress and pigtails (who I later found out was Mama Lola's granddaughter) took my hand, let me in, and asked me to wait in the living room. I'd never been in a house quite like it. From floor to ceiling the living room was jammed with stuff: dolls, toys, papers, books, knickknacks. There was a dusty TV that must have been my age playing *Jerry Springer*. I waited primly, my back straight and hands folded in my lap. What had I gotten myself into?

Eventually Mama Lola came in. She was in her seventies, wearing a long caftan and a turban with big gold hoop earrings. Her nails were long and decorated with rhinestones. I know the Hollywood version of voodoo has nothing to do with the real religious practice, but Mama Lola was straight from the movies.

Mama Lola sat down with me. She called me Cory. After a few times I stopped correcting her.

"Why have you come to me, Cory?" she asked. Her voice was deep and serious. She had a thick accent. *Um, I thought it would be fun? It might make a good chapter in a memoir someday?* I said, "I think maybe someone put an evil eye on me."

"An evil eye?" That got her attention. "Is it a cleansing you want, Cory?" A cleansing. I didn't know. That sounded nice and harmless, like a spiritual colonic. "Sure," I said. "A cleansing."

We were on the parlor floor of the brownstone. Mama Lola went to what I thought must be a closet door and opened it. Instead, I saw a set of concrete stairs leading into darkness. By candlelight we walked down the stairs. Along the way the walls were decorated with little alcoves hosting shrunken heads, more candles, idols with big phalluses, and crosses. It looked to me like the set decorator had overdone it. Mama Lola kissed all of them as she descended. Then we went down another dark flight of stairs into a subbasement, and she let me into a little room the size of a broom closet. Inside sat three milk crates on the bare floor. Mama Lola gestured for me to sit on one of them. On various surfaces were mason jars full of unidentifiable liquids. A few flies buzzed around. For all Mama Lola's warmth, this was like the setting of a horror film. There was absolutely no doubt in my mind that I was about to be mercilessly slaughtered. Only the certainty that at this point my fate was already sealed and there was no escape kept me from panicking.

Mama Lola sat across from me with a wobbly crate table between us. She told me that the first step of a cleansing was a reading. Okay, that sounded harmless. I waited for tarot cards or for her to look at my palm, but she started laying out a deck of regular cards. She said, "Yes. I see someone. I don't know who it is, but I see this person and I see jewelry." I knew it. My mother. (I mean, yes, I had a jewelry line with Mehran. But Mehran wasn't exactly out to get me. I mean, sure, he still hasn't gotten over my crimped bangs in the nineties, but I don't think he'd put a curse on me for that. Nothing identified my mother more than her jewels. It had to be her!) Mama Lola started going on about how I had really bad energy surrounding me. I needed to be cleansed, big-time.

I guess this wasn't the kind of thing antibiotics could handle. First there would be a "bad" cleansing bath to clear away the evil eye, then a "good" bath to help me go forward. She wouldn't be ready to do the bad bath until tomorrow. Tomorrow? I was supposed to work all day with my *So NoTORIous* writers. But this might be my only chance, ever, to free myself from a curse! It could change my whole life. Work would have to wait. As I left, Mama Lola said, "I don't tell people they need a cleansing if they don't. I don't charge for this. If you want to donate to me, give whatever you see fit. But you don't have to pay me—just tell me if I'm right." First Terence Trent D'Arby, now Mama Lola. None of my spiritual guides wanted anything but to help me move forward.

When for some reason I went back the next day, the same little girl silently guided me into the brownstone. Mama Lola greeted me by asking, "Did you bring the perfume?" I had no idea what she was talking about. She said, "Don't worry. I'll lend you a perfume." Then she said, "I have to cook," and she left. But she was very nice, popping her head in now and then to check on me. Once she asked, "Are you okay with chicken?" I said yes, thinking maybe she was cooking chicken? Then she said, "You're not scared?" Scared of *chicken*? I was already scared of so many things: dolls, planes, being alone, confrontation, those little shrunken heads on the stairwell—the more I thought about them, the more I wondered whose heads they actually were. Was I supposed to be scared of chicken, too? I said, "A live chicken? No, I'm not scared." Then I realized exactly what was going on. How could I have been so oblivious! It was obvious. The adorable little girl. The cluttered house. The men with phalluses. The chicken. I was totally being *Punk'd*.

I called Chris, one of the *So NoTORIous* writers and, whispering in the phone, told him what was going on. I said, "There's voodoo and rituals and they're talking about a chicken. I think I'm being *Punk'd*." His advice: "Make sure you look good."

Finally, after Mama Lola, her granddaughter, and I spent an hour watching *Jerry Springer*, Mama Lola's daughter came in carrying a crate. I heard clucking. There was a chicken, for real. I said, "I'm a huge animal activist. You're not going to hurt a chicken, right?" Mama Lola said, "You'll be fine."

We went back to the basement, where Mama Lola and her daughter started putting newspaper all over the floor. She told me to take off all of my clothes except my underwear. Then I stood in my G-string in the middle of the newspaper reading from a sheet of paper that said something like, "I, Tori Spelling, cast off any harm that's come my way." When I had to fill in the blanks of who put the evil eye on me, I named my mother and Mark.

Then they brought a cute little white chicken up to me. Mama Lola and her daughter walked around me saying things—it's something of a blur—but all I recall is that ultimately, she began to clutch the poor chicken's neck. I started crying and begging her not to kill the chicken. She said sternly, "Her life for your life. This has to be done." I pleaded with her, but what was I going to do—grab the chicken and flee in my Cosabella thong?

Then she really did break the chicken's neck. Next blood was everywhere, and she wiped it on me, drawing a bloody cross on my forehead. (I'm Jewish!) She put something in my hands—I'm pretty sure it was the chicken's heart, though I refused to open my eyes. This was definitely not *Punk'd*. *Punk'd* wouldn't kill a chicken. Killing a chicken was, I was fairly certain, against the American Humane Association's Guidelines for the Safe Use of Animals in Filmed Media.

Mama Lola smeared some sort of bean and vegetable slop on my body—and what's a three-course meal on my skin without drinks?—so next she raised a huge Costco-size jug of clear alcohol, took a swig, and spit it in my face. Then she came over with a bottle of Jean Naté. (It was the drugstore perfume Nanny used to wear, with its spherical black top. It took me briefly to a happy place.) Now I smelled like chicken entrails, gin, and Jean Naté. If Mehran and I ever branched from fashion into scent, this was not the direction I had in mind.

After all of this was over, she gave me three handkerchiefs to clean myself. Then she had me take off my underwear and give it to her. She had to bury it with the chicken. Sure. Of course she did. I wasn't asking questions. I just wanted it to be over.

When I got in the car to head back to work, I felt like the sole survivor at the end of a horror movie. I sat dazed, my eyes blank, speeding away from the scene of terror and death. I'd escaped.

The writers were furious. They'd flown to New York to work with me, and I was two hours late. I said, "You guys, you don't understand. She killed a chicken, ripped its heart out, and smeared it on me." Then, over lunch, one of them said, "What's on your face?" We were in a nice restaurant. I picked up a spoon to look and saw that there were flecks of dried blood all over my forehead. Chicken blood.

I didn't want to go back, but I was afraid I'd be cursed forever if I didn't have the good bath. My manager went online and Googled Mama Lola. She reported back, "You know, she's pretty reputable. She's big in the voodoo priestess world. She gives seminars. I think you're okay." So the next day I went back. It was the same day I was supposed to leave for Ottawa, so the limo took me to Brooklyn before I headed north.

It was my third day at Mama Lola's, and for all my fear, I was starting to know and like her family. There were several generations living in the house. While I was chatting with them, the young granddaughter ran in and said, "There's a car mansion sitting outside our house!" She'd never seen a limo before. I was trying to explain about Ottawa when Mama Lola said to her other granddaughter, who was about twenty years old, "Just ask her! No one's embarrassed here." Then Mama Lola turned to me and said, "She said you're on a TV show."

I said, "Yeah, I was on a show. *90210.*"

And then Mama Lola said, "They tell me your dad is that producer, Aaron Spelling. You think he can get me on one of those shows?"

I said, "Which show?"

She said, "*Extreme Makeover: Home Edition.*" She was onto some-thing there. Her house could've used a helping hand.

But all I said was, "Well, I'm sorry, but that's not one of his shows."

The second bath was simple. It was a milk bath, with more chanting and gesturing. I gave Mama Lola two hundred dollars and thanked her. I felt exhausted and traumatized. I still didn't really know what to think. As I was leaving she gave me her business card. It read: MAMA LOLA. HIGH VOODOO PRIESTESS.

Safe in the limo, I IM'd Kelley. My message said, *Um. I went to Mama Lola. I'm just wondering. Did your cleansing and reading involve killing a live chicken? She covered me with beans and rice, spit gin in my face, drenched me in Jean Naté, smeared blood on me, and had me hold the chicken's heart.* Kelley quickly IM'd back. She said, *No—she just walked around me with some candles and made me recite some stuff.* I guess my evil eye was really, really evil.

My visit to Mama Lola made it into *So NoTORIous,* so at least the writers' time wasn't completely wasted. Whoopi Goldberg played a character inspired by Mama Lola, but it was not without some trepida-tion. She was concerned that Mama Lola would put a curse on her. But now that I have some distance, I don't think Mama Lola is the kind of priestess to issue revenge curses. And if you're reading this, Mama Lola, please know that I retell this story with gratitude. Let's give credit where credit is (possibly?) due: After my cleansing . . . everything changed.

*CHAPTER THIRTEEN*

# The Real Fairy Tale

I almost turned *Mind over Murder* down. There were a few good reasons not to do the movie. First of all, the pay was less than my quote (the standard amount an actor commands for a role). Secondly, it was shooting in Ottawa—eastern Canada. Ottawa? It wasn't exactly Vancouver, which is less than two hours by plane from L.A. Thirdly, we were going into preproduction on *So NoTORIous*. I was supposed to be home hashing out ideas for the season. But TV movies have been my bread and butter. If I'm offered a TV movie I like, I'll find some way to squeeze it into my schedule.

I read the script for *Mind over Murder*. It was a thriller/romantic comedy, and the part they had in mind for me was an assistant district attorney. Tori Spelling as an ADA? Wasn't that kind of ridiculous? Would people be able to buy me playing a lawyer? I couldn't picture myself in court—whether in movies or in real life. (I'm a good girl, remember? I don't shoplift, drink and drive, violate parole, or go clubbing baring the beave). Still, it was a quirky, funny character, different from anything I'd done before. It'd be nice to make some money. But *So NoTORIous* was all I could think about. I wavered until it was down to the wire. Finally Charlie read the script and weighed in. He thought it was a good role for me and encouraged me to take it. I'm so indecisive that if someone has a strong opinion, I feel like I should follow it. I signed on at the last minute. If I hadn't, I never would have met Dean, and who knows what would have become of me.

The *Mind over Murder* producer told me that in Ottawa I'd be staying at a hotel called the Cartier Place. It sounded fancy. Plus, they'd booked me the penthouse. Woo hoo! I was going to live it up, Canada-style. I arrived late on a Wednesday night in the beginning of August. My penthouse was large, yes. But nice? Not so much. It was a two-bedroom with roof access, but there were push-button shampoo dispensers in the shower and the comforter felt like paper. It was like a very large room at the Holiday Inn. Oh well. So much for movie-star luxury.

The next day I had to do wardrobe fittings and get a physical exam, then on Saturday we were going to start filming. In the wardrobe room there were head shots of all the cast on the wall. The woman who was taking my measurements said, "Do you want to see your leading man?" I realized I had no idea what my costar, Dean McDermott, looked like. Usually, whenever I was about to meet a new leading man, I'd look him up on IMDb.com (the Internet Movie Database) so I could see if he was cute. Even if I was in a relationship, I always checked out my leading men. Now it hit me that for the first time ever I hadn't IMDb-stalked this Dean McDermott. It hadn't even occurred to me.

I have to admit that I was a little disappointed when I saw Dean's head shot. He looked older than I, kind of conservative, and not supercute. But he was playing a detective in the movie. Maybe a straitlaced look was good for that. Whatever, it was no big deal. I was there to work. And, hello, I was married anyway!

Later that morning I had a meeting with the director, Chris Leitch. We were talking across his desk when he looked past me and said, "Your leading man is here. You two should meet." I turned around, and Dean was standing in the doorway. He looked nothing like his head shot. He was tall and handsome, wearing jeans and boots, with a sexy scruff. My first thought was, *Oh my God, he's so hot.* My second thought was, *I must look terrible.* I hadn't put on makeup or done my hair.

Dean came across the room. We shook hands. I've been instantly attracted to men before, but this was different. It was love at first sight. I am fully aware of how ridiculous that sounds, and I still mean it. Who believes in love at first sight? Sure, it's all very cute when you're a little girl playing princess or a teenager watching John Hughes movies. Then you get older and wiser and live enough of life to know that love at first sight doesn't exist except in fairy tales. And then, all of a sudden, this moment. All my accumulated cynicism dissipated. There was such thing as true love. I fell so hard.

That night the producers had invited me to a big cast and producers' dinner. I was supposed to meet them in the lobby of the illustrious Cartier Place so we could all shuttle to the restaurant in a van. When the elevator doors opened, Dean was standing there. The first thing he said to me was, "Great purse." It was the new Chloé bag, a large cobalt blue Silverado. I'd splurged on it in New York—a present to myself for *So NoTORIous* and the movie. I couldn't believe a straight man was complimenting me on my purse. Mehran would approve. I was impressed.

Dinner that night was in a private room at a place called e18hteen, a cool, chic, new restaurant-lounge in downtown Ottawa. The producers put me and Dean next to each other at the long banquet table. I remember every detail of that night because when I look back, it seems that if one little thing had been different—the casting, the timing, the weather, the seating arrangement, the Ottawan elections that year—everything might not have happened. But things were what they were. It was so meant to be.

Usually when I first meet a boy, I can't eat in front of him. I'm too worried about having something green in my teeth or talking with food in my mouth. But that night I ate every morsel on my plate. Dean said he was impressed that a tiny girl like me ate so much. But I'm a total foodie. *If* I'm comfortable. During dinner the director asked from across the table if we were getting along. Dean replied, "We're getting along famously." No question, we were hitting it off. We had everything in common—and this time it wasn't because I was trying to be whomever he wanted me to be. I was, I realized, completely myself around him. I wasn't afraid to be obnoxious or crass. I could be funny, and he responded. I was pretty sure he thought I was charming and hilarious. He told me I was "tragically cute," and I thought that was adorable. Then I noticed that he had a wedding ring on. When someone asked, he pulled out photos of his children.

And—oh, yeah—I had a husband too. It was fun to flirt, but I knew nothing would happen. It was a nonissue.

But: Dean and I went to a bar after dinner. And we spent that night together at the Cartier Place.

My publicist would want me to say what all celebrities say when they hook up on the set of movies. We were just friends at first. A relationship developed over time. We didn't get together until we'd both left our spouses. But that's not true.

Dean and I spent the first night we met together, but hear me out. Before that night I had never cheated on Charlie. I'd worked with numerous attractive actors in the course of our relationship. I'd had men hit on me. There were plenty of opportunities with guys who were interesting and great. But I was married. It never occurred to me to do such a thing to my husband. I wasn't in that mode. I didn't want to hurt him. This was totally out of character. It was testament to how powerful my connection with Dean was.

Tellingly, the following day when I woke up next to Dean, I had no regrets. Something was really wrong with my marriage. Not only because I slept with this guy—although that certainly wasn't a positive sign one year into a marriage—but because I didn't regret it.

It was Friday morning. The hair colorist for the movie was coming over at ten a.m. I told Dean he had to leave before the colorist got there, and that felt icky. I didn't like having to hide something that felt right. But the real kicker was that Charlie was arriving that night. It was a four-week shoot, and I'd come straight from two weeks in New York. That meant I was going to be away from L.A. for a total of six weeks. Without my dogs. How could I leave Mimi and Ferris for so long? Charlie had gone home after our New

York trip. Now, with my then-assistant (and now close friend), Marcel, he was flying them to Ottawa so they could be with me. I didn't want Charlie to come. I didn't want the dogs to come. Actually, I did want the dogs to come. I really missed the dogs. But my relationship with them was much less complicated. Mostly, I spent all day feeling like a kid in high school, wondering if Dean was going to call.

That night when I got home from work, there was a voice mail from Dean. He called me "T," like lots of my friends. That felt right. But he called himself "Deano," which seemed like more of a buddy nickname. Did he actually like me? Or was it an obligatory phone call—he knew he had to work with me and wanted to smooth things over? I must have listened to it a hundred times, trying to analyze his voice inflection. I was excited and nervous, and I twisted it all different ways, trying to unravel the real story.

But the reality was that my husband was arriving in three hours. I had to erase the message. I couldn't tell my friends. I'd cheated on my husband.

When Charlie arrived late that night, I was still wide awake, wired from the drama, but I pretended to be asleep. The next morning I had an early call. Charlie stirred as I was leaving and told me he'd come meet me for lunch.

The movie was being shot near a high school, so lunch was served in the school's cafeteria. Charlie, Marcel, the dogs, and I sat at one of the long lunch tables. Then, out of the corner of my eye, I caught someone looking over at me. It was Dean, sitting with the director, Chris. It was his day off, but he'd come for lunch. We were in a high school cafeteria, so what did I do? I pretended I didn't see him. I pretended I was just scanning the room. I let my eyes float right past him. Hello, seventh grade.

After lunch Charlie, Marcel, and I went outside and were standing around talking. Soon Dean walked out, and I introduced him to Charlie. That was the weirdest experience of my entire life. Dean I'd only known for a day. I felt like I was in love with him, and I doubted that was possible. Charlie was my husband, but I doubted that love too. And there I was introducing the two of them as if there were no conflict or doubt.

Later Dean told me that he was shocked when he saw Charlie. He said, "I expected him to look like . . . well . . . me. I figured I was your type." It made me remember a conversation I'd had with Jenny about a month before my wedding. Charlie and his writing partner had written a movie based on an idea I had. We were having a staged reading to try to get investors. My friend Scout, a casting director, had lined up actors for the event. I was reading the lead role and the colead was being done by Matt Davis, the hot guy from *Legally Blonde* and *Blue Crush*.

The next week I was at dinner with Jenny and a couple friends. Jenny said that Matt Davis was my type. He was tall, good-looking, cool. She said she always thought I'd end up with someone like that. I was taken aback. Why was she talking about what my type was right before my wedding? Besides, it was shallow. I wasn't marrying for looks. Jenny backpedaled immediately. "Of course," she said, "Charlie's not your type, but he's really good for you."

So Dean wasn't off the mark. Charlie's not my physical type and Dean is. He's very tall, with blue eyes and light hair. And I've always thought that noses on men are very important. (I mean, I had the gene pool of my future children to consider, didn't I?) Dean's nose is cute and perky. He's Canadian, and Canadian men have the best noses.

Charlie stayed for the weekend. Nothing was discussed. I knew my marriage was over, but it wouldn't be right to just dump that on him (and we all know I wasn't brave enough anyway). I just wanted to get through the weekend without talking. Luckily, I was working every day. Afterward we'd go to dinner with Marcel. We didn't have sex—our sex life had waned anyway, to say the least, and I wasn't about to resuscitate it.

On set with Dean, I was nervous, confused, and suddenly shy. I didn't know him. I didn't know if he hooked up with all his costars. On set the girls liked him. When I was getting makeup and hair done, I'd hear them talking about how cute he was and whether he was available. They'd say it in front of me—they had no idea. And I could see that he liked the attention he got from the ladies. I figured, *He probably isn't happy at home. Maybe whenever he does a movie, he finds someone to sleep with. I'm just another girl in a long line of conquests.* I kept asking myself, *If that's all it was, just a hookup, then do you have regrets?* But I still didn't. It had been magical.

The night Charlie left, Monday, Dean asked me to get a drink. I invited Marcel along, and the three of us had a great time. We all came back to the hotel, and Marcel went to bed. Dean and I were talking in the living room of my not-so-fab suite. I fished for whether this was his MO, saying, "You're probably just going to flirt with girls the whole time." ("Flirt" was my euphemism for "hook up.") He asked, "Is that what you think? I just do this all the time?" I said, "Yeah, maybe." He said, "Well, I don't." He, like me, had never done it before.

Even if he wasn't a philanderer, he was married and had a family. At the very beginning of the shoot, before I'd even seen Dean's head shot, I had a meeting with the director, Chris. In the movie my character is sleeping with a married man. There's a scene when I call the house and he's dismissive of me on the phone because his wife is there. I hang up, upset. I told Chris, "In movies women are always dating married men, and they always think the men are going to leave their wives. But they're just deluded. Married men never leave their wives for their lovers." Chris disagreed. He said he'd known men to leave their wives. I said, "It never works out." If you were going to have an affair, you should know what you were getting into. Each woman thinks her situation is special. I wasn't about to fall into that trap. I assumed it couldn't go anywhere.

I didn't want to be naive. Nonetheless, from that day forward we were inseparable. I'd never had a relationship develop so quickly. There were no uncomfortable first stages of dating. It felt like we'd been together our whole lives. We practically lived together since we were staying at the same hotel. Funny thing is, I had a huge penthouse suite while Dean had a regular room, but 90 percent of the time we stayed in his room. I liked it because it was smaller. Like the laundry cupboard of my youth.

Dean and I hid our relationship from the cast and crew. I'd just learned how to text on my BlackBerry, and I taught Dean how to use his cell to respond. Texting was the medium of our early love notes. He was writing me poems in between takes, and nobody on set knew. Now, time moves differently when you're falling in love. (Or maybe it's just that time moves differently on movie sets, but that's not quite so romantic, is it? So let's say when you're falling in love.) All I know is that only twelve days had passed when we were out to dinner with the producers and Marcel. Dean was across the table from me. Everything seemed fine, when I glanced down at my BlackBerry. Dean had texted me: *I'm in big trouble.* (Actually, it probably said *I'm in bjg trouble,* but who can blame him—secret texting is an acquired skill.) I looked up at Dean. He was staring at me but gave no indication that something was wrong. Did someone find out? A crew member? His wife? Much as I was dying to know, I didn't want to pull out my BlackBerry and give us away. Later that night I finally asked him, "Why are you in big trouble?"

He said, "Because I'm in love with you."

I said, "I love you too."

It hit home. We'd been living in our own reality where we were together and we were meant to be together. We'd put the world beyond on hold. I hadn't even talked to my closest friends in the world. Jenny, Mehran, and Zack (who played Mehran in *So NoTORIous*) would text me to ask how the filming was going. I was scared to tell them the truth, so I sent them responses like, *I love it here. I never want to leave Ottawa.* They were understandably confused. Ottawa? What was so great about Ottawa? (I'd really come around to Ottawa.) Eventually I ended up telling my friends what was going on. By text. That's pretty much how I communicate.

In the beginning of the filming I called Charlie every night, but now I called him less and less. I'd e-mail him from Dean's room to say it was late and I was going to bed. Dean and I had talked about our marriages and shared how and why they weren't working. I told him everything I've told you about how I wasn't myself with Charlie and how I worked so hard to convince myself it was right because

I'd made so many bad choices in the past. As for Dean, his past isn't mine to tell. All I'll say is that he was unhappy in his marriage, but he loved his children deeply. Ottawa wouldn't go on forever. In fact, Ottawa would last only fourteen more days. And then what? What were we going to do? This wasn't home. There were other people and other hearts involved. I started counting down. At some point I had to deal with this.

After three weeks of shooting we finally had a whole weekend off. The movie producer was going back to his hometown—Montreal—and invited me, Marcel, and Dean to join him.

That weekend in Montreal something happened: Dean and I had our first talk about what would happen when we went home. He wanted to be with me and to spend the rest of his life with me, but because of certain circumstances with his family, he thought we should wait six months. His reasons, which I won't discuss, made sense to me. But six months was going to be hard.

I kept asking myself, *How do I know? How do I know we'll be together?* I didn't want to be played for a fool. And it was so hard for me to imagine that I could actually end up happily married. Saturday night in our hotel room we were drunk and being silly. I told him that when I was little, our neighbor in Malibu was Lloyd Bridges. I used to play with his grandson—Beau Bridges's son, Jordan—on the beach. When I was maybe four years old, we pretended we were getting married. We built our wedding cake out of sand, and he made me a wedding ring out of string. I knew it was a silly childhood dream, but I told Dean I'd take anything as a sign that this was real and we were committed. I said, "I just wish I had a promise ring, a string, *anything* around my finger so I could look down and know that it was all going to work out one day." As if a ring would make a difference. Wasn't I that foolish girl having the affair with a married man?

After we talked about a promise ring and parting ways for six months, Dean fell asleep. I went out to the living room of our suite and sat there for an hour, crying quietly. I was crying because I'd met the right person for the first, the only, time in my life, and I didn't think it would work out. We were both married. And even though I knew I had to leave Charlie, Dean would go back home to his family and realize he belonged there. Even if this felt real and right, it was going to disappear.

After Montreal my hours on the movie kept me on the set later than Dean. The plan was for Dean to bring dinner over to my penthouse. When he appeared, he told me that he had something for me. It was my "unengagement ring," the promise ring I'd asked for. It was only made out of yarn, but he'd worked hard on it. There was a braided black linen wool string—like the kind of string you'd use for gift-wrapping—and he'd sewn pink thread, my favorite color, through to accent it. (Remember, this is a guy who knows a fabulous bag when he sees one.) Where he tied the ends together, he frayed them out into a spray to look like a ring top. A string ring, a very slightly upgraded version of the one Jordan Bridges made me on the beach in Malibu.

Dean told me that this was my promise ring, the symbol that he was going to marry me one day. When I saw the string ring, I started crying so hard, and I thought about how when Charlie and I got engaged, he'd put together such an elaborate, romantic night and it didn't affect me this powerfully. Now I was in a jenky hotel room with burgers and fries and a ring made of string, and I was crying with hope and joy and love. This unengagement meant the world to me.

It was almost the end of the movie shoot when we decided to tell the director, Chris. He and Dean were friends—they'd worked together before—and we'd hung out with him a lot over the course of the filming. We figured he probably knew already. We were both giggling when we said, "We're in love." Chris said, "In the movie?" We said, "No! In real life!" He didn't believe us (or he acted like he didn't). He said, "For real? But you're both married." That sobered us up a bit. We told him, "We're going to leave our spouses. We're going to be together." He said, "You're both in for a lot of hurt. This is not an easy thing. It's going to be hard for everyone." Our bliss clashed—not for the first time—with harsh reality. We looked at each other and said, "Yeah, we know." Then Dean said, "I'm in love with her. I have to be with her." I said, "Me too."

The night we wrapped the movie, everyone went out for drinks. At the bar we sat close to each other. Dean was on my right and my makeup artist, Sarah, was to my left. Dean looked at me and said, "Here's me. Here's you. I love you." Right as he said it, I turned to my left and Sarah had a huge grin on her face. "I knew it!" she said. "I'm so happy! You two are so cute together." She said that everyone knew. So much for all our efforts at subtlety.

Our work on the movie was done, but we weren't leaving for two days, so I had a Hawaiian-themed wrap party in my penthouse and rooftop digs. Dean and I decided we'd just be together at the party. We were done hiding. We were in love. It was that simple. In Ottawa, at least. During the party I was dancing, and the ring that

Dean made for me flew off. It was dark out. The entire rooftop was covered in little beige rocks. It was like looking for a needle in a haystack. I was devastated. My engagement ring! I lost my engagement ring! Dean promised me we'd find it in the morning.

Because the hotel was in a residential neighborhood, we had to shut down our party at ten. Everyone was still feeling celebratory, so we headed to a bar. At the bar there was a private back room, and we knew everyone there—it was just cast and crew—so I was sitting on Dean's lap, and at some point we were intertwined in a chair. Then I noticed that a cast member had two unfamiliar girls with him. One of the girls was taking photos with a disposable camera. She'd strategically positioned her friend to hide the camera. Clearly she was taking pictures of me and Dean in compromising positions. I went over to confront her. That's right. Me! I wanted to show Dean how tough I could be.

"Excuse me, are you taking pictures of us?" I asked, in what for me was a pretty accusatory tone. She said, "No, I'm taking pictures of my friend. What do you want me to do, give you my camera?" Whoa. She was defensive. I backed right down. "Oh, sorry, I was just asking. It's fine," I said meekly. (Do I really need to tell you that those pictures would come back to haunt me?)

The next morning I was obsessed with finding my string ring before we flew home. It had been so meaningful to me that I was afraid losing it was equally meaningful. Maybe Dean and I weren't meant to be. Our friends, Dean, and I all searched until we were in danger of missing our flight. Everyone except Dean headed inside to finish packing. Half an hour later Dean came in. He had the ring. He put it on me. Maybe it was meant to be after all.

The flight home was our last five hours together. Dean and I sat next to each other. It started off happy. Dean pulled out our airplane sick bags and we took turns writing down all the things we wanted to do together in life.

I wrote: *I want to go wine-tasting in Napa and eat at French Laundry with you.*

He wrote: *I want to get a place at a beach in California with you.*

I wrote: *I want to learn Spanish with you.*

He wrote: *I want to travel the world with you.*

I wrote: *I want us to go to Maui together.*

He wrote: *I want to open a bar with you.*

I wrote: *We promise never to be apart for more than three days.*

He wrote: *I want us to keep in touch with our Ottawa friends.*

I wrote: *To love each other madly.*

He wrote: *To love our children madly.*

As the plane descended, so did reality. I started crying. Again. Love was sure making me cry a lot. Dean said, "You have to believe. We're going to be happy and be together and have lots of children together." But I knew we had some painful confrontations between here and there.

## CHAPTER FOURTEEN

## Breaking News

Charlie wanted to come pick me up at the airport, but I wanted to be able to say good-bye to Dean. So I lied to Charlie and told him I was coming home a day later. (When you've already broken your wedding vows, lying about a flight arrival isn't such a big deal.)

My relationship with Charlie was already strained. I'd stopped calling and e-mailing regularly. Before I left, he made it clear that he wanted us to call or e-mail every single day. The tone of the request was more practical than romantic. He said, "We're married. You have to make that effort to make a relationship work." He reminded me of that agreement in an e-mail to Ottawa. It said that he'd been trying to contact me for three or four days and only got short e-mails in return. He reminded me that relationships take work and I wasn't working on ours. I just apologized.

When Dean and I landed, each of us had a car waiting. Our good-bye was short. We hugged and said we loved each other. He and his family were heading to Palm Springs the next day for a weeklong family vacation with another couple. He said, "I promise I'll text you. I'll call you when I can." We parted.

Charlie was in his office on the computer when I came in a day earlier than he expected me. "Surprise!" I gave him a hug, then told him I had a headache from the flight (I often get migraines when I fly) and went straight to bed. Exhaustion. Avoidance. The two had completely blended in my head.

When I woke up, all I knew was that I had to get out of the house. I met up with Jenny and Mehran at the W Hotel in Westwood. Out on the patio I told them the entire story, down to the pink thread in the string ring. Neither of them seemed particularly surprised that my marriage had bombed in such short order. When Jenny said, "Well, we all knew it wasn't right," I had to respond, "Why didn't you tell me?!" You sort of think that if you're making the biggest mistake of your life, one of your lifelong best friends who have been surrogate family for years will stop you. But Mehran reminded me that he'd tried to tell me in subtle and not-so-subtle ways (yeah, I guess planning our dramatic helicopter escape from the wedding should have been a clue). It was then that they explained that Jenny had told Mehran to let me figure it out for myself. Something about that sounded so parental—protective and supportive, but, I don't know, kind of like I was a baby bird they were pushing out of the nest.

The next day I told my other two best friends, Amy and Sara. Jenny and Mehran joined us for a summit on the patio of the Four Seasons. Again, no one was surprised. But they were wary of the

fact that Dean was married with kids and that I was telling them
we wanted to get married as soon as our divorces were final. Why so
fast? What was the rush? We knew we were supposed to be together
from the moment we met. We'd waited our whole lives to find each
other, and we were hurting other people in the process. Why dilly-
dally? My friends were suspicious and wanted to meet him. I wanted
them to meet him too, but all I could do was show them photos of
Dean and his kids—they were a part of him, and I loved them for
that before I ever met them. But Jenny claims that even as I told
them how much I loved him, I kept saying, "I know he's not going
to leave his wife. I know this isn't going to work out."

Three days passed during which I avoided Charlie as much as
possible, staying out all day shopping with Jenny and Mehran, then
pleading exhaustion and forcing myself to crash at nine p.m.—not
an easy feat for a night owl. Dean was texting and leaving me messages, reassuring me whenever he got a free moment. Nothing had
changed. He was still in love with me. He felt as miserable and duplici-
tous as I did. Then, in one instant, everything changed. Mehran and
I were hanging out, and my phone rang. It was Dean. He said, "I left
her. I just left her. I'm on my way back from Palm Springs." I'd been
expecting to live this lie for six months. It had only been three days
and here was Dean saying, "I have to see you. Can you meet me?"

Of course. Of course I wanted to see him right away. But my
head was spinning. Oh my God, was this really happening? Oh my
God, I had to leave Charlie. How would I tell him? What would I
tell him? I knew it was unavoidable. I had already checked out. I
couldn't look him in the eye. In my head it was done, and there was
no way I could spend six more months with him and then leave.

I'd been so focused on worrying that it wouldn't work out, that I'd lose Dean. Now I started dreading the confrontation with Charlie. I wanted it to be over with. Through the dizzy rush of hope and dread I heard Dean on the other end of the line saying, "Where are you going to be?"

I'm not one for a tête-à-tête. I do better surrounded by my faithful support team. Besides, I needed my friends to meet Dean. No part of me thought I was making another mistake, but I wanted them to meet him, to see us, and to—well, to give me their blessing. So I told Dean to meet me and Mehran on the patio of the Chateau Marmont on the Sunset Strip. (I seem to conduct all my powwows on the patios of hotel bars.) I called Amy and Marcel (whom Dean knew well from Ottawa) to join us.

As we waited on the patio, I kept looking at the doorway. I was nervous. Ottawa was one thing. We'd always have Ottawa, et cetera, et cetera. But now we were at home. Would seeing him through my friends' eyes change how I felt? Would everything be different? Suddenly Dean appeared. As soon as I saw him, the fear drained right out of me. It all came rushing back. This was my love. He'd come for me. That imaginary prince I'd given up on years ago had finally shown up. This was right. It did and didn't matter what my friends thought, but they all felt completely comfortable with him. It seemed like a natural fit, but they didn't like the situation. They were worried about how it would all shake down, and so was I.

That night Dean and I stayed in a room at the Chateau. To my relief our connection wasn't geographically confined to Ottawa. It was magical. At some point I called Charlie and told him I wasn't coming home that night, making up something about staying over at my friend Sara's. Charlie said it was fine, but he said, "Tomorrow night we're having sex. It's important for our relationship." That said it all to me. Our marriage was mechanical. Whether he knew it or not, we were both just going through the motions.

The next morning Dean spoke on the phone with the husband of the couple his family had been vacationing with in Palm Springs. By now I knew what had gone down in Palm Springs. His wife had noticed that he was acting distant. She started asking questions and he told her the truth. She asked him to leave. Now, on the phone, Dean was apologizing to his friend for ruining their vacation. He asked how his family was doing. Whatever was said, when Dean got off the phone, he started to cry. He said, "I don't know what to do. I don't want to lose my kids." I couldn't bear to see him like that. I said, "I can't do this. I can't come between you and your children. Maybe you need to be with your family even if you're not in a happy marriage." But he said, "No. We're in love. I have to find a way to work this out." I didn't want anyone to be hurt. Not Dean's family, not Charlie. But Dean and I were meant to be together.

That afternoon during a lunch for the writing staff of *So NoTORIous,* there was a lot going on in my head. I hated leaving Dean feeling so sad. And I was supposed to be professional and together as executive producer of this show. I'd worked so hard to make it happen, and now I couldn't even focus. Maybe it doesn't speak well for my acting ability, but I wasn't very good at faking it.

That night my friends had put together a welcome home get-together for me on the patio (always the patio!) of the Crescent Hotel in Beverly Hills. Before it started, I met up with Dean at the nearby L'Hermitage Hotel for a drink. I was dreading the encounter with Charlie so much that I was forty-five minutes late. Not very cool when you're the guest of honor. Amy was texting me, asking, *Where are you?*

When I finally forced myself to go, the party wasn't as torturous as I'd anticipated. It was easy to avoid my husband—we weren't the kind of couple who stayed close together when we were socializing, particularly with my friends. We'd go our separate ways, then converge at the end of the night. I thought that's what married people did. During the party, in the hotel bathroom, I told some of my other friends what was going on—that I was going to leave Charlie. The more people I told, the more I noticed the same response. Nobody seemed shocked. But I still hadn't told the person who was least likely to have that response. That weighed on me at every moment. But I was not a brave person, and it was a lot easier to tell a friend in a hotel bathroom than to figure out how I was going to tell Charlie our marriage was over when he didn't even seem to know I was unhappy in it.

As the night progressed, I got increasingly nervous. Charlie had made it clear to me that he wanted to have sex with me that night. We hadn't been intimate since I'd gotten home. But if anything was clear to me, it was that I couldn't have sex with Charlie. The fact of my affair was bad enough, but to physically go back and forth between two men seemed like it would compound the offense. It would be a disservice to Charlie. And, significantly, it felt like cheating on Dean. I absolutely couldn't do it. Just to be clear, this wasn't exactly in the forefront of my conscience. It was more like a jumble of anxiety somewhere in the back of my head while I chatted and joked with friends I hadn't seen all summer. So when my friend

Gueran texted me from the other end of the long table to say, *We're going to Fubar. Want to go?* the answer was easy. I texted back, *I'm in.* Fubar was a gay bar where I knew for sure I'd be completely safe from heterosexual wifely duties.

I didn't know it, but down at the opposite end of the table Charlie was reading over Gueran's shoulder. He came up to me and said, "It's getting late. Time to go home. I want to go home with my wife." I said I didn't want to go. We went back and forth like that a little. And then, subconsciously, I kind of realized that if Charlie and I fought, I wouldn't have to go home with him. So, as my friend James, who played Pete on *So NoTORIous*, likes to remind me, "It was so genius. You screamed, 'I'm going to Fubar!' across the patio."

The table got quiet. There was an uncomfortable pause. Then Charlie, jokingly, said, "If you go to Fubar, our marriage is over." And suddenly we were closer to the truth than I'd anticipated. In a light, tipsy way I said, "Well, I want to go out with my gays. I'm going to Fubar." That was my code for *I wish everything had happened differently, and I've gone about this wrong, and I'm sorry, but the truth is that our marriage is over.* Apparently, Charlie didn't know the code. He said, "Can we talk about this in private?"

Charlie drew me aside, into the tiny lobby of the hotel. He said, "What are you doing? What is wrong with you? You've been distant since you've been home. I want to be with my wife." As we all know, this was a completely reasonable line of questioning. But I was doing what guilty parties do best: picking a fight. This was the path toward not going home, and I wasn't about to change directions. I said, "I just got home. I want to be with my friends, and you're trying to control me and tell me when we're leaving." We hadn't fought much in our relationship. I hadn't expressed myself. Now I was on a roll. "You know," I said, "maybe we just don't have that much in common. Maybe we want different things. Maybe we're at different points in our lives." It was the exact same fight we'd had on my birthday right before our wedding. But this time there was no upcoming wedding volunteering itself as a rug to sweep the fight under.

Charlie said, "Maybe we *are* too different." Now I was getting somewhere. Maybe when it came down to it, he'd understand. I said, "This makes me not want to go home with you."

In the small lobby our friends were quietly filtering past, clearing the scene because some couple was fighting in public. Our friends Suzanne and Marcel were roommates. They lived close to the Crescent Hotel. When I saw them approaching, I told Charlie I wasn't going to Fubar but that I was going to crash at their house. I walked out.

Dean picked me up from Suzanne and Marcel's, and we went to a hotel called the Farmer's Daughter that night. It was the second in what would be a series of nights in random hotels. When we woke up the next morning, I said, "I'm not going back home. I'm not going back." I didn't have any clothes—just the heels, rolled-up shorts, and tank top I'd worn to the bar the night before. We went to Urban Outfitters. It was nine thirty. They weren't open yet, but the salesman recognized me. Through the glass door I told him, "I just need pants and flats. It's an emergency." I bought gaucho pants, a couple shirts, some flats, and some flip-flops. Then we drove to Dean's house. I waited in the car a few blocks away while he packed a suitcase. Then we were . . . homeless.

At some point in those first crazy homeless days I got in touch with my therapist. I needed to talk to Charlie, to tell him I wanted to separate, and I just couldn't do it. Part of me was afraid that if I told him in person, I'd let him talk me out of it. Guilt is a powerful emotion. What if I found myself agreeing to stay and work on the relationship when I really wanted to leave him no matter what? My therapist knew how nonconfrontational I was. She suggested that Charlie and I meet and talk in her office. She wouldn't take sides. She'd just be a mediator and help me tell him. It sounded like my best option.

Even though my friends admitted they'd never thought Charlie was my match, they weren't exactly gung ho on the current situation. When I called Jenny, wanting to bring Dean over to meet her, Norm—Jenny's husband—was hesitant. He cared about Charlie and didn't want to just blindly accept Dean in his place. I understood, but I tried to explain myself. I told him I wasn't having an affair. I was ending my marriage. Dean was the person I wanted to be with, the person I had to be with. When he heard how serious I was, how it felt from my perspective, he got it. Of course, he still didn't like the way it had come about—neither did I—but he saw that I wasn't hurting Charlie for no good reason.

Then Mehran called. He said that Charlie had called and that he had no idea what was going on. It wasn't right. Mehran said I had to call him.

I couldn't summon the courage, so Jenny helped me compose an e-mail to Charlie saying that I was sorry for the way I'd behaved at the Crescent Hotel. I wrote that I was out of line but that it came from something real. I told him we needed to talk but that I didn't want to come home. I asked him to meet me Monday morning at my therapist's office. In the e-mail I said, *Please know that I love you.* I hesitated to write it. I didn't want to give him false hope, but I wasn't heartless. I did love him. I just wasn't in love with him. At any rate, it was an e-mail. Hardly the best way to communicate.

That night I had dinner at the Hotel Bel-Air. Jenny, Norm, Amy, Dean, and I sat outside at the restaurant having dinner. It was the same hotel where I'd gotten ready for my wedding to Charlie, but I wasn't thinking about that. I was trying hard not to imagine what Charlie must be going through. His wife had picked a fight with him without provocation, then disappeared. It wasn't a pretty self-portrait. On the other hand, I was with the man I loved and the friends who meant so much to me. Charlie aside (and to be honest, that's where I was pushing him), I was in total bliss.

Then, during dinner at the Bel-Air, Amy and I went to the bathroom. I asked her if she liked Dean. She said, "I think I do." This gave me pause. I said, "What do you mean?" I didn't want my friends to keep quiet this time around. I'd missed my opportunity to hear their concerns about Charlie. This time I wanted to face every doubt head-on. Amy said that Dean seemed great, but she was worried about the situation. She wanted us to take it slow. Amy is a good friend. She was being protective, and I'm grateful for that. But I was sure about Dean. I wouldn't have caused so much trouble if I hadn't been. This was my first—maybe my only—chance at true love. I couldn't let it go.

The end was in place. The location and time were set. All that remained was for me to go through with it. It was Labor Day weekend. We checked into the Casa del Mar, a big hotel on the beach in Santa Monica. On Monday morning Amy showed up to drive me to the appointment. I managed to haul myself into the car, but it was the longest drive ever. My heart was pounding. I didn't want to go. I couldn't do it. I was sure I couldn't do it.

And yet, there I was, waiting in the therapist's office when Charlie came in. He saw me and started to cry. He said, "I'm not going to let you get rid of me. I love you." We hugged and sat down. With some prodding from the therapist, I started talking. I focused on why I was leaving Charlie, not on Dean. I told him that I wasn't in love with him. I told him that I'd never been in love with him. I loved him and he'd been a friend to me, but I married him because he was a great guy, a nice guy, a guy who took care of me. Finding someone who loved me seemed like enough. I thought you either were in love or you loved each other, but I didn't realize they could coexist. Charlie didn't want to hear it or believe it. He kept saying, "You're happy. Where's this all coming from? We have a perfect relationship."

I pushed onward, telling him that my whole life all I wanted was to be a mom, but that in the course of our marriage I had stopped wanting children and didn't know why. It was true. I hadn't known what it was. I thought it was me, that I'd changed. But now I knew the real reason: I didn't want kids with *him*. I explained this to him. And that I wasn't sexually attracted to him. That I wasn't happy in the marriage. That it wasn't right for me.

It wasn't sinking in. Charlie could be blind to things he didn't want to see. Our mutual friend Suzanne had been his friend for fifteen years and lived with him when she first moved to L.A. Back in happier times we were all going to a barbecue, and she said to Charlie, "Tell T to bring her pipe." Charlie said, "What pipe?" He didn't know that I occasionally smoked pot. As soon as Suzanne got off the phone with him, she called me to apologize for busting me. She said, "Why doesn't Charlie know you smoke pot?" I didn't smoke pot very often, but when I did, I hid it from him. I wasn't scared of his reaction—he was a gentle person—but I knew he wouldn't approve and I didn't want to deal. It was easier not to mention it. But even after Suzanne mentioned the existence of my pipe to him, he never asked me about it. He turned a blind eye. The whole relationship was like that. I hid certain things about myself— that was my fault. But I think part of him wanted me to hide them. He was blindsided because he was blind.

Now, in front of the therapist, he resisted hearing what I was saying. Finally the therapist stepped in: "She's trying to separate. She's saying she doesn't want to be in this marriage." Then she went on to say, "Tori is saying she isn't in love with you. She doesn't have that weak-in-the-knees feeling." Charlie said, "Movie romance doesn't exist. It's a fairy tale. It isn't real. We're happy." Then he turned to me. "Is this about someone else? Did you cheat on me?"

I said yes.

He said, "It was with Dean, wasn't it?"

I said yes.

He said, "I should have known."

I made sure to tell him that I'd felt this way throughout the whole relationship. I wasn't leaving him because of the affair. I kept saying, "I'm sorry, I'm really sorry. I didn't mean to hurt you. I didn't mean for this to happen." And that was pretty much it. We agreed to talk again; he left angry and hurt, and I felt sorry and sad.

When a marriage fails, the story of the relationship changes. The best parts, the parts that made you think getting married was a good idea, fade from memory. I'm sure I haven't done justice to Charlie. We had fun. We had good laughs. He adored my dogs and we'd take them on hikes together. He had no qualms about carrying Mimi in a backpack on his back, on his chest like a baby in a Bjorn, or in her pink carrier that said MIMI LA RUE in pink rhinestones. I haven't done him justice if people wonder, *If she was so miserable, why didn't she leave sooner?* Charlie made me happy. He was good to me. He made me feel safe. He shared his family with me. We supported each other. Something about it did work for a while. I wasn't miserable, but it wasn't right. I didn't know what "right" felt like until I met Dean.

When I came down from the therapist's office, Amy was waiting for me with Jenny and her baby, Delilah. As soon as I got in the car, I started crying. I was destroyed.

My manager at the time, who'd been my manager since I was eighteen and took Charlie on when we did *Maybe Baby* together, was becoming something of a mediator between the two of us. In the next days she called me to let me know that Charlie wasn't going to come to our next scheduled meeting with the therapist. Instead, he was flying east to see his family. Then I knew he understood. There wouldn't be any more talking it over. Charlie was gone—or so it seemed. He was still living in my apartment—really my mother's apartment. There would be a divorce, and there would be press. But it was over.

It needed to end, but it could have happened in a nicer way. I wish I'd been able to communicate with Charlie from the very beginning of our relationship. And I should have handled things differently at the end. He's a sensitive, kind person. I know he would have listened. If I'd let our differences reveal themselves earlier . . . well, we might never have gotten married.

It doesn't fix the past, but at least I learned from my mistakes. From the minute Dean and I met, I took thirty-two years of being passive and nonconfrontational and changed, like *that*. Leaving our marriages—it was a rough road. We cared about our spouses. I'd hear Dean on the phone with his wife discussing the children. When he hung up, I'd have withdrawn. He'd ask what was wrong, and my first instinct was to say, *Nothing, nothing's wrong. I'm tired. I have a headache.* But I decided to break that habit. I always told Dean the truth. I'd say, "I feel like you're going to go back to her." It was scary, making myself vulnerable like that, but I was determined not to repeat my past. I've been honest like that ever since.

## CHAPTER FIFTEEN

## Safe at Last

Dean and I stayed at Casa del Mar for a week, but it was getting expensive. We'd conducted most of our relationship in hotels, and it was time to make our own bed and lie in it. We rented a furnished apartment in a building called The Marlowe in Hancock Park, on the east side of L.A. Hancock Park is a leafy, upscale neighborhood, but it was a world away from the mansions of Beverly Hills.

The Marlowe was not what I was used to. In my old building, The Wilshire, you drove up to the front door and handed your car keys to the valet. In The Marlowe you drove into an open lot and picked a spot if there happened to be one. In The Wilshire the elevator opened onto my private entry hall. In The Marlowe you walked through a lobby to the one elevator that everyone shared. Then you walked through hallways where you actually saw your neighbors. From the half-open hallways you could look down into the outside courtyard. It was a regular apartment building. I felt like I was living in Melrose Place (and you know your sense of reality is whacked when the best image you have of "normal" life is a television drama that your father invented).

Our apartment was a one-thousand-square-foot two-bedroom. The front door opened into the kitchen. It was modest in size but comfortably furnished. I had a little bag of the clothes I'd bought at Urban Outfitters, plus a single suitcase of stuff that Marcel had brought over from my apartment. Soon we would pick up the dogs. That was it. I couldn't think of anything else I needed. My life was suddenly so simple, so small, so happy. To that point I was the happiest I'd ever been.

Nonetheless, there was an outside world that refused to disappear. My agent and manager wanted me to "take a meeting," as we say in Hollywood, to "strategize." I wasn't just separated from Charlie in our private life. Soon enough, they knew, the press would be onto the story and there would be tabloid covers with photos of us torn in half saying SPLIT! (Seriously, can't they think of any other eye-catching breakup image?) There was a lunch full of talk about how we had to be "very careful" about this in the press. They were worried what VH1 would think because my image on *So NoTORIous* was like everyone else's: normal, nice, and likeable (we hoped). Now they reminded me (as if they had to) that I had cheated on my husband with a guy who left his wife and kids for me. They feared people were going to hate me. They told me to keep a low profile. If I'd been in a better mood, I might have made a joke about my nose job (my profile still wasn't low enough?), but I just wanted the meeting to end, let the chips fall where they might.

Not a week later we received word that the *Enquirer* had bought photos of the two of us in Ottawa. Remember those two girls who were taking pictures of each other at the wrap party? The ones I tried to confront? Thank God we'd already told our spouses. At least they heard it from us.

I had no idea what exactly the pictures showed, but my publicist found out that they were pretty intense and made it clear that we were together. Word spread quickly. My publicist started getting calls from *People* magazine and other weekly magazines asking if it was true that I'd fallen in love with my costar and that we'd both left our spouses. My publicist told me that we had to issue a statement. I didn't want to. She said that if we didn't say anything, I was going to come across as a terrible homewrecker. But was telling my side of the story really going to change that? Apparently, what they tell celebrities to do in situations like this is to release a joint statement saying, *We've separated and it's mutual. Please respect our privacy.* My manager talked to Charlie about releasing the statement together, but he wasn't interested. He thought it was just for my image, and (who can blame him?) he didn't care much what people thought of me.

Ultimately, my publicist put out a statement I wasn't totally happy with. It was a lie or, at very best, a manipulation of the truth. She wrote that Charlie and I split up (true), that we had been living separate lives since the beginning of August (sort of, since I'd gone to Ottawa on August 3), and that we had decided to separate ("we"— definitely not true). My publicist put the statement out on the AP wire. The next day it was picked up everywhere.

Right before the press release went out, I e-mailed my mother, saying, *I need to talk to you about something that's happened in my life. I want you to be aware of it before you hear about it. Please let me know a good time to call you.* My mother e-mailed back, saying, *Try me tomorrow. Know that I love you and I'm always here for you.* I tried her the next day, and we started playing phone tag. I finally reached my father the afternoon the news broke. He said, "Don't worry. I love you. Do whatever you need to do that's right for you." He'd probably already heard the news that morning, but at least we got to talk about it a little.

A few days passed, and I gave up on reaching my mother. By now there was no doubt that she knew what had happened and wasn't desperate to be in touch. But then, right after we'd announced the separation, her sixtieth birthday rolled around. There was a big party for her at Il Cielo in Beverly Hills. I was in the middle of filming *So NoTORIous*. Yes, I could have shown up at the party late, after work, but we were still in the middle of the press storm. I couldn't imagine walking into a party full of all my mother's friends who'd just been at my wedding. I didn't know how to deal. People think it's easy for the person who leaves the marriage, but I felt like I couldn't win. If I went and put on a happy face, people would say I was heartless. If I acted serious and shamed, they'd say I was self-absorbed. So I just didn't go.

I felt terrible for missing a milestone birthday, so (in the spirit of my parents' "bigger is better" birthday approach) I ordered a massive arrangement of flowers to be delivered to her at the party. It was the largest, most elaborate flower arrangement I've ever seen. On the card I said how sorry I was that I couldn't be there, and I backed it up with a longer e-mail to my mom explaining that I was filming, but also that it was a difficult time to go to a public event.

My mother sent an e-mail thanking me for the flowers. It said that the party was wonderful. She wrote, *It was a great night. Everyone who cares about me came out to celebrate my birthday.* Message received, loud and clear.

Not long after that I got an e-mail from my mother's business manager saying something like, *Your mother feels it is a good time investment-wise to put the condo up for sale. You have until March to find a new residence.* Holy filicide (yes, I had to look that word up), I was being evicted. There was no mother-daughter conversation about it. Just the e-mail telling me to move. Word came back to me that she was angry to hear that I'd let Charlie stay in her apartment while we worked out the divorce, but that was third-hand information. Maybe that was the reason. Maybe it was the realization that *So NoTORIous* was going forward without her approval. Who knows? I didn't understand it, but I accepted the date. I'd lived there for ten years. It was autumn. Charlie would leave when we settled the divorce. I'd get my stuff out by early spring.

Meanwhile, Charlie was furious at all the press. This was between us, and he thought it should stay that way. Not surprisingly, he took issue with my press release. As far as he was concerned, our separation wasn't even official yet. I imagine he was sick of finding out the status of our relationship in therapists' offices and tabloids: Charlie filed for divorce on October 15. The press picked up on it right away since filings like that are a matter of public record. It was my turn to learn private news in a public forum. But to his credit Charlie didn't talk to the press for a long time. He could have sold his side of the story, but he wasn't that kind of person. I respected that.

In spite of his anger, Charlie e-mailed asking to have one last meeting face-to-face. He wanted closure. He said he wanted to say good-bye while he still remembered why he loved me. He wrote, *I know your fears—you're scared to be alone with me.* He suggested a quiet restaurant. He was right. I was scared. Like a coward, I e-mailed him trying to change the date. He responded saying, *Actually, the more I think about this, the more it's clearly not a good idea.* He canceled.

One of my biggest regrets is not having that last meeting with Charlie. I owed him that. We had been so close for so long. I wish I'd been brave enough to say good-bye.

I never got to say a real good-bye to Charlie's family, the warm, welcoming family who I knew must hate me for wronging and hurting their son. One family member wrote me to say, *I have no interest in talking to you or having any interaction with you at all.* Another young relative with whom I'd been close wrote to say, *All these years when people said Tori Spelling's a whore, I defended you. At least I don't have to anymore.* I didn't write back to her. And that was it. There was no contact ever again.

As for the divorce settlement, well, remember how my mother threatened to call off the wedding if we didn't sign the prenup by the end of the day? Charlie and I joked at the time that he had signed it under duress. Now the prenup was coming into play far sooner than anyone had anticipated, and there was risk he'd contest it because of the time pressure we'd been under. My mother's efforts to "protect" me had backfired. We negotiated a divorce. Needless to say, I was the one who had to pay the settlement, not her.

Making such a big change was hard and messy. But Dean was

worth it. And, though it took me some time to realize, there was a transformation beyond finally being with the right person. I'd always been so scared of change. When I was little, if my mom got a new rug or coffee table (which happened fairly often), it took me weeks to adjust. And change wasn't the only thing that scared me. I was a mess of irrational fears. Maybe it started with the Madame Alexander dolls, who stared at me with empty, haunted eyes as I fell asleep as a child. Or maybe it was the horror movies I watched with my mother from a young age. Whatever caused it, I invented nightmarish scenarios in my head. Every time I went to a movie theater, I thought I was going to be shot. When I walked down the street, I'd imagine that someone was following me. I was scared to sit with my back to a window in restaurants.

Then there was airplane travel. When I flew, I had to bring along a slew of good-luck items. There was the bag of crystals that my brother gave me. I had to have one crystal in each hand at takeoff. Then there were the good-luck teddy bears who had to sit out on the seat with me, and if one teddy bear looked particularly alone as I left the house, I'd have to add him to the bunch. If I flew wearing a specific necklace and the plane didn't crash, then I'd have to wear that necklace on every plane I went on thereafter. But sometimes as I was putting on the first good-luck necklace, another necklace would catch my eye. Then I'd wonder, *Why did I notice that necklace? It must be fate.* And I'd have to wear that one, too. I was so bejeweled when I flew, I looked like Mr. T. If we'd crashed over water, I certainly would have sunk like a stone.

Yeah, you might call me a little OCD. Like how if I'm eating potatoes, I won't leave one potato alone on the plate. I'll cut it in half so it has a friend. If there are three beans left on my plate, I'll eat one so there are two and they can be friends. I know it's weird and crazy, but I feel sorry for the food. I don't like things to be alone.

Now that I was with Dean, things were different. In the course of a single week I had left my whole life behind. I met change head-on. I felt open to everything that was happening. Me, who'd grown up with live-in security guards and a high-tech surveillance system in a secluded, gated fortress. Me, who couldn't handle it if an ashtray got moved. In the first two years together we would live in six different places. It didn't matter. I was finally safe, safe with Dean.

A lot of the OCD stuff stopped when I met Dean. I used to get all kinds of free swag, so I always had a bunch of different shampoos and conditioners in my shower. When I got out, I'd have to make sure they were all facing out because if they were facing the wrong way, I felt uneasy that they couldn't see. And they'd have to all be touching so they'd be equal. *And* I used to have to tap a toe of each foot in the shower before I got all the way in or out. I remember coming back to my apartment in L.A. after meeting Dean in Ottawa. The first time I took a shower, I went to straighten all the shampoo bottles, and then I stopped myself. This was crazy. I got out of the shower and never did it again.

In spite of the shadows of my former life, I was so happy with Dean. I was finally living a smaller, more normal existence. It wasn't exactly the laundry-room closet I'd craved, but my life was considerably simplified. I'd accumulated so much crap living in that condo for ten years, so much that I didn't need. Here I had nothing and wanted nothing. I was free. I was starting over with Dean. I was starting a whole new life.

We were lying low at The Marlowe. Sometimes I'd pass people in the halls, which was ridiculously exciting to me. I'd never had proper neighbors before. One time a woman saw me and said, "What are you doing here?" I said, "I live here." She said, "Why would you live here? Don't you have a mansion?" She was so perplexed. She couldn't fathom that I'd live where she lived. It was a very nice building! I just said, "I like it here." There was a building barbecue by the pool every Sunday. Dean and I couldn't wait to go.

CHAPTER SIXTEEN

# Is That a Knife in Your Purse or Are You Just Glad to See Me?

While Dean and I played house, I was busy being the star, a producer, and one of the writers on *So NoTORIous*. VH1 started putting money into a big publicity campaign. Then they told me that they were going to do billboards for the show. There was going to be a building with my face on it! A gigantic photo of me and Mimi La Rue for all of L.A. to see. On the day of the photo shoot, in the flats of Beverly Hills, I got the full star treatment. I had my own trailer (which everyone knows makes you a big shot). My hair was set in curls, my makeup was high-fashion glam, and I was dressed in Marc Jacobs and Manolo Blahniks. I came out of the trailer and stood on the street corner while the cameramen finished setting up. It was a beautiful January day. There was a slight breeze, but not enough to blow my hair into my lipstick. Things were going my way. Uh-oh— remember what happens when things are going my way?

As I stood on the corner, all dolled up, a car drove by. A man leaned out of the driver's window. I smiled, expecting a catcall. But instead, he sneered and neighed at me. He neighed like a horse. It was a horsecall. This wasn't new to me. I knew exactly what he was trying to say. He was calling me "Horseface," as some bloggers have in the past. I froze for a moment, then just started laughing. Of course. It was so my life. Give me a high moment, and someone will always be there to neigh at me. But I was in love and I loved my work, and this time I wasn't about to let anything bring me down.

For Christmas, Dean and I planned to go to Canada. I was going to meet his family in Collingwood, a little town two hours outside Toronto where two of his three sisters live. We (along with Mimi and Ferris, our faithful companions) started the trip by spending a few days in Toronto, where I met all of Dean's friends. Then, on the afternoon of Christmas Eve, we drove up to Collingwood. On the way there Dean said, "My sisters are so excited to meet you." They both worked at a ski resort in town, and he told me that they'd arranged for us to take a carriage ride through a Christmas tree farm. A carriage ride through a Christmas tree farm sounded idyllic—now why hadn't my father imported *that* winter wonderland to our back-yard in L.A.?

In Collingwood there were a couple inches of snow coating the ground. We barely got our bags in the house when Dean packed a bottle of wine and a couple of glasses and hurried us off to the carriage ride.

Needless to say, I'd never seen a Christmas tree farm. I sort of pictured a big parking lot with a bunch of trees leaning in rows. I figured you wandered around, picked a tree, they'd wrap it, and you'd head home. But apparently, in Canada (and possibly in all parts of the world where places exist that call themselves "Christmas tree farms") the trees are actually in the ground. You pick the one you want, and they chop it down right in front of you. (Note to self: Never go to a "Thanksgiving turkey farm.")

I would have been happy to wander through the winter wonderland, but we weren't there to pick a tree. Instead, we found our carriage. It was an open, horse-drawn number, driven by an old man and woman who looked suspiciously like Santa and Mrs. Claus. I felt like I was at some amusement park about to go on "Jingle Bells: The Ride." It was starting to rain, but they cheerfully bundled us up in the backseat and we set off.

The path through the snow was dimly lit by hurricane candles and moonlight. The flickering candlelight reflecting off the snow gave everything an ethereal glow. All you could see were miles and miles of trees. As we drove, I started talking to the couple. I asked if they were married. They said they'd been married for forty-four years. It was the cutest thing—this little old couple doing carriage rides together all winter long. I said to Dean, "I hope that's us." I was only thirty-two and Dean was thirty-eight. It wasn't unreasonable to hope that we still had at least forty-four good years to spend together.

Then the carriage came to a stop. The Clauses said, "Okay, this is where we let you off." I was a little confused. Were we being held for ransom? But Dean said, "I think my sisters set something up for us." We walked through the grove and came to a little table in the middle of a clearing. It was surrounded with hurricane candles. There were two chairs and a bottle of Veuve Clicquot, my favorite champagne. All the surrounding trees were decorated with Christmas ornaments.

We sat down at the table. Dean said, "Oh my God, my sisters really went overboard." I was thinking, *Hmm, does Dean have the best sisters in the entire world, or is he going to ask me to marry him?* And my next thought was, *Now? I'm freezing and soaked. I must look like a drowned rat.* We opened the champagne and shared a toast. Then Dean dropped on one knee in the snow, pulled out a ring, and asked me to marry him. I started laughing and full-on bawling simultaneously. As I said yes, I could barely breathe. My heart was like a cartoon heart, beating so hard, it was bursting out of my chest. I felt elated and overwhelmingly in love. It was the greatest moment ever. Then it hit me. Oh. This was what it was supposed to feel like the first time. Every time I had an experience with Dean that I'd been through with Charlie was a lesson in how it was supposed to feel. Maybe I should have known Charlie wasn't right. But only now could I look back and see a million stop signs that I had failed to recognize. I'd had nothing to compare it to.

My hair was in pigtails, absolutely drenched. We took a picture of ourselves, with me showing off the ring, so happy. It was a ring I'd seen once before.

Dean and I left our spouses to be together. Neither of us went into it thinking we'd take things slowly and just see what happened. We wanted to get married right away. Even as early as the day we were leaving Ottawa, we talked about our wedding. I didn't know if it was going to work out, but the wedding I imagined was the opposite of my first. Everything I wanted the first time around had made the wedding feel like a play—the costumey gown, the onstage vows, the elaborate scene-setting, the large cast and extras. The two-carat diamond ring. It was all too fussy for me. Now it seemed like a contrived production—the wedding I was supposed to have for the person I was supposed to be.

Now that Dean and I were going to be together, it wasn't about show. It wasn't about spinning a fairy tale. This marriage was about who I was and what I wanted in my heart. And yes, that vision included an engagement ring.

I knew from the start that I wanted an antique ring. My first ring, which I gave back to Charlie, was platinum with a solitary diamond. I imagined something two-toned, with yellow gold and platinum, and another stone besides a diamond. Back in L.A. we'd gone to look at engagement rings at a place in Beverly Hills called Antiquarius. It's a big building where lots of different antique dealers have booths. Dean kept pointing to diamond rings, but none of them exactly fit my vision. Then we got to the ring. I said, "There it is. That's the ring I envisioned." It had a gold band with platinum around it. There was a diamond and a sapphire. Dean played it down. He said, "It's good that I know kind of what you want, but it's only our first day of looking. . . ."

Of course he'd given me the ring I'd picked. It was a beautiful, glorious, freezing, romantic moment. At some point Dean shouted, "She said yes!" It echoed and echoed through the trees. Then, completely unexpectedly, there were fireworks. Neither Dean nor his amazing sisters could take credit for those—they were Christmas Eve fireworks from a nearby town—but we decided to take them personally.

Eventually our carriage came back to get us. We rode back through the parallel rows of hurricane candles (which I later found out Dean's nieces had lit themselves, staying out of sight just ahead of the carriage, running for a mile to light every single candle all the way to the table in the woods). Mrs. Claus twisted around in her seat and said, "I've been meaning to tell you. We've been married for forty-six years, not forty-four." I nudged Dean. We had a new goal. Then she said, "Oh, what a blessing that it's raining. It's like a baptism. The rain is a symbol of cleansing, and the future is yours to create. Everything that starts from now on is about the two of you." I like to believe she had no idea who I was and that the subtext of her message wasn't *Congratulations, you're no longer a homewrecker.*

Dean and I were having such a great time in Collingwood that I didn't sit down and call my friends one by one with our news. The only notification I gave my beloved friends who were always there for me was a group e-mail telling them what had happened. (By the time I got home two weeks later—years in the tabloid world—they'd all read the details in *Us Weekly* anyway.)

I was on top of the world and nothing could interfere with that, but, as always, all my silver moments have cloudy linings. My relationship with my mother had been cool since my wedding to Charlie. We never got in touch about the divorce. I missed her sixtieth birthday party. We weren't officially in a fight or not speaking, but we weren't exactly bosom buddies. And yet she was the only person I reached out to when Dean and I got engaged. With friends, if you keep making an effort to reach out and you keep getting hurt, you eventually stop trying. But it's much harder to give up on family. Somewhere deep down you want it to work so badly that you keep making the same mistake over and over again.

I sat down and wrote my mother a long e-mail. Dean was asleep. I'd taken an Ambien, so maybe my judgment wasn't perfect, but I poured out my heart in that e-mail. I told her that I was so happy, so in love. I'd finally found real love, and I wanted to share it with her, to share it with my family. I wrote, *I want you to know and love Dean. I want us all to get together when we get home.* In the back of my head somewhere I suspected that she wouldn't want to hear that I was really happy and in love. Because she wasn't happy. She didn't have that kind of love in her life. But I thought, *I'm being truthful. She's my mother. She should want me to be happy. I want her to be part of it.*

I had a slew of e-mails with *Congratulations!* in the subject line sitting in my inbox on AOL. But my mother's response didn't come for four days. We were both on AOL, so I knew she'd opened and read the e-mail. Silence.

Finally a reply appeared. It was a brief e-mail. It said, *Congratulations on your engagement. Daddy and I are very happy for you. Love, Mom.* It went on to say, *P.S. We've decided to sell the condo sooner than anticipated, and we need you out of it by January 30th. That gives you one month.*

I laughed. Then I cried. Then I laughed again. Here it was. Documented for history. This was our relationship. Even though I hadn't called—I'd sent an e-mail—it was the best I could do with her. I'd poured out my heart.

I had lived in that condo for ten years. Charlie was still in the apartment—he'd be there until the beginning of January, and let's just say Charlie was not in an accommodating mood. We were due home from Canada on January 4. I started back up on *So NoTORIous* three days later, and we were in the heart of production. I had work every single day, and they were bound to be fifteen-hour days. I had been planning to move in March when *So NoTORIous* went on break. Now everything was going to have to go to storage. My mother was evicting me.

That night over dinner with Dean's sisters and our new friends, someone suggested that I e-mail my mother and ask for an extension. But I refused. I thought she wanted a reaction, and I wasn't going to give her the satisfaction. I didn't want to ask for anything from her again. I'd rather go way into debt. In fact, with the divorce and the hotels and the wild shopping compulsion I'd indulged before I met Dean, I already was in debt. Hiring movers to pack and store ten years of my life in record time cost me ten thousand dollars. I think of that as my mother's engagement present to us.

Not long after we came home from Canada, Dean and his soon-to-be-ex-wife started having custody issues. The details, again, aren't my story to tell. But one subject that emerged in their conversations was Dean's dream that, for the sake of the children, we'd all get along eventually. He pictured us all having dinner together not long down the line. Probably in hope of moving the custody dispute along, his wife, Mary Jo, said she wanted to meet me. Dean called me at my office at *So NoTORIous* to tell me that she wanted to meet with me over the upcoming weekend. The way it was presented was that she wanted to talk to me about being a stepmom. He said she wanted to make sure we were on the same page, that we agreed about behavior, bedtime, and eating—normal day-to-day stuff.

This was a hundred times worse than facing Charlie. I mean, put all my nonconfrontational past aside and you've still got me sitting face-to-face with a woman whose husband of twelve years and father

of her children left her for me four months ago. And I'm supposed
to have a civil conversation about whether I should feed her son peas
or carrots for dinner? Oh. My. God.

I know I said that Dean quelled all my irrational fears. But I had
to wonder: Was it irrational to be terrified of her? She had every right
to be angry at me. And for her wouldn't it be a simple, logical jump
from *This woman destroyed my marriage* to *And so I must destroy her*?
These things happen. Especially in TV movies. In fact, I'd probably
starred in this one. His ex-wife would murder me, and all the papers
would say was TV MOVIE QUEEN TORI SPELLING MURDERED AGAIN—
THIS TIME FOR REAL!

I told Dean I didn't want to do it. He was upset. He was trying so
hard to make everything okay. We went back and forth on it all day
long. In between phone calls I told my producers what was going on.
They said, "What? No, he's not seeing straight. You can't go see this
woman. Nothing good can come out of it." But if you do go, they
said, Dean should go with you. I suggested this to Dean, but he said,
"No. She wants to meet with you alone." Of course she wanted me
to come alone! She wanted to kill me!

Finally he told me it had nothing to do with him or me. It was
something I should do for his son. So I agreed. I figured worst-case
scenario: I die. And then Dean would feel bad. But I was going to be
brave. If I survived, it would be the bravest thing I'd ever done.

I was the Other Woman. I didn't want to be threatening, so I
dressed in jeans, a baggy sweater, and tennis shoes. I didn't wear
makeup. I put my hair in pigtails (possibly a mistake since she's
twelve years older than I am). Oh, and one more thing. At the last
minute before I walked out the door, I turned around and grabbed

the biggest kitchen knife out of the knife block. I stuffed it into my
purse. I wasn't going down without a fight.

Mary Jo welcomed me into her house with a gracious smile. She
was pretty and pleasant. As soon as I came in, she said that she'd just
put water on for tea, and would I like some? I was so taken aback at
her warmth that I rolled over like a puppy dog. "Great, great. That's
perfect."

As we sat down to talk, I made two potentially fatal mistakes right
off the bat: One, out of habit I'd deposited my purse on the dining room table. Now we were in the living room. I was completely
defenseless. And two, she brought me tea I hadn't seen her make.
And I drank it. Had I learned nothing from my TV movies? But
as the minutes passed and my vision didn't go all blurry, I finally
relaxed a little.

We sat there for three hours. Conversation didn't exactly flow. She
made limited eye contact. Even so, she set a sort of old-girlfriend
chitchat vibe, as if we'd gone to school together and hadn't seen each
other for five or six years. She led the conversation, filling me in on
her life and kind of giving me "tips" on Dean in a confiding but
somewhat ominous way, saying things like, "Oh, he has the worst
temper . . . but you'll see that eventually." I kept trying to steer the
conversation toward my responsibilities as a stepmom, but she had
other things on her mind.

We left on a nice note. She thanked me. We even hugged. I
grabbed my hidden Cutco weapon off the table and said good-bye.
When I got in my car, there were two main feelings swirling in my
head. The first was pride. For once in my life I had tackled my fear
head-on. (Sure, I had to come armed, but let's not kid ourselves.

Even if I'd pulled out that knife in self-defense, I wouldn't have had the first clue what to do with it.) It haunted me that I'd never had that final meeting with Charlie. It still keeps me up at night. But this time I'd actually done it.

The second feeling I had was doubt. I was going home to Dean, and somehow she'd put questions in my head. I loved him. I knew that. But how well did I know him? She seemed so warm and sincere, and yet in talking about Dean, she had described a man I didn't know. Things were going too well—someone had to rain on my parade.

I have a pretty detailed short-term memory. I can read a script through once and remember all my lines—for the next day at least. That night I walked Dean through every detail, every line of dialogue from my afternoon with Mary Jo. He was floored. He said, "I can't believe I sent you into a meeting where you'd come back doubting our relationship." But the doubts were short-lived. And no matter how stupid Dean felt, I didn't regret that meeting one bit. It was the bravest thing I'd ever done, even if I had to do it with a Balenciaga-sheathed knife in hand.

## CHAPTER SEVENTEEN

# What? It Doesn't Grow on Trees?

Blood, sweat, tears, and hair-extension maintenance. I worked around the clock on *So NoTORIous*. Sometimes I'd come to the set to start filming at five or six in the morning. I'd wrap at eight at night and head to the writers' trailer to brainstorm new episodes until midnight. Then the next morning I'd be back on set. It was my total career fantasy finally come true.

Being in the writers' room felt like therapy. I'd sit there recounting stories, and the other writers would chime in with their own stories or ideas about how to make mine funnier. It felt good to get all that stuff out and to laugh about it. Playing myself on the show was scary at first. Usually, I have a character to build around, but when that character was me, was I just supposed to say everything the way I'd say it, or was I supposed to act like . . . me? Of course, just because it was loosely based on my life didn't mean that the character was exactly me. I'm a little more grounded. It was more like me in my younger, *90210* days, even though the show was supposed to be taking place post-*90210*.

Then there was the executive producer side of the job. I was in charge on set. That had never happened before. Acting was great but familiar. What was new to me was sitting with each script, seeing jokes that I wrote, and planning shots. I had a say in wardrobe; I approved locations and sets; I did casting sessions for the costars and guest stars; I went to budget meetings. When we worked on the pilot, sometimes we'd be in the editing bay until three a.m. There were moments when I stepped back and realized that we were working on a set that was supposed to be my apartment. The characters were supposed to be my friends. The story was supposed to be my life. I was literally reliving some of the most memorable moments from my past, but this time I was miked and there was better lighting. And it was all because of an idea I had. I made this happen, and I loved every second of it.

Loni Anderson played my mother, and she eventually became like a cool mother figure to me—so much so that at some point she said, "I'm sad for your mother. She has no idea what an amazing daughter she has. She doesn't even know you. It's her loss."

Originally, when I pitched the show, the network loved the story about Farrah Fawcett wanting to borrow a potato, and it fell on me to ask her if she'd do a cameo on the show. I still lived next door to her at the time, so I went across the elevator bank and slipped a script under her door. A few days later she called. Apparently, her mother had just passed away—I had no idea. She said she'd been going through some hard times but that she read the script on the plane coming home from the funeral and laughed through the whole thing. She was still chuckling as she said, "I remember that. It must have seemed so bizarre. I really just wanted a potato." She did the part.

Before the show even aired, we started getting reviews. I've (noTORIously) never gotten good reviews—some backhanded compliments for *Maybe Baby, It's You* and *Trick,* but with TV? Never. I had no idea what critics would make of the show. But as the reviews came in, they were the best I'd ever gotten. The *LA Times* ran a feature saying, "*Beverly Hills, 90210* alumna, tabloid regular, gay icon and plucky Hollywood heiress, [Tori Spelling] has her fans, but in the 16 years she's been working as an actress, the 32-year-old has been subjected to what even the most poisonous observer of pop culture would have to admit is more than her fair share of vitriol and ridicule." They went on to say, "While this sort of thing has been done before . . . it has been done here exceedingly well. . . . She is a comedian, not a starlet, and if she is made for no other comedies than this one, she has landed for now in the exact right place. Little Tori, happy at last." The *New York Post* described the show as "very witty, sometimes brilliant, insightful hybrid sitcom *So NoTORIous*—a *Curb Your Enthusiasm* for the under-40 set," and the writer went on to say, "What I didn't know about Tori Spelling is that she's also smart. And funny. Very." Even the *Hollywood Reporter* had to admit, "She creates an appealing character despite all the preconceptions, many of which are acknowledged and dispensed with in the first few scenes."

The show hadn't aired, and the producers were already taking the reviews to the frame shop. I should have known it was the kiss of death. It's the "build me up to break me down" curse. Whenever there's a sign of hope, I know the crash is coming soon. It's the "Horseface" comment. It's the lead role in *Scary Movie 2*. It's being the "indie queen" and starring in *Maybe Baby* and all the pilots I did after *90210*. The night *So NoTORIous* premiered, Dean and I had a little party at our house for the cast, producers, and our agents. The ratings were at best mediocre.

Our premiere fell on the evening that daylight saving time kicked in, so there was hope that the time change had caused a mix-up, but the next week it was the same thing. Blah ratings. At first VH1 said not to worry, so we all hoped the ratings would pick up in the second season. Some shows are like that. The show was a critical success. It was a good, smart show. We felt blindsided when VH1 changed their tune and didn't give us a second season. The reason they gave for canceling the show was that it was too expensive. It cost a million dollars to make a single episode, and they could spend two hundred thousand dollars per episode on a reality show and get better ratings. They said, "Maybe we're just not ready for scripted TV." We met with the head of VH1 and offered to cut the budget in half. I said I'd take half of my salary. He said, "I guess I'm going to lose my standing in the gay community if I cancel"—the show had a cultish following, particularly among gay men—but then he canceled it anyway.

VH1 went silent. All the people we'd been friends with there disappeared. It was like a breakup—we never heard from them again.

I was thirty-three years old at the time; I'd been working almost consistently since high school; and I had nothing to show for it. When all my friends were kicking back in college, being supported by their parents while they partied every night and squeezed in a little schoolwork on the side, I was working seventeen hours a day, five days a week. When the cast of *90210* took off on summer and Christmas breaks, I filmed as many TV movies as I could.

All actors know that you need to strike when the iron's hot. You never turn down work. So I worked all through my twenties and sacrificed love, friends, relaxation, a college education. Now after all that I was two hundred thousand dollars in debt, almost bankrupt. And every time I tried out for a part or pitched a new show, it was like I was back at square one. It never got easier. Don't most careers get somewhat easier as you have more experience under your belt? All I wanted was to stop constantly making calls and taking meetings and strategizing relationships. It would be so nice to be able to relax and coast, with some idea where my next job was coming from.

Yeah, about that whole debt thing. How did a girl like me end up in debt? Well, I guess it starts with how I grew up. You remember the birthday parties. My godfather, Dean Martin, would give me a money tree blossoming with twenty-dollar bills, and where would that money go after everyone oohed and aahed? I have no idea. I didn't have a bank account. Not then and not later, when I scooped poo with my father to earn an allowance. I had a piggy bank, but to my memory all the piggy had in its belly was a few breakfasts' worth of coins. I didn't ask my parents for money because I never had to. I wasn't allowed to go anywhere alone—I was always with Nanny or our driver. In high school other kids would get dropped off in Westwood—the neighborhood of shops and restaurants surrounding UCLA—to walk around, but I always had a chaperone. The one time I went to a mall with a friend after school, I got in big trouble.

Even when I was sixteen years old and working full-time on *90210,* my financial independence took the form of a credit card. The bill went straight to my business manager. I didn't give a second thought to how much something cost and had absolutely no idea what my bill was every month.

I came from money. But I didn't exactly expect to be supported, now or in the future. I'd been living independently since I moved out of the Manor, except that I paid rent to my mother for the ten years before she evicted me. I hadn't even gotten a money tree from Dean Martin since the mid-eighties. Before my father got sick, before I sold *So NoTORIous*, I had lunch with my dad at his office once a week or every couple weeks. Eventually people who were pretty high up at his office started telling me that he was starting to fade. He was a little out of it, and they said in no uncertain terms that they thought I should talk to him about the contents of his will before he was any further gone.

It felt gross and wrong, but my father's colleagues were emphatic enough that I eventually summoned the nerve to broach the subject with my father.

At one of our lunches I said, "I hate to bring this up, Dad, but I know you love me and Randy, and I know you'd want to protect us and your future grandchildren. I'm not asking for anything, but I just want to make sure you know what your will says about me and Randy." I said, "I don't want to get into details, but I want you to make sure that everything's set up the way you want it to be." He said, "Let me find out. I'll talk to my business manager."

I didn't have to ask again. The next time we had lunch, he said, "Babe, I talked to the business manager about the will. You and Randy are going to be fine. You guys are totally set up. Don't worry. You're getting just under a million. You'll be fine." And he believed it.

I have no idea what the actual number is, but reports had it that my father was worth $500 million. I realized in that moment that my father knew nothing about money. Of course I know a million dollars is a lot of money. But was it in my family? My father would buy my mother a million-dollar necklace for Mother's Day without blinking. At the same time I believe he was totally sincere when he thought I was beyond set for life. I thought, *God, okay. It is what it is.* In that same conversation my father said, "I know you need money right now, and I want to help you out. If I give you something today, will you promise me to just accept it?" I thought he was going to write me a check. He didn't know the extent of my debt, but anything would help. Instead, he went with Aunt Renate, his assistant of forty years, to his safe. When he came back, he handed me five one-hundred-dollar bills, saying ceremoniously, "This should help you out for a while." I shouldn't have been surprised. Often when I saw him, he'd slip me a twenty-dollar bill and say, "Don't tell your mother."

This was my dad at a restaurant: Eat the meal. Add the tip to the check. Hand the struggling actor/waiter a hundred dollars. And then there was me. He never said a single word about wanting us to make it on our own. He never did anything to teach us about the value of money. He never talked about wanting us to be independent. But there you have it. Just because someone has a lot of money doesn't mean they spend much time thinking about it.

So, getting back to the question at hand, how did I find myself in debt? What about all those years on *90210,* all those TV movies? Where was my nest egg? I guess the best answer is that I didn't think about it. I wasn't raised to think about money. I had no idea how to manage it or how to put myself on a budget. I was born into a millionaire lifestyle, and I had no idea how to live any other way. If my mother liked a shirt in a catalog, she'd order it in six colors. I went from that way of living with my parents to working on *90210,* where for a while I was able to maintain it without their help. I didn't live in a mansion, but if I walked into Barneys and saw a cashmere sweater I liked, I'd take it in multiple colors, just like I'd learned from my mom. I never looked at the price tag. Mehran always calls those the "glory days." He says, "We'd walk into Dolce and Gabbana; they'd see you, close down the store, and bring out the champagne. You'd drop fifty thousand dollars. We were on top of the world." As recently as right before I met Dean, my shopping was at an all-time high. I was obsessed with Internet shopping. I didn't want to be in the living room with Charlie, and I didn't have work, so I'd disappear into my office and shop online for hours. I was on eBay constantly. Not a day went by when boxes didn't arrive at the door. I wouldn't even open them. The boxes would just pile up in the dining room.

Now things were different. Years had gone by where I still bought whatever I wanted to buy. I lived the high life, but my income was unstable and fluctuating. I wasn't making millions. Dean and I hit reality. We had to start thinking about our budget.

I'm a fashion whore and I love clothing, but I had to change where I shopped. I became the girl who looks for the bargain. My friend Jenny buys a lot of her clothes at a fancy boutique called Calypso. She'll spend four hundred dollars on a sundress. I used to spend that without blinking. Now I'll spend twenty-five dollars at Forever 21 and be just as satisfied. Once you change, I think you change forever. I don't think I could ever go back to spending money so easily. That's not to say that I don't still indulge, but I'll buy a good piece that I know will last me for years to come. And I still have a serious weakness for Christian Louboutin shoes. But you can wear shoes over and over again!

Right—that's another thing. I get photographed a lot. Last year I was on the cover of *Us Weekly* four times. Even if the reasons why are different, sometimes it seems I'm photographed by the media as often as big stars like Jennifer Aniston and Angelina Jolie. But stars like that don't have to pay for most of their clothes, especially red-carpet dresses. I go out, I'm photographed in a dress, and (unless I want to be mocked by the press—which maybe someday I'll be brave enough to invite upon myself, but don't I get mocked enough already?) I can't wear it again.

The other thing about all that publicity is privacy. Jennifer Aniston and Angelina Jolie can afford ten-million-dollar homes with driveways, gates, and security guards. I grew up with that, and it sure would be nice to feel safe and have a refuge from the paparazzi, but I can't afford to buy such a house. In a weird way much of my life seems to be dealing with megastar issues on a microstar's budget.

Look, I'm not complaining; I'm just trying to explain what it feels like to think about money for the first time in your thirties. Adjusting my lifestyle has been, for the most part, a good learning experience. Dean made a lot of what had seemed important to me stop mattering. Having nothing felt amazing. Everything was so simple. All the weight was gone. I loved it. We lived in six places in two years. If we didn't have furniture, we could sleep on a mattress. The day I met Dean, my whole world changed for the better. I could go with the flow. Love made all the other stuff unimportant.

CHAPTER EIGHTEEN

# A New Family

When it came time to plan my wedding to Dean, I contacted the only travel agent I knew: the one who arranged my honeymoon with Charlie. It was kind of an awkward e-mail to send: *Hi, um, a year ago I asked you to plan my honeymoon, and now I'm asking you to find a place for my next wedding.* But business is business—she didn't complain.

Dean and I fell in love alone. We'd both had big weddings the first time around. Now we wanted to get married alone. We told the travel agent that we wanted to be married on a tropical beach. We wanted privacy. It should be secluded and spiritual. Other than that we were open to anything. A couple days went by, and then a packet from the travel agent arrived in the mail. I opened it with excitement, ready to explore our options, but there was only one slim brochure inside. It was for a place called the Wakaya Club in Fiji.

Planning my first wedding was all about decisions. I had to look at one hundred flowers to select the right three. The food at the first tasting was delicious, but I had to do four more. I was focused on getting the wedding perfect, but what about the marriage? Now I looked down at the Wakaya Club brochure. Shouldn't there be options? What about Tahiti? Everyone was always talking about Tahitian huts with glass floors over the ocean. And here our travel agent was telling us, "I can send you other brochures, but this is the place." She was so firm. And how could it be the wrong place when I was with the right man? We decided to take a leap of faith. We booked it.

Two weddings in two years, and the only thing they had in common was me. For the second wedding I didn't want a classic wedding dress. We were getting married on the beach. In Dolce & Gabbana, I found a fitted white eyelet summer dress. It wasn't a wedding dress, but it had a short train. It was perfect.

It was a ten-hour flight to Fiji. As I've mentioned, I inherited my fear of flying from my father, who came by it honestly. He served in the U.S. Air Force and was on his way from Fort Worth, Texas, to an air base in Ohio when he came down with the flu. The flight surgeon pulled him off the plane—he was too sick to fly. That plane to Ohio crashed, and everyone on it was killed. My father rented a car and drove straight from Fort Worth to Dallas to see his parents. But when he entered his childhood home, his mother opened the door and immediately fainted. The authorities had telephoned to tell the family that my father was dead. When she came to, she made him swear he'd never fly again. He promised. He was eighteen, and he never got on an airplane again. Growing up, every time I traveled by plane, he'd cry and I'd cry. You wonder why planes give me migraines?

Someone from the Wakaya Club met the plane in Fiji. Then we had to go get a marriage license. At the airport a sweet couple recognized us and said, "We're getting married—what are you guys doing here?" The paparazzi had been on a "Tori and Dean Wedding Watch" for weeks, and we didn't want to be busted. We were so paranoid that we just said, "Oh, vacationing." Then we went to the Fijian equivalent of city hall to get our wedding license and ran into the same couple getting theirs. They were definitely onto us. But of all the couples marrying in Fiji, what were the chances that the one couple we encountered would be the kind of people who would spend part of their wedding trip calling the *Enquirer* to sell information about another marrying couple? (Answer: 100 percent. We later found out they called the tabloid immediately. I guess they figured it would pay for their honeymoon.)

Now was the hard part. Wakaya Club is on its very own island in Fiji. To get there, we had to take a four-person puddle jumper from Fiji to Wakaya Island. It was my worst fear, but I was done letting fear stand in my way. I guess they'd heard about my fear of flying because our escorts offered us warm wine. I downed a glass. The flight was terrifying. The pilot, who was two feet in front of us, kept turning around to give me a thumbs-up. *Eyes on the road, buddy, eyes on the road!*

After what seemed like a lifetime but I'm told was less than an hour, we landed on a unpaved clearing the size of a postage stamp. Overshoot and you'd go off a cliff. Enough with the drama, people. I got it. We were secluded. Would an actual runway have killed anyone? At the time I wasn't negotiating for a runway. I was too busy kissing the unpaved ground and cheering, "I made it, I made it!"

There were ten little cottage suites, called *bures,* lining the beach. Basically little huts, but five-star huts. And that was it. No shopping. No restaurants. No village. Just the visitors, and a community of Fijians who live and work at the resort. We stayed in the "Governor's Bure," which was the fanciest of their suites. It was very Tommy Bahama, with woven bamboo walls and timber floors. There were two rooms, a master bedroom, and a living room. It was the ideal blend of primitive luxury: an open-air lava rock shower and a flat-screen TV. A waterfall in the private garden and a four-poster bed with fine sheets.

We spent our first couple days at Wakaya just hanging out. I love seashells—I have ever since I found the beautiful ones my mother hid for me in Malibu. But now that the jig was up, I couldn't fathom finding real ones just sitting there in the sand. But the beaches were absolutely covered with all sorts of shells. I was so excited. I became obsessed. I even put on snorkel gear to crouch in two inches of water looking for sea treasures. No shell was too small or broken for me. All of Dean's photos are of me, in a bikini and sunglasses, stooped over peering intently at the sand. Dean just lay on the beach staring at me with a content smile on his face. He said, "You're like a little girl, full of sheer joy." I was. I felt totally free.

True to our two-person wedding plan, the traditional rehearsal dinner held for out-of-town guests had two attendees: me and Dean. The table was strewn with Fijian flowers, and a Fijian band played drums for us. We ate authentic food. But there were some other guests whose presence wasn't physical.

I know I've said it before, but Nanny was a mother to me. She died three months before I married Charlie. I have regrets that I didn't spend enough time with her in her last few years. I'm just not good at phoning. She'd leave me messages saying, "It's Nanny. Call me back! I've called twice now!" I'd call to apologize and she'd say, "I don't care, but call your dad. He gets sad when you don't call him." Toward the end she was diabetic, on dialysis, and in and out of the hospital. When she was in the hospital for the last time with an infection they couldn't locate, I was there every day. The doctor said, "Margaret's a miracle." He couldn't believe how strong she was—up until the end she was talking about how she planned to wear lavender to my wedding but didn't trust a friend to pick out a dress for her. When the time came at my first wedding, I placed a lavender rose on a front-row chair to save a seat for Nanny.

When I arrived at her bedside on the day she died, the nurse said, "Wake up, your baby's here. Tori's here." Nanny said "Baby" to me—that's what she called me—so I guess she knew I was there. But while I was there, she took a turn for the worse. When I called my mother to update her, I was in hysterics. She told me to go home. She said, "I made my peace yesterday. I said my good-bye. You've made your peace. You should go home now." But I wanted to stay with Nanny through the end. My biggest fan, Nanny watched every single TV show I ever was on. I had taped *The Ellen Degeneres Show* the day before, and it was on that day. We told her I was going to be on and turned up the volume on the TV. She literally hung on until the show was over, and then she passed. When she died, I was holding one of her hands, my brother was holding the other.

My brother and I helped organize her funeral, and I wrote a eulogy for her. In the days after her death we spent a couple days going through her apartment—she'd left instructions that she wanted me and Randy to take anything we wanted to remember her. The whole apartment was full of photos of us growing up. On the bookshelves were album after album. Tori: first grade; Tori: second grade; Tori: graduation. She had saved every picture I ever drew. When the woman next door saw me, she said, "Are you Tori? Margaret's daughter? I've heard so much about you. She was so proud of you." It dawned on me that I'd only really known Nanny in the context of our lives. I'd spent time with her in Crenshaw, but I didn't know her personal life when we weren't around. In her apartment I felt like I saw more clearly what our relationship had been. She wasn't just a mother to me. I was a daughter to her.

May 7, the date of the wedding, was the day Dean's father had died the year before. His mother died when Dean was fifteen. We liked to say that his parents and Nanny teamed up in the afterlife to make sure our paths collided. They were and are our angels. At our "rehearsal" dinner Dean and I wanted to celebrate them. After a private dinner in our hut we went out to the beach where there was a little bonfire waiting for us. We wrote letters to his parents and Nanny expressing love and thanking them—our closest family—for bringing us together and looking out for us. We invited them to be a part of our wedding. Then we put the letters in the fire and watched the smoke rise up into the night.

*People* magazine had an exclusive on our wedding photos and sent a high-end fashion photographer. He brought his girlfriend and a two-person crew. Not a bad gig, flying to a deluxe resort in remote Fiji to photograph the world's smallest wedding. Soon after we arrived, we got a fax warning us that the wedding had been leaked to the *Enquirer* (thanks to that couple at the airport). The letter told us that everyone knew we were getting married in Fiji. They'd dispatched teams of paparazzi and were flying them to Fiji to come find us. This was not good news. We just wanted to be alone. I knew what it was like to have helicopters drowning out the ceremony, and it was exactly what I wanted to avoid.

Freaking out, we told the resort manager what was going on. He smiled, perfectly calm, and said, "No worries. Nothing will happen." I thought it was sweet, how he thought his island was so isolated, but I said, "You don't understand. These people always find a way to get their money shots." But the manager told us that in his twenty years there not one picture had ever gotten out. He said he'd spoken to his friends who ran the various tourist businesses on Fiji. No boats would come near the island. No planes would fly over the island. No helicopters would venture near the airspace. No one would get a picture of us. It sounded crazy and impossible. But we never heard a single helicopter. I had to hand it to the travel agent. She was beyond right about the privacy.

The next morning was our wedding day. We woke up to pouring rain. Rain! In Fiji! We had no backup plan, so we just moved ahead. They told us they'd decorate the spa *bure* for us. I was disappointed, but oh well. What could we do? Besides, as Dean reminded me, it rained when we got engaged and Mrs. Claus told us it was a baptism. After a decadent breakfast, we got a couples' massage. Then, two hours before the wedding, the sun burst through the clouds. It was a gorgeous day.

There wasn't much for me to do to get ready. I put my hair in braids and let it dry naturally. When I took the braids out, I had wavy, beachy hair. I did my makeup and slipped on my dress, and I was done, dressed, and ready to wed before my husband-to-be. It took twenty minutes from start to finish. Somebody notify the *Guinness Book of World Records.*

When I walked out of our *bure,* I felt content, beautiful, and so at peace. I was completely, 100 percent happy. It was effortless. For my first wedding everything was perfectly staged. I was so carefully made up and coiffed. I moved like I was back in that heavy Marie Antoinette costume. Now all I wanted was to look pretty for Dean. My hair was flowing in the wind. I barely had any makeup on. I felt the sand moving between my bare toes as I walked outside. Amazing!

Before Dean saw me, we got in separate Jeeps to head to a beach we'd chosen for the wedding ceremony the day before. We drove through the wilderness of the tiny island on winding dirt trails, passing deer and wild boar. As I stepped out of the Jeep, I was greeted by a guy in warrior regalia. He blew into a conch shell to announce my arrival, and I followed a path of white frangipani petals around the trees to where Dean was standing near the water's edge.

I was carrying a bouquet of white orchids. The stems were wrapped in ribbon, and dangling from that were narrow ribbons with little sepia photos of Dean's mom and dad and Nanny. Our guests. Dean was in place next to the officiant, who held our two rings in a shell full of sand and seawater. The *People* photographer was there with his crew, and we'd also brought along a kit to make our own non-traditional wedding video. We used eight-millimeter film, so our wedding video would be silent, grainy, and rough-cut, like a home movie from the seventies. For the wedding itself, we hired a local videographer to do the filming.

It was my second time walking down the aisle, but it was a completely new experience. The first time my nose was running, my dad was standing on my train, and I had my best bride face on. This time I was looking straight ahead, thinking, *I love this man so much*.

The *People* photographer was getting his shots. The videographer was backing down the aisle as I walked toward Dean. And the officiant was standing in place with the seashell holding our rings. Dean and I took each other's hands and stood there beaming at each other. I just wanted to stay in that moment forever, and I did my best to memorize it. I can still remember the exact look in Dean's eyes as he looked at me. We took a few moments. Then we were pretty much done taking it in, and it seemed like the ceremony should be starting, but nothing was happening. We looked over at the officiant and saw that everyone was on their hands and knees: the officiant, the various cameramen, the warrior with the horn. The videographer had bumped into the officiant, spilling the rings out of their little baptismal shell. The rings were gone. Dean stalked off, upset. I followed him, and he said, "We've been through so much. We planned this out. You look so beautiful. And now the rings are lost!" I was totally calm. I'd lost one of Dean's rings before, on the roof of our hotel in Ottawa. I knew we'd still be in love and, eventually, married, with or without those rings.

If finding my string ring on that gravel roof in Ottawa was looking for a needle in a haystack, then this was looking for . . . rings on the beach. Then they found Dean's ring. That was half the battle. Almost. I wear a size 3½ ring. It was so small, I knew there was no hope of finding it. But the ever-calm, "don't worry, it's all taken care of" hotel manager sent a couple of his guys away, and moments later they came back with sand sifters. Sand sifters! They weren't metal detectors, but I was still impressed. I made a mental note to borrow them for shelling. Fifteen, twenty minutes went by, then someone shouted, "I got it!" Phew. We *were* meant to be after all.

Dean wanted to start over from the beginning, so I went back to the Jeep and waited until the warrior guy blew his conch shell. I walked down the beach to Dean. We read the vows that we'd written ourselves. I said, "I promise to live with you and laugh with you; to stand by your side, and to sleep in your arms; to be joy to your heart, and food for your soul; to always make you, you." Dean said, "I promise to worship and adore you each and every minute of every day. I promise to protect you with my life and promise to give of myself till time's end." The vows were a little longer than that, but they were still short but sweet. And that was it. The photographer was Dean's witness, and his girlfriend was my witness. We were man and wife. We kissed, and all five of the other people there clapped. Then Dean said, "I'm going to take my wife for a walk down the beach."

This was our most private moment in a very private ceremony. Later I'd compare it to the "intimate" moment Charlie and I were supposed to have after our ceremony, when various attendants milled around as I had my hair and makeup touched up and had my portrait done. But there, on the beach, I wasn't making comparisons. Dean was my family now. We walked and talked about how magical it was. Everything we said was just love, love, love.

We drove back to the "cocktail hour" in a Fijian Jeep that said *Just*

*Married* in Fijian and was decorated with palm fronds and coconut shells instead of aluminum cans. At my first wedding I missed both the cocktail hours. This time I was 50 percent of the guest list. Out on the beach in front of our *bure,* they'd set up a lounge area for us: a couch with ottomans and pillows. There were tiki torches and flowers everywhere. They played a special CD we had brought with us, and we ate shrimp skewers served on leaves, sushi, dumplings, rose champagne—all our favorite things.

Before dinner we had our first dance. Dean led me into the shallow water, where the eyelet train of my dress spread out behind me, wet and sandy. Dean rolled his pants up, and we danced in water up to our shins. The song we danced to was Lonestar's "Amazed." It had come on the radio once when I was pulling out of a parking lot. I stopped my car. It reminded me of Dean. My whole life I'd known fairy tales, seen romance movies, and heard love songs, wanting them to resonate, wanting them to feel real. I'd always wanted a fairy-tale wedding. This time around, all my attention was on the real prince who stood before me. *This* was the fairy tale.

After we danced, the photographers and staff went off to have their dinner and left us alone for ours. They served us a five-course meal in a four-poster bed set up on the beach. By the time our third course came, we were getting drowsy. The photographer had to wake us up when they brought out the cake. It was a beautiful cake decorated with fresh orchids. He took his shot of us cutting the cake and left. It's a good thing, because the photos of us tasting the cake might not have come out so picture-perfect. Apparently, they'd used salted butter to make the cake. Then added more salt. It was like a salt lick. It was terrible. We were too blissed out to care.

I took my bouquet to the water's edge. The little photos of Nanny and Dean's parents dangled against my wrist. I stood with my back to the ocean and said a silent prayer to them. Then I tossed the bouquet into the ocean, and we watched it float away.

As for our wedding night, well, after a long day together I couldn't wait to have sex with my new husband.

## CHAPTER NINETEEN

# You Can Never Go Home Again

Six weeks after our wedding Dean and I were in a Toronto burger joint with another couple when I glanced down at my Black-Berry and saw an e-mail from a friend saying, *I just heard about your dad. I'm so sorry.* I was perplexed. My friend worked at ABC News. Did she know something I didn't know? I checked my next e-mail. It was from Chris, a creator of *So NoTORIous*. It read, *I'm sorry. I know you were trying to get home in time to see him.* I looked up at Dean and said, "I think my dad just died."

As we left the restaurant, my phone started to ring. My publicist, my manager, one friend after the next. Everyone in my life was call-ing to express their sympathy. My father had passed. But it was four hours before I heard from anyone in my family. My brother finally called.

A couple weeks earlier I'd gone to see my father for the first time in nine months. I can't say exactly why it had been so long. There was no fight, just an increasing list of alienating moments: My mother didn't call back when I told her I was getting divorced; she told me I had to move out of her apartment when I told her I was engaged. Then *So NoTORIous* started airing a couple months before Dean and I got married, and I was pretty sure that hadn't helped matters. The character of my mother in that show was, well, somewhat in the *Mommie Dearest* vein. We showed her selling my possessions on eBay, leaving my brother on a cruise ship, and putting an evil eye on me. Even though it was fictionalized, a lot of what happened in the show was loosely based on stories and behaviors that I described to the writers and that my mother surely recognized in some form, regardless of how warped she thought the retelling to be. Although I saw my mother interviewed at a red-carpet event saying, "It doesn't bother me. It's a comedy," it's not like she called to congratulate me.

But as far as I'm concerned, the biggest reason for my alienation from my parents was Mark. My mom spent all her time with him. They went out every night. Dad said he didn't want to go to functions and was happy for Mark to go. I didn't buy it. Then I started hearing stories—I'd been told she went to Paris on a private jet with her girlfriends, but someone I knew saw Mark flying to Paris on a commercial plane the same day. Mom would have movie night and would tell my father everyone who was there except Mark. I'd say, "You know Mark is down there too," and he'd say, "Oh, maybe she told me but I forgot."

I don't think my father had to die so soon. Yes, he had a stroke, but for two years before that—years when he could have recovered from throat cancer—he gave up on life. He never saw daylight. He rarely got out of bed. Or walked around his property. Or ate. He'd drink Ensure out of a can. He felt useless at work. His shows were running themselves and nobody needed him there. And his wife went out every night without him.

When we were in Fiji, one of the writers from *So NoTORIous* e-mailed and said that my mother had closed my father's office and sold its contents. He told me to look at Perez Hilton's website. I saw that it said a high-profile Hollywood producer had sold his office furniture at an online auction site. Then I saw the photos. It was his stuff, still in the office I recognized as his. There was a lamp for sixty dollars. A coffee table for two hundred dollars. Even the hideous fish windmill that Ed McMahon had given him, which he proudly displayed on his office patio for years. That undeservedly beloved fish windmill was listed for twenty dollars (far more, I'm sure, than its actual value). But that summed it up for me. I felt that selling my father's office was essentially stripping his life of meaning. I couldn't bear to watch it happen, to watch him cared for by nurses while my mother and Mark controlled the house. His fire was gone. But I'll always regret that I missed nine months with my dad that I can never retrieve.

Before my dad died, my brother told me he wasn't doing well, but I didn't believe it. Maybe I didn't want to deal with it. But mostly, I thought that my mother and Mark wanted him to seem like an old, feeble man so they had an excuse for their behavior.

Finally my brother called in tears. He wanted me to come see Dad, to introduce him to Dean. Mom and Mark were in Vegas, and my father was at home with a nurse. It had been so long. We'd had maybe two strained conversations on the phone in those nine months. I didn't know how he'd react to seeing me. But Randy told me that Dad wouldn't remember how long it had been. And Randy said he'd come with me. I'll always be grateful to him for that. It would be the last time I saw my father alive.

My father was in bed, looking frail but not terrible. When he saw me, he lit up, and just like that, it was as if no time had passed: I was Daddy's little girl again. He was with it but not sharp, happy to just watch sports. I sat at the foot of the bed pretending to care about football, and at some point he said, "So what's our next project? What are we gonna produce together?" He was meeting my new husband for the first time, but this was how he best related to me—what could he do for me, what could he give me, what show could he put me in? He might have asked about my dogs, but never about my life.

After a couple hours Randy, Dean, and I left. On the way out I went into my mother's upstairs den, where she keeps photo books. I said to Dean, "This is the last time I'll ever be in this house." I opened up my travel Balenciaga. It was a huge bag, but thankfully, Nicole Richie and Mary-Kate and Ashley Olsen made it fashionable to carry weekend bags everywhere; otherwise, the guards might have busted me. I took the photo books from when I was a baby, including one with my birth certificate. Then we went downstairs, and I took some cookbooks that had Nanny's recipes in her handwriting. That's all I wanted. Somewhere deep down I had to be aware that I was saying good-bye to my dad. And I knew when my mother came back, I wouldn't be welcome.

What happened next was my fault.

At a social event I talked to someone who worked for a weekly magazine. We were among friends, and I didn't think of the conversation as a press interview. But of course you can't blame the media for doing their jobs. So I was catching my friends up, and I mentioned that my father and I had reconciled but that I wasn't seeing my mother because she was having a relationship that I didn't approve of. Surprise, surprise, two weeks later it appeared in the magazine. I didn't know it then, but that would be the beginning of the press war between me and my mom.

Right after I saw my father for the last time, Dean and I went to Toronto. I called my father twice, the first time was on Father's Day. He was hard to understand, and I told Dean that it sounded like he'd had a stroke, but nobody told me anything. The next time I called turned out to be three days before he died. I was in the middle of doing press for *So NoTORIous,* but I'd also just found out that the show had been canceled. When I asked for my father, my mother got on the phone. She said, "Hi, Tori. It's Mom. Your father has had a stroke, so he can't really talk. This is a private matter. We'd appreciate it if you didn't go to the press with this information." I insisted on talking to my father, and when he got on the phone, I heard him say, "Hey, babe, I love you." He was pretty out of it and hard to understand, but I was happy that he knew I'd called.

When I got off the phone, I was furious at my mother. I know she was responding to my indiscretion in the press, and I can't say I blame her, but at the time all I could think about was that what I'd said was true—her relationship with Mark was disturbing, and I thought it had taken a toll on my father when his health was in jeopardy. My whole life, through all my conflict with my mother, I'd never really had it out with her. I never spoke back to her. Usually, I'd do something passive-aggressive like bringing the birthday cake for Nanny even though I knew she was against it. What she said wasn't totally unfair, I get it, but for some reason that phone call was the final straw. I wrote an e-mail saying something like, *Keep what out of publication, Mother? The truth about you and Mark? You disappoint me to no end. You should never have been wife to a man so generous and loving. You never deserved him. You never deserved to have children like me and Randy. The greatest lesson you taught me is how* not *to be a mother and wife. Without Nanny (the best gift you ever gave us) we would not be the down-to-earth people we are today.* I knew my dad was going to die, and I put it all out there. I wrote the e-mail out of anger, but I didn't send it blindly. I reread it three times, although I did press send from a bar. It was an e-mail that had been building up for thirty-three years. It was a relationship-ending e-mail.

She never responded. Three days later my dad passed away.

In Toronto, the night my father passed, everyone in my life called me except my family. Finally my brother called at one thirty in the morning. He'd been on a plane from Miami, had gotten the news when he landed, and had gone straight to the Manor. Randy and I consoled each other.

Shortly after I spoke to Randy, I heard my mother's statement on the news. It confirmed my father's death and said that my mother and Randy were by his side when he passed. I knew it wasn't true—that Randy had been on a plane. It seemed my mother's first message about my father's death was a public condemnation of my absence.

The next morning Dean and I were at the airport on our way home when my publicist sent me an e-mail with my mother's press release. It was from "Candy and Randy Spelling," and it said that they were both grieving a great man. They thanked everyone who had reached out. If my mother's first statement was a snub, this was a deliberate slap in the face. My publicist was already getting calls asking why I hadn't been included in the statement. It made it sound like I wasn't part of the family or even sad about losing my father! So now I had to issue my own statement saying, *I'm obviously heartbroken that my father has passed. . . .* In the middle of this airport-based press-release composition, I ran into the former Dodgers manager Tommy Lasorda. When he gave me his condolences, he said, "At least you have your family. Give your mom my love." Yeah, right.

When we landed at LAX, there was a covert operation to get us out of the airport—the paparazzi had been staking it out all day waiting for our return. We snuck out some back exit and headed to our house, where all our friends came over to be with us. The big topic was my mother. It had happened again—like the night Charlie asked for my parents' blessing, like the brunch after my first wedding, like so many times in my life. Somehow every big moment in my life was all about my mother, even if she wasn't in attendance.

The funeral was on Sunday. I pulled myself together and focused on my dad. The point was to honor him and his life. I wanted to be there with Dean, of course, and Jenny, Pete, and Mehran, who had grown up with my dad, to close this chapter. We arrived at the funeral service before my mom, Mark, and Randy. It was a small, private room, with maybe thirty chairs set up in rows. The front row was empty and, I assumed, reserved for immediate family members. Since I didn't know where I stood in the family, I didn't know where to sit—I didn't want to be presumptuous. He was her husband. If she didn't want to sit next to me, I wanted to respect that. So Dean and I slid into the next available row.

My mother, Mark, Randy, and my uncle Danny came in together. (I later found out they'd been viewing the body and saying their good-byes. I tell myself I wouldn't have wanted to see my father in that state, but I, ahem, would have liked the option.) My mother and Mark greeted the guests together, looking to all appearances like a couple together bidding farewell to one of their parents. Mark was taking charge as he had taken charge at my first wedding. My brother hugged me, took my hand, and guided me to the first row. It was the permission I needed.

My father had an incredible life. He produced more than fifty TV series, made ten movies and almost one hundred fifty TV movies, and won two Emmys and many other awards. A small group of family, friends, and longtime business associates was gathered at a funeral parlor for a closed-casket service on that quiet summer day. It was a somber scene. But the rabbi's eulogy—I am not kidding—went something like this: "If Aaron could see all his friends and family here today, it would mean so much to him. It would almost be like he was in . . . *7th Heaven*. When Aaron started out, he met wonderful people and moved up in the business, but when he met Candy he was on . . . *The Love Boat*." He wove all of the shows my father produced, and probably even a few that he didn't, into his speech. Then he talked briefly about the important people in my dad's life: Candy. Tori. Randy. And his good friend Mark Nathanson. Mark was in the eulogy. The deceased's wife was sitting in the front row of his funeral next to the man with whom she was having an affair, and this rabbi—an old friend of Mark's?—was going on about what a great friend Mark was to my father. We heard actual snickers from the crowd. Jenny and Mehran were sitting next to a business associate of my father's, a man who really cared about him. He muttered, "This is so not right."

Then it was over. We went to the Manor for the reception. As we came in, that same business associate of my father's was hurrying out the door. He said, "Out of respect for Aaron, I'm leaving. This is just wrong. I can't do it." My little group walked inside. Uncle Danny greeted us, crying. He said to me, "Go make up with your mother. All your dad would want is for you to be together. Promise me." Then Mehran found me and said, "I just talked to your mom. She says she's happy you're here, and she wants to meet Dean."

I was scared, but my mother was gracious. She hugged me, and I thanked her for having us, and she shook Dean's hand. That was us. Pretending my venomous e-mail and the passive-aggressive press releases didn't exist. I would have liked to believe that my father's death trivialized everything else, but I knew too well that this stuff didn't disappear. It just got buried beneath a thin layer of artifice before surfacing again.

Mark herded us into a room for a prayer. Randy, my mother, my uncle Danny, and I stood at the front. I felt a little better. Then I glanced over at Dean, and he, the tallest man in a room full of Jews, was wearing his yarmulke on the front of his head like a Conehead. Randy and I looked at each other and burst out laughing.

After the prayer Uncle Danny asked the family to gather in a hug. We had a moment. Then he asked me and my mother to say we loved each other, so we did. Uncle Danny said, "I'm so happy. This is what Aaron would have wanted."

That would have made a nice ending, but the truth is that there was awkwardness at the ongoing reception. I ran into Aunt Renate, my father's longtime assistant. She was off to the side, crying, and she said she had to leave. That's when she told me that she'd been fired six months earlier. As I looked around, people seemed like scared mice, walking on eggshells. It was creepy. I told Dean and my friends that I just wanted to go home, where we could sit around and share stories about my dad. But I didn't want to have to say good-bye to my mother and Mark. Which meant I didn't want to walk from the garden back through the house. I absolutely refused. So the five of us approached the bushes in the back of the house. Dean boosted me up to the top of the manicured hedges. One by one we dropped onto the three-inch deep pea gravel below, James Bond–style. Then, giggling, we ran to our car. It was a perfect, Lucy-esque exit. I'm sure the security cameras caught the whole escape on video. The guards probably had a good laugh over that one.

Back at our house we sat our version of shiva. For the next week my friends came over every day. Mehran brought food from Baja Fresh. Jenny brought Chin Chin. It was the same as when Nanny died and the same as when Jeremy died. Nanny was my mother, and my friends are my extended family. It made sense to sit shiva with them, eating Roscoe's chicken and waffles and reminiscing.

As soon as the funeral was over, the press craziness between me and my mother resumed. A reporter from a weekly magazine told me that they were doing a tribute cover story about my father and asked me for some quotes. I talked about what it was like growing up with my dad. I told him about how we'd act out fairy tales and pick up dog poo together. People might have known about the fake snow, but they didn't know about small father-daughter moments around the house. Then I talked about how his actors weren't just actors to him. They were friends and family who could call him anytime about anything. If you worked with him once, he'd hire you over and over again. He was loyal. It didn't matter if you were a big actor or a makeup artist or in craft services—he always seemed to remember you. He'd talk to you, hug you, and make you feel as important as Joan Collins. He may not have had emotionally deep relationships with anyone, but he was still infinitely loving and supportive. I tried to share nice stories. I tried to show the kind of person he was. Of course the reporter asked me questions about the funeral and my relationship with my mother. I told him where the funeral had taken place and didn't think I said much else. *But . . .*

Cut to the cover of the magazine. It wasn't a tribute to my father. It was a big photo of me. This was not what I wanted. A legend had died, and there I was, taking center stage. Just as bad, the lead quote for the story was, "I was surprised that my mother didn't tell me herself when he passed." I'd said it in an e-mail to someone. The article was a compilation of various interviews I'd given over the years, pulling together everything I'd ever said about my mother and my family issues. But if you didn't pay attention to the dates, it looked like I'd given a full-blown interview about the "estrangement" immediately after my dad's death. There I was, thinking I was honoring my father's life. They barely used any of the tribute memories I'd shared. It was an embarrassment.

Apparently, that article so outraged Mark that he decided to tell his side of the story in a competing weekly. Then, as these magazines are wont to do, they called my publicist, told her that Mark's interview didn't put me in a good light, and asked if I wanted to comment. They told me that Mark had said that the real reason my father died was of a broken heart, that I was the apple of his eye and when I'd cut him out of my life, he slowly died. Meanwhile, word came to me through a "source close to the magazine" (as the weeklies would say) that Mark had called the magazine volunteering to give an interview about me. He was angry, screaming, and on a rampage about me. I refused to say anything other than to pay respect to my father's life. But my publicist went a step further. She said to the reporter, "Do your research. Google this man. He's a convicted felon." She asked, "Why is Mark Nathanson speaking on behalf of the Spelling family? Who is he?" She implored him to think about what he was writing. Ultimately, they did mention in passing that he was a convicted felon, but I still think it's amazing that in light of what was happening, for all the rumors that were flying back and forth, the press didn't pay much attention to my mother's new boyfriend and what their relationship was. It was all about our feud.

Next there was another statement issued from my mother. It was such a joke. We were using the media to communicate. *Us Weekly* followed up by putting me on the cover with the headline HER MOTHER'S REVENGE. At this point my publicist just told me to leave it be. Right. It was good advice. I should have taken it a lot earlier. All I can say in my own defense is that those reporters are excellent at their jobs. They tell you that you've been wronged and you need to set the record straight. Your side of the story needs to be heard. But our issues needed years of therapy. They'd never work themselves out on the printed page. Which I guess is what made it such good fodder.

Most of my father's shows were on ABC. At one point he was the producer of seven out of twenty-one of ABC's prime-time hours

(*T.J. Hooker, Dynasty, Hotel, Love Boat, Fantasy Island,* et cetera). Insiders started jokingly referring to ABC as "Aaron's Broadcasting Company." A week after my dad's death ABC contacted my manager and agent to say they wanted to put together a special tribute for my father. They asked me to host and executive produce. I met with them and loved what I heard. They were looking to do a two-hour special that truly honored him. I told them I wanted to interview the people who were important to my dad: not just actors, but the cameraman, the transportation guy, the fans, some of his family left in Texas. We were going to show the house where he was born. The tribute would reveal him to be more than the wealthy, big producer people imagined. It would show him as a person. ABC was completely on board.

Dean and I had to go to Ottawa for work, but the production company flew there to meet with me and begin formatting the tribute. They started interviewing people like E. Duke Vincent, who was my father's producing partner and had known him for fifty years; Nolan Miller, who designed all those *Dynasty* gowns (and my Halloween costumes); and Heather Locklear.

We were well into production when ABC looked into licensing clips from my father's shows. When Spelling Productions was sold to Paramount, they became the owners of the clips. Ordinarily, licensing clips is a matter of paperwork. But this time Les Moonves, head of CBS and a friend of my parents, stepped in. Word came back through the lawyers that Les Moonves wanted Candy Spelling's blessing before licensing anything. I thought, *Oh, shit. Watch this. It's going to be a nightmare.* And, indeed, my mother said no. She said there was going to be a tribute to my father at the Emmys, so there was no reason to do it. That was the reason she gave: oversaturation. Without the clips, the project was dead.

The Emmy tribute was thirty seconds long. They showed some clips from his shows, then the Angels said, "We'll miss you, Aaron."

My father would have loved a full-scale tribute with the people he cared about, and he would have loved that I was producing it. I still felt guilty about being out of touch for those nine months. I wanted to give something back to him.

Dean and I were in Ottawa to do a movie together. It was basically the same setup as *Mind over Murder*, the movie we'd met on one year earlier. This one was called *The House Sitter*. It was with the same producers, the same director, and the same crew. Dean and I were executive producing and starring in it. We were even staying in the same hotel, the Cartier Place, in my old penthouse suite.

Ottawa was where Dean and I met and fell in love. During the filming of this movie it became the place where our son, Liam, was conceived, in what was for us a setting of pure love. We'd been trying ever since I had a failed pregnancy after we got engaged. Now the timing—right after my dad died—made me feel like he had a hand in it, that part of my father's spirit had passed into the baby who was growing inside me. My father was an angel, and he'd given me my angel.

I was in my trailer when I got word about my father's will. Of course I remembered how he'd told me that Randy and I were well taken care of—that we'd each get almost a million dollars, so I wasn't surprised to learn that $800,000 (actually, a little more than half that after estate taxes) was coming my way.

Still, to be completely honest, I was let down when I heard that nothing had changed. Yes, $800,000 is a lot of money. But from what I heard in the press, my father was worth half a billion dollars. It was his money. I hadn't worked for it and no part of me thought I *deserved* it. But, come on, if your father had $500 million, wouldn't you hope for, oh, just a paltry $10 million? If you had a golden ticket waved in front of your face your whole life, wouldn't you want it? I cried a little bit in my trailer, and then I felt guilty and disappointed in myself for crying. I'd always taken care of myself. Why was I crying like a spoiled little girl? Certainly I hadn't been banking on the money. But part of me (the pregnant, hormonal part) wanted to enjoy having a baby and being a mom without having to work my butt off. My father had helped so many people throughout his life. Meanwhile, I'd been working hard to support myself since I was sixteen. In a blink he could have given me the opportunity to be a stay-at-home mom and wife, to play with my child and cook dinner for my family instead of jetting off to Germany for two days when I was four months pregnant to do a personal appearance in order to help pay off my credit card bill. Now, with the announcement of the will, I knew for sure that there was no pot of gold. I'd been reared rich, with no education about money and a high standard of living. Even if I worked really hard, I'd never earn the type of money that he could have just given me.

Oh, boo hoo. I know. But give me this, at least: I got crap my whole life for being a spoiled, rich daddy's girl. Now I wasn't that at all, but it's not like the lifetime of crap disappeared along with my theoretical inheritance. Plus, I was grieving and hormonal.

The funeral for my father had been small, around thirty people, but my mother's publicist had announced that there was going to be a large public memorial service for my father, possibly at the Television Academy, later in the month.

My dad loved people. He never believed he was as big and important as he was. I imagined him looking down and getting a kick out of how many people would show up at his memorial service. But then, inexplicably, it was canceled. I read the news in the paper. It said that it was too soon and my mom was still grieving, but that she would reschedule for later that year. It never happened. Nanny was gone, my father was gone, and my relationship with my mother was in pieces. My brother was in the middle, torn and wanting to keep the peace. The family I'd been born into was, effectively, gone. But I had Dean and I was pregnant. Something new was growing.

*CHAPTER TWENTY*

# B and B . . . and B

The idea to open a bed-and-breakfast was also conceived in Ottawa. For one week out of the three-week shoot, we filmed at an old house an hour away from downtown Ottawa. They told us we could either drive all the way back to our hotel every night or we could stay in a bed-and-breakfast a minute away from where we were shooting. I was kind of curious—I'd never stayed at a B and B. Five-star hotels, yes. The *Queen Elizabeth II*, yes. Vegas casinos, yes. Bed and breakfast? Never. My makeup artist was vehemently against it. She said that B and B's were musty, dusty, and filled with old people's crap. It sounded ominous, but we went to take a look.

This particular B and B was a Victorian house on a nice piece of land with a gorgeous lake. There were bicycles and a canoe for fishing on the lake. A lovely old couple showed us their best room. It was the "teddy bear" suite. There were stuffed teddy bears and needlepoint "collectibles" featuring teddy bears sitting on every surface and in every corner. It triggered memories of my early-childhood Madame Alexander doll trauma. But we decided that overall it was romantic and cute, and we're both suckers for a charming old couple, so we decided to stay.

The proprietress was determined to prove to me that my fame meant nothing to her. Every morning she reminded me that she had never seen *90210,* wasn't interested in television, and knew nothing. Then she'd bring me breakfast and say, "These berries, they come from my neighbor. I told her I was making Tori Spelling's breakfast. You like them? I'll tell her Tori Spelling liked her berries."

The charm and novelty won out until the night we filmed until five in the morning. We returned to the house and crashed, hoping to get some much-needed sleep before our three p.m. call for the next day's work. But at eleven a.m. our hostess banged on the door and told us to vacate our room so the maids could clean it. We tried to decline maid service, but moments later her husband pounded on the door insisting that we clear out. So we did. For good.

But we loved the idea that travelers could feel like they were weekend house guests at a country estate. It felt so personal and intimate, but what if it were run by cool young people and didn't have scary pillows shaped like cats and samplers saying THERE ARE NO STRANGERS HERE, ONLY FRIENDS WE HAVEN'T MET? We pictured a modest, modern house where guests could get the kind of attention that they wouldn't find at a big hotel.

We knew we wanted to start a B and B. Then we had the idea that the process of launching the business as a husband-wife team might make a fun reality show. That's when Dean and I started making the rounds, pitching *Tori & Dean: Inn Love*. My pregnancy was part of the pitch—we told them we hatched an idea for a B and B . . . and B. Yes, I sucked it up and went in to VH1, even though they dropped *So NoTORIous* like a hot brick. Business is business. But it really killed me when the response from VH1 was something like, "Can they put themselves on tape so we can see what their personalities are like?" They had just produced a whole show based on my life! They knew me! And Dean had been around for the whole time. It was dumbfounding, but thankfully, Oxygen was into the show. We had a deal!

We found a house in Fallbrook, California. Fallbrook, the self-proclaimed Avocado Capital of the World, is in San Diego County, about fifteen minutes from the ocean. We bought the house (well, leased with an option to buy) with a ticking time clock. We had to renovate the house to meet our fantasy of a young, modern B and B, open it up to guests, and shoot the entire first season before the baby came. I would have liked to take more time to shop for a house, to shop for furnishings, to shop for . . . shopping's sake, but everything was rushed. In some ways it was the least perfect time to make a big move. How crazy were we to move out of L.A. and embark on a new business venture in the middle of my pregnancy? But in another way the timing was also perfect. The two of us were finally setting up house together. We were starting a business that we hoped would support our family. We were creating a life in a place that was new to both of us. Our baby would be born into a fresh start.

When we first moved in and I walked around our property in Fallbrook, it felt like a childhood fantasy come true. It was a picturesque house with a green yard and a white picket fence. There were flowers everywhere, and there was even an idyllic pond. It was springtime. I had a perfect husband, and I was going to have a baby. It was easy to flash forward to strolling the land with Dean while our three kids tumbled along beside us. It all made sense . . . except, that is, when it came to waiting on guests hand and foot at all hours every day.

Running the inn was anything but a fantasy. I didn't anticipate the guests taking surprise photos of us while we tried to clean the house or prepare breakfast. I didn't know there would be vandals and Peeping Toms. I never want to plunge another toilet again. And, for all that hope and sweat, the inn wasn't exactly raking in the big bucks. We didn't know what the future held.

Regardless, I was looking forward to being the mother I had missed. But it wasn't just about me as a mom or Dean as a dad. It was important for us to be parents together. My father had always doted on me, often in ways that I later realized were damaging to the family. One of my earliest memories is being at my dad's bedside when I was about five. He wasn't feeling well, and I was visiting him. He told me I was his angel and that he loved me more than anything in the whole world. I asked, "What about Mommy?" And he replied, "No, I love you the most. I love you more than Mommy." When he said that, I looked up and saw that my mother was standing in the doorway. From the look on her face I knew that what he'd said was wrong, but I was too young to have any idea why. Now I think that sort of comment set the tone for my relationship with my mother.

His ranking of us in the hierarchy of his love wasn't the only problem. When I showed my dad my schoolwork, it was like I invented Wite-Out. I could do no wrong. But his response was so over the top that, comparatively, my mom's reaction was never enough.

My whole life I always blamed her for our relationship. Now I know that he fanned the flame. He set her up to fail. As I got older, my mother tried to explain some of this to me. She told me that he made her the bad cop. He'd tell her not to let me do something. She'd tell me no. Then I'd go to him and beg, and he'd say yes. He villainized her.

My mother reached out first. Some time after the crazy, grief-laden, anger-filled mess that played out in the tabloids, my mother sent me an e-mail. It was a really nice e-mail saying that she knew I was pregnant and I was going through one of the most special moments of my life right now. She said she would always love me. She wanted to be a part of this time in my life and would like to get together. The end said, *I love you.* It was a heartfelt e-mail, and it filled me with hope.

At the time she e-mailed, I'd just found out that she and Mark had broken up. I was sure it wasn't a coincidence. It was easier for him when we didn't get along. Before writing back, I took the time to think carefully. I certainly didn't like all the drama and conflict, but I also felt very calm and happy in my life. Was I ready to reopen that door? Wouldn't it just happen all over again? This was our pattern: She hurt me; I backed away; she acted nice; I started to think she'd changed; we got close again; I got hurt again; and so on like that. At what point do you decide a relationship is just plain bad for you? But soon I'd be having a baby. I wanted my mom to see me pregnant. I wanted her to be part of the baby's life. I craved her love and influence. That overpowered the reality of our relationship.

Dean and I talked about it. Together, we decided that I'd e-mail her back. But I had to do so knowing that I'd have to accept her for everything she was and everything she wasn't. Taking her back on my terms? We knew that wasn't an option. I wrote back thanking her and telling her how much her note meant to me. We were up in Fallbrook. We'd just remodeled our inn and were about to welcome our first guests. It was such a joyful, crazy time in my life. I was nine months' pregnant, blissfully happy with my husband, and about to be a mom. I suggested that we meet the next time I was back in L.A. I didn't want to dredge up all the bad stuff to get to the good stuff. But I knew we had to hash some of it out. How else could we move forward?

But our plans to meet were interrupted. Liam made an early arrival.

We hadn't quite finished shooting the first season of *Inn Love* when my water broke. It was the middle of the night. I woke Dean up and showed him the sheets. He said, "Yeah, seems like it." As we drove to the hospital I couldn't stop wondering what our son was doing in there without my amniotic fluid. I figured he was flopping around like a fish out of water, slowly dying. Okay, so I wasn't the most calm, optimistic mother-to-be.

To me pain was part of the childbirth experience. I didn't want to be the kind of person who said, *Oh, yeah, I got my epidural. Never felt a contraction.* But after hours at the hospital I texted Jenny to say, *You didn't tell me contractions hurt this bad!* Bring on the painkillers. Meanwhile, Jenny was texting me to ask, *What are you going to do about your mother?* Did I want her at the hospital for the birth? We still hadn't seen each other or talked about anything. I had no plan.

Jenny offered to leave a message for my mom and brother that I'd gone to the hospital.

At some point Dean slipped out of the labor and delivery room, and talked to my mother. They decided that she'd come to the hospital. He wanted to surprise me, but one of the nurses told me she was on her way. "Don't leave us alone!" was my first reaction. I texted Jenny and told her she had to come.

For whatever reason, my mom didn't show up for four hours. Dean was pacing. I was contracting. Jenny and Mehran had arrived and were trying to keep me calm—we were anxiously awaiting the arrival of . . . my mother. Of course. A big moment in my life and—I know she didn't plan it that way—it was about her.

And then, at long last, my mother appeared. I started to cry when I saw her. Excluding my father's funeral, it had really been a year since we'd been in the same room. I realized in that moment that this was exactly what I wanted and needed. I wanted her to see my belly before I gave birth. I wanted my mother to be with me in that moment.

We were waiting for me to dilate when Jenny said to my mother, "Do you know what the baby's name is?" It was then that I realized my mother hadn't asked. Mom said, "No, they haven't told me." That didn't sound like a question to me, so I said, "Mom, do you want to know his name? It's Liam." There was silence. Everyone looked at one another. Dean jumped in and said, "Liam Aaron McDermott." There was still no comment.

The only explanation I can offer is that my mother likes to be included. She likes to feel like part of the process. If I'm right, she was upset that she hadn't been told. If she had to ask, she wasn't going to ask. At that moment something changed in her face. It was as if she'd remembered what it is about me that offends her.

Oh, right, and about the baby who was struggling to enter this world? He wasn't responding well to my contractions. His heart rate was dropping, and I had stopped dilating. It eventually became clear that a C-section was in order.

It didn't seem like I'd been in surgery long when the doctor said, "Thirty more seconds—here he comes!" Then I heard Liam's first cry. That's when it all became real to me. Liam became real when I heard his voice. For nine months we'd waited, and I thought about who he would be and what it would be like to have a baby. But as real as it was and felt, I didn't connect the two until I heard his voice. It took my breath away. I was overwhelmed with love. My whole world changed. Dean said, "Oh my God, he's gorgeous," and brought him over so I could see him. I looked down at my baby and said, "Oh, he is. And thank God he has a good nose."

The next day when my mom came to visit me in the recovery room, a crowd had gathered. Dean's son was there with Dean's sister Dale and her husband, Stuart. A couple friends—Jenny, Amy, Sara, and Mehran—were also there. My mother's cell phone rang. She sat down in a chair in the corner of the room and said into her phone, "I don't know, there's *all* these people here. I might just call the driver to come pick me up." All those people were Dean's family, and my family, and Liam's family. For all my mixed emotions about my mom, I wanted Dale to think she was great. But nobody in Dean's family reacted to the comment. Dale just gave her a warm hug. Later she said, "No matter who she is, that's not who you are. She doesn't reflect on you."

That day Mehran reported that during my delivery my mother said, "It's great that we've made up, but she and I have a lot to talk about. That whole *So NoTORIous* thing really hurt me." Jenny, always protective, was angry at him for telling me, but Mehran said he'd never keep anything from me. I wasn't surprised that they were of different opinions. Mehran reveled in the crowd in the hospital room. Jenny thought Dean, Liam, and I needed space. That's why Jenny and Mehran are such amazing friends to me. They both take care of me. If Mehran is my husband (second to Dean), then Jenny is my mother and sister all in one.

When you have a baby of your own, it makes you realize a lot. The feeling that I had when I first heard Liam's cry—I can't help but think that somewhere deep down my mother feels that same way about me. She's my mother. She loves me. How do we work as mother and daughter? We haven't figured it out yet. We may never figure it out. We're not a good fit. We may go back and forth forever. There's no tidy, perfect bow like the ones that my mother crafts in her gift-wrapping room. But Liam's birth changed things. It may not have brought us closer, but it connected us.

Back home Dean and I settled into life as new parents. For any parent, I imagine, there are too many amazing moments that can't really be described. But what I loved the most was when the three of us took a nap together in our bed, with Liam safely tucked between me and Dean. Liam completed us. I'm a mom and a wife, and I'm happy. I have a family. I always wanted to be a mother. But meeting Dean added another element to that desire. Being a mom also meant creating a life that was part me and part Dean. I'd always wanted a baby, but I'd never given much thought to the love that would foster that child. Being a parent with the man I love fulfills me.

When *Tori & Dean: Inn Love* premiered, it scored the highest ratings with women aged eighteen to forty-nine in Oxygen's history. Still, I was sure it wouldn't get picked up. *Just watch,* I thought. *It's the story of my life.* But then Oxygen ordered a second season. Finally.

Even more rewarding was the response people were having to the show. Dean and I put up a page on MySpace, and I started reading the comments and responding to viewers. The biggest response seemed to be people saying, "You're so normal. You're just like everyone else. You have a normal relationship. You could be my neighbor." A friend of mine said shattering my image as a spoiled rich girl was making a mistake. But it meant the world to me. For once in my life what people saw matched up with how I saw myself.

Not long ago Mehran said to me, "Look where you are now. Can you believe it? You're married. You have a baby." I knew what he was saying. For a while there it looked pretty unlikely. When I got together with Dean, my friends thought, *Here we go again with Tori.* Jenny, Suzanne, Sara, Amy, Jennifer—they've all now said individually, "Look where you are." For once my instincts were right. It worked out. Dean is my soul mate. For all the mistakes I know I've made, it's hard to have deep regrets when things turn out so right. It starts to feel like destiny. Dean, Liam, our work, wherever it may lead us, our lives together—it feels safe, protected by the love we have for each other.

Most parents want their kids to lead a better life, growing up with more advantages and opportunities than they had. I was born into a family that seemed to have everything. But I hope if I've made anything clear in this book, it's that perception and reality aren't always the same. I am who I am because of and in spite of all of those impressions. We are not defined by the family into which we're born, but the one we choose and create. We are not born, we become. The biggest thing I want for Liam—and any other children Dean and I have—is a family in which he knows it's okay to talk about stuff. I want to find the right balance between knowing about his life and not being overbearing. I want to find a happy medium. (And when I say "happy medium," I'm not talking about Mama Lola. For all my respect for her, my maternal instincts compel me to protect Liam from chicken-blood baths and the like.) I want him to know that I care about his day-to-day world. I want him to be happy and feel loved (and not to have a paparazzo camera in his face every time he leaves the house).

My whole life I wanted to be normal. Everybody knows there's no such thing as normal. There is no black-and-white definition of normal. Normal is subjective. There's only a messy, inconsistent, silly, hopeful version of how we feel most at home in our own lives. But when I think about what I have now, what I strived to reach my whole life, it's not the biggest or best or easiest or prettiest or most anything. It's not the Manor or the laundry closet. Not the multi-million dollar inheritance or the poorhouse. It's not superstardom or unemployment. It's family and love and safety. It's bravery and hope. It's work and laughter and imperfection. It's my normal.

# Acknowledgments

There's no awards ceremony music to pull me offstage here, and I want to thank so many family, friends, and colleagues for their love and support, so here I go:

My daddy: I'll always be a daddy's girl, and I miss him every day. I hope I continue to make you proud. Nanny, who made me the woman and mom I have become. I miss you so much. Mom, we have our ups and downs, but I'll always love you. Randy, who was born my little brother but has often guided me as a big brother. Uncle Danny, who has been a second father to me. Jack, I believe there's no "step" in "son," and our relationship is a happy testament to that. Aunt Kay, who has always been such a positive and fun influence in my life.

Jenny, my best friend and sister, whose love and support proved to me that family is what you create. Mehi, my gay husband and best friend, we've been through bad and amazing times together, and I would go through them all again just to be with you. Amy, Sara, and Jennifer, thanks for being the understanding and caring best friends that you are. We get one another, support one another, and will always be one another's family. Bill and Scout, whose generosity and friendship mean the world. You are always there for my family, and I can't picture our lives without you. Geordie, Marcel, and Suzanne, whose humor, loyalty, and honesty make them amazing friends. I cherish our individual friendships with all my heart. Jeremy, whose cynical humor and shared laughter I miss. You got me and I got you. I'll always hold you in my heart. Kevin and Tammy, thank you for being lifelong friends.

Ruthanne, my friend, who believed in me when most didn't. Thank you for seeing me through good times and bad times and for taking a personal interest way beyond an agent's call of duty. Gueran, my hardworking agent and one of my closest friends, without whose perseverance and loyalty this book would not have been possible. You turned it all around for me and my family in many ways. Meghan and Jill, who, like two angels, came into my life and career when I needed them. Thanks for being unbelievable publicists but even better friends. Jamie, my lawyer and friend, thank you for your loyalty, honesty, and continued guidance all these years. Jacob, Lee, Jonathan, Jo, and Carlos, my wonderful agents at UTA, thank you for supporting me and being there for me. Chris and Mike, who brilliantly executed my vision and dream. The best thing I got out of *So NoTORIous* was gaining you as friends. Jennie, it's been eighteen years since *90210* started, and we're still close. Zach and James, with whom in a short period of time I found friendships I hope to maintain forever. Loni, who became a true "Mom" and friend to me. I will cherish forever our talks and your sage advice. Dan, who found this book a home. Patrick, who believed in this book, edited it brilliantly, and remembers more about *90210* than I do. Hilary, without whom this book and my story wouldn't have been anything. Sometimes fate works out, and it did when I met you. Randy and Fenton, who make "reality" more fun than I ever imagined. Thank you for producing and being as passionate about *Tori & Dean: Inn Love* as I am.

Dr. Jason Rothbart, who brought Liam, my most precious gift, into this world. Dr. Ann Wexler, who made me face my truths. I hope you are proud of how far I've come and the person I've become. You had a huge part in that. Isabel, my dear Isabel, who has taken loving care of me and my babies for the past fifteen years. We would have been lost without you. Doreen and David, who I know are watching over our family. Thank you, our angels, for bringing your son, Dean, into my life. My Canadian family, who so quickly embraced me. I thank you for giving me what I've always wanted—a big, loving, close family. And I love all your hugs! Uncle Nolan, whom I'm glad to have back in my life. Aunt Renate, who has always been such a wonderful mothering figure in my life. Mama Lola, who I believe changed the course of my life and allowed me to find true happiness with Dean. Patsy, who loves my little man so much. You are and always will be family to us.

Mimi La Rue, diva, princess, and fashionista. You'll always be my number one (fur) baby. Ferris and Chiquita, who both came from Much Love Animal Rescue, quickly stole my heart and found a place in my family. You demonstrate why rescue is so rewarding. Much Love Animal Rescue, all of you are amazing and give so much of yourselves. I am proud to be a part of your amazing organization, which I shamelessly promote: www.muchlove.org.

And to gay men everywhere, I'd be nowhere without your support.

This book is dedicated to Dean, who showed me what true love is, and Liam, my angel, who made us a family. I love you both to no end. You are my world.

Love,
Tori